A Pilgrimage to the World of

Peace and Nonviolence

Integration of Spiritual, Social and Political Consideration of Doctrines
related to Peace and Nonviolence

Indian Edition

Chandan Sukumar Sengupta

Creative Commons Series

A Pilgrimage to Peace and Nonviolence

Indian Edition
Chandan Sukumar Sengupta.

First Publication: December 2022

Revised Edition: September 2024

Place of Publication: Bankura, West Bengal, India

It is true that we are passing through a critical situation during which entire society is getting divided into class and section day by day on the basis of different types of superficial parameters. Such differences are so prominent that they even hamper the normal acculturation process of early schooling and socialisation of individuals through which newly introduced fellows are allowed to gain a perfect pitching in the multi-plural community. Service oriented life of modern world is also moving on with such kind of toss and twist giving birth to regional as well as global tension of different degree and radial expansion. It is also becoming difficult for us to overcome the situation due to its deeper impression in the mind-set of individual coming out from the isolated segments of restricted mechanism of acculturation. Main objective of our discussion and analysis is to cultivate a balanced process of educational, social as well as economic acculturation which will be suitable enough for ensuring implementation and continuation of world Peace.

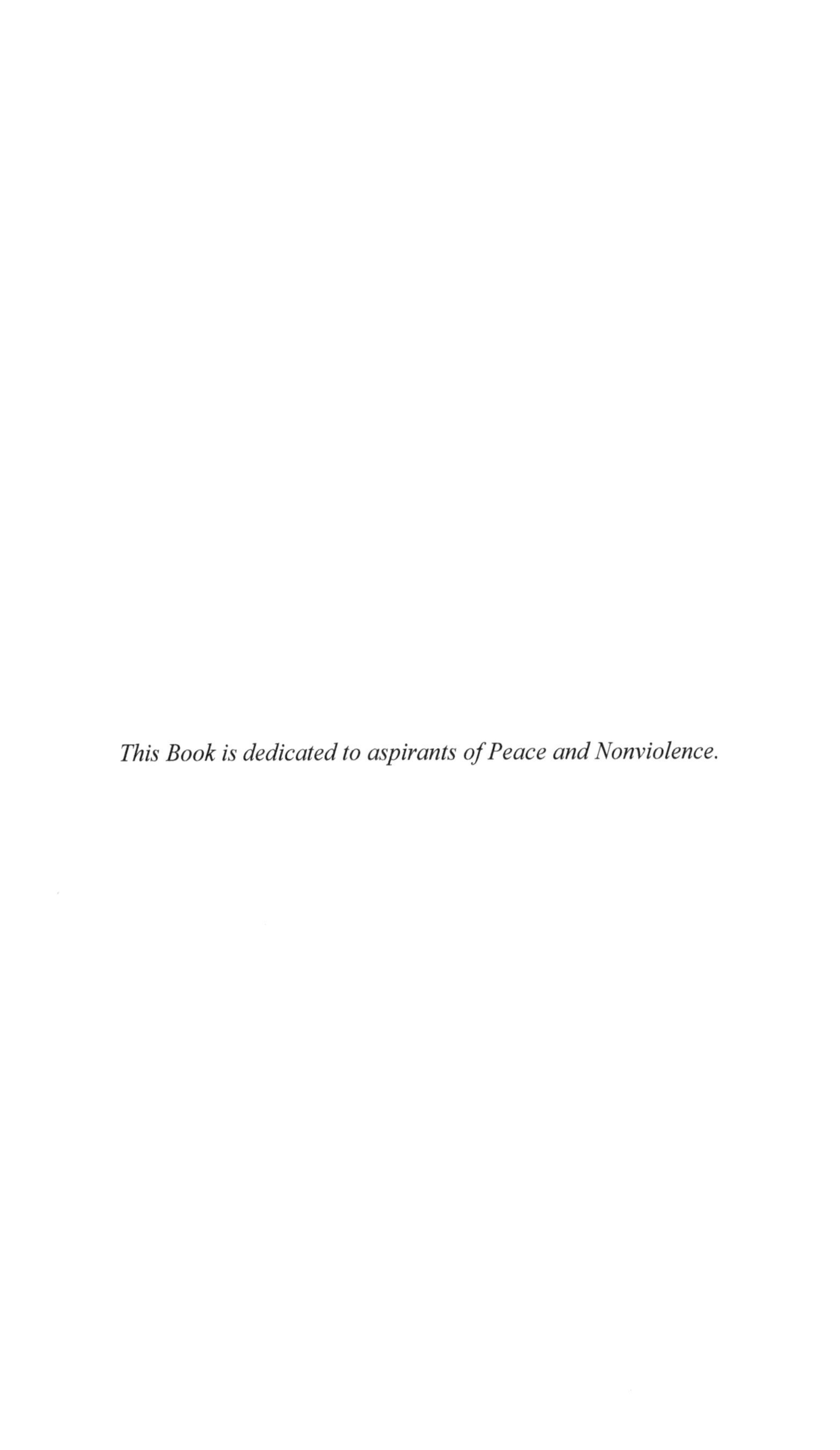

This Book is dedicated to aspirants of Peace and Nonviolence.

Contents

Foreword

Peace can be maintained by actualising state of mental and spiritual status of an individual or a surrounding in which a smooth functioning of other entities is duly observed. We can consider Pilgrimage as a journey where an individual goes in search of some expanded meaning about their good self, about others, divine, or to explore some higher meaning of life through gaining experiences.[1] It often involves a journey primarily meant for searching moral or spiritual significance of life. The person associated to such kind of focused movement is called a pilgrim. Pilgrimage is also associated to biological, social, spiritual and psychological therapeutic benefits,[2] for it provides a spiritual enrichment to a pilgrim, for it ensures the advancement of the knowledge base of a pilgrim by exposing the individual to some higher order of attainment of experiences, for it becomes helpful for an individual in the path of spiritual, social and psychological actualisation of the soul.

Pilgrimage to Peace and Nonviolence always contains faith expectancy and search for wholeness. Because of that reason this type of pilgrimage does not require any tourism. It does not mean that we restrict ourselves from visiting sacred places and hermitage of saints[3]. We also move through some experience sharing to make ourselves enriched.

After incorporating justice in larger concept of peace the theory of "Active Peace" is proposed.[4] An idea of restoration of peace is advanced according to which the involvement of local community and locally

---

[1] *Plate, S. Brent (September 2009). "The Varieties of Contemporary Pilgrimage". CrossCurrents. 59 (3): 260–267. doi:10.1111/j.1939-3881.2009.00078.x*
[2] *Warfield, Heather A.; Baker, Stanley B.; Foxx, Sejal B. Parikh (14 September 2014). "The therapeutic value of pilgrimage: a grounded theory study". Mental Health, Religion & Culture. 17 (8): 860–875. doi:10.1080/13674676.2014.936845. ISSN 1367-4676. S2CID 143623445.*
[3] *Werner, Karel (1994). A popular dictionary of Hinduism. Richmond, Surrey: Curzon. ISBN 0700702792. Retrieved 30 October 2016.*
[4] *"The Theory of Active Peace". internationalpeaceandconflict.org. Archived from the original on 25 July 2015.*

active administrative units are considered as an important component to be considered as unavoidable conditions.[5]

Pilgrimage to Peace and Nonviolence confers the journey of an individual from ground level of understanding of concepts and propositions related to Peace and Nonviolence to a higher level of self actualisation, for such kind of spiritual and intellectual advancement will ensure the capability of a person with which omnipresence of the Divine can be felt, for a better understanding of the conceptual and practical nature of the doctrines related to Peace and Nonviolence can be felt with better understanding. We consider this work as a pilgrimage as it ensures our spiritual, intellectual and psychological understanding of the doctrines of Peace and Nonviolence. It will also confer our adequate alignment towards the rituals associated to the doctrines of Peace and Nonviolence.

It is also recommended that entire portion of this work are arranged in such a way that they lead person towards a balanced understanding of doctrines of Peace and Nonviolence so as to ensure the perfect and ensured progression of an individual from small purpose of life to a higher purpose of life. Socialisation and acculturation is a pair of effort with which participants of a society explore their aspirations in a better way for making efforts more result oriented.

---

[5] *Jyot Hosagrahar: Culture: at the heart of SDGs. UNESCO-Kurier, April-Juni 2017; Rick Szostak: The Causes of Economic Growth: Interdisciplinary Perspectives. Springer Science & Business Media, 2009, ISBN 9783540922827.*

Preface

Peace and Nonviolence is actually a pair of inseparable doctrine with which personality refinement is perpetually accelerated. There is a conception in Yoga Philosophy which proposes the relevance of Peace and Nonviolence in life without which progression through the path of Spiritual advancement cannot be ensured.

There are different approaches of addressing the situation which people expect in ground, or perfectly to say in reality, because of the implements of Peace and Nonviolence. Peace of a forest, for an example to understand the physical situation, is disturbed when any violent attack of any predator is pounded upon any group of grazers. Peace of a specific area is disturbed when some kind of unwanted activities taken up by any group of performers, or any natural calamity is advanced by the nature, or any disturbing elements come in action for taking some sort of non-desirous acts and conducts, or during the situation when two armed forces come in the fore front and remain engaged in encounters. There are examples in plenty having no mental, spiritual or psychological sanction of mind for which peace of the surrounding and that of the spiritual, mental, psychological and some other set up of an individual is disturbed. There exists situation when an individual feel that peaceful situation is disturbed. Saints from Indian origin maintain their view regarding the establishment of peace in and around the context which also depends upon the mind-set and knowledge base of the person who is trying to feel the situation. Feelings have direct link with senses and senses are governed by neural control. This neural control is the subject of the proper adjustment of sensory and motor mechanism regulated and impacted through proper and timely adjustment of the memory and intellect.

The situation can be elaborated by taking a small example from our daily life. We regularly follow news through several popular channels. If, say merely for an example, a train accident took 300 lives, a bus accident, and 34 casualties etc. the immediate response, or reaction to these types of news, which often appears in our mind, will be: "Only 300 deaths! The figure may go on increasing. Channel people often hide figures; railway department is not taking care of tracks; drivers are not sincere; ...." Some other reactions start coming on the basis of the approach and knowledge base of the mental and spiritual set up. But regarding the news of any mishap in which our nearer ones and dearer ones were traveling will make us completely disturbed. We start following ways out to address the situation. It the second situation we can say that peaceful mental set up is disturbed.

Regarding the nature of nonviolence also there exist different types of approaches with which the doctrines related to this ritual are addressed. The term "nonviolence (AHIMSA in accord to Indian Scriptures)" is addressed by thinkers and philosophers of different origin from the context of the feelings of violence. This term, specifically to say AHIMSA, is addressed in Yoga, Vedanta and Sankhya Philosophy as a state of mental and spiritual situation of an individual being aligned to which hatred, agony and enemy-like feelings are casted off. The context in which all beings start living like members of a family we feel that the situation of nonviolence is established. It is a multi---dimensional concept which maintains the omnipresence of Divine in every creation because of which one should pay respect to all the creations and start getting adjusted with all such entity remaining functional in the context.[6]

The non-cooperation campaign meant primarily for Indian independence led by Mahatma Gandhi and his fellow associates, the Civil Rights Movement in the United States, and the People's Power Revolution duly experienced by people in the Philippines are some of the initiatives through which non-violent approaches of social and political movements came in practice. Most prominently of all such movements the freedom struggle considerations adopted by right wing of Indian leaders can be considered as an approach which was planned keeping the doctrines of Peace and Nonviolence at the base. Mechanism duly adopted for isolating sinners from sins is the act through which possibility (or

---

[6] *John Arapura in K. R. Sundararajan and Bithika Mukerji Ed. (1997), Hindu spirituality: Postclassical and modern, ISBN 978-81-208-1937-5; see Chapter 20, pages 392–417*

probability) of attaining changes in the attitude of sinners can be ensured. This mechanism will also infuse some sort of re-adjustment of thinking and attitudinal conducts to ensure their participation in the context of freshly restored human relations.[7]

There exists evidence from epics and other ancient scriptures which permits taking support of violence by warriors and rulers, but strictly rejects taking support of violence at any cost by a hermit.[8] Without any universal consensus applicability of AHIMSA to non-human beings is advanced in epics and scriptures.[9] A hunter, as depicted in epics, defends his profession in a long course.[10] Even hermits were urged to live on fruits and other farm yields to avoid destruction of natural greenery and wildlife.[11] Tirukkural, often considered as Tamil Veda, dedicates Chapters 26, 32 and 33 of Book 1 to the virtue of ahimsa and also maintains a view that AHIMSA is applicable to all life forms.[12]

There are several other approaches through which the rituals and doctrines associated to peace and nonviolence can be addressed in some of the practical ways. It can be advanced that all the approaches refer directly or indirectly towards the process of acculturation for addressing the issue. Jainism and Buddhism consider any life form out of passions as Himsa (violence) and keeping oneself isolated from such acts is considered as nonviolence.[13] Truth plays a vital role by safeguarding peace and nonviolence. According to Jain tradition, which is also applicable to Saints like Mahavratis, the vegetarianism or veganism is

---

[7] *King, Martin Luther Jr. (2010-01-01). Stride Toward Freedom: The Montgomery Story. Beacon Press. p. 114. ISBN 978-0-8070-0070-0.*

[8] *Manu Smriti 5.30, 5.32, 5.39 and 5.44; Mahabharata 3.199 (3.207), 3.199.5 (3.207.5), 3.199.19–29 (3.207.19), 3.199.23–24 (3.207.23–24), 13.116.15–18, 14.28; Ramayana 1-2-8:19*

[9] *Mahabharata 3.199.11–12 (3.199 is 3.207 elsewhere); 13.115; 13.116.26; 13.148.17; Bhagavata Purana (11.5.13–14), and the Chandogya Upanishad (8.15.1).*

[10] *Mahabharata 3.199 (3.199 is 3.207 according to another count).*

[11] *Rod Preece, Animals and Nature: Cultural Myths, Cultural Realities, ISBN 978-0-7748-0725-8, University of British Columbia Press, pages 212–217*

[12] *Tirukkuṛaḷ Translated by V.V.R. Aiyar, Tirupparaithurai: Sri Ramakrishna Tapovanam (1998)*

[13] *Jain, Vijay K. (2012), Acharya Amritchandra's Purushartha Siddhyupaya: Realization of the Pure Self, With Hindi and English Translation, Vikalp, ISBN 978-81-903639-4-5, Public Domain This article incorporates text from this source, which is in the public domain.*

considered mandatory.[14] Not to injure plants and animals in everyday life as far as possible is perfectly advanced by all the prominent religious schools of Indian origin.

We will discuss the other relevant issues having direct or indirect linkages with vows of Peace and Nonviolence. First chapter will focus on analysis of the context followed by development of "Care Management" mechanism. Third chapter will describe the nature of "Knowledge" and the ways through which people attain it, along with attainment of capabilities of correlating memory & intellect. Fourth chapter will focus on citizenship rights and duties of an individual to the nation-state. Fifth chapter is designed to address issues related to the ultimate gain for which all the human beings are duly assigned by the Divine. Philosophy of ANTYODAYA (addressing aspirations of poorest of the poor and disadvantaged class at the beginning) is the terminal point of discussion which can be considered as the foremost requirement of a conscious society having aspirations of moving along the path of Peace and Nonviolence. It is expected that all the parts of forthcoming discussions will enable an individual to actualise their own approaches with which address to issues and concerns of society and nation are advanced. It will also provide an ample scope of self actualisation to individuals having eagerness to attain prosperity while maintaining vows of Peace and Nonviolence in a best way possible.

---

[14] *Dundas pp. 158–159, 189–192; Laidlaw pp. 173–175, 179; Religious Vegetarianism, ed. Kerry S. Walters and Lisa Portmess, Albany 2001, p. 43–46 (translation of the First Great Vow).*

Source of Inspiration

The idea of this publication is developed to focus on the approaches with which development of the context is felt progressive. A prolonged service line of thinkers and philosophers are considered to work out a convergent approach of actualising the concepts and propositions related to the spiritual, psychological and social aspects of peace and nonviolence.

Truth resides at the base of peace and nonviolence. This truth can be addressed through proper understanding of the context for which peace and nonviolence will provide a spiritual and intellectual base. We also expect that all the individuals living under certain jurisdictions of nations-state should follow the doctrines of peace and nonviolence for ensuring their access to the spiritual and intellectual truth. Respect to animals, plants and rest of the other parts of the nature is the principal dogmatic blend of Jainism, Buddhism and Vedantic Philosophy which also implies adequate emphasis of advocacy of vegetarianism.[15] Even Biblical ethics advance the spiritual aspects of accommodation of peace and nonviolence in life by advancing a concept: A person shall be perfect as the Divine is perfect[16]. The ethical concept of AHIMSA is evolved in Vedic Scriptures[17]. Being a doctrine with its parallel alignment with Peace is developed during later Vedic age as an obligatory practice for saintly individuals and is expected the same to be practiced by other individuals having eagerness to gain an advancement on the same track of attainment of spiritual and intellectual bliss. Such kind of effort leading an individual towards attainment of the spiritual bliss by

---

[15] *"Animal, Vegetable, Mineral: The Making of Buddhist Texts" (12 July 2014). University of Cambridge (www.Cam.ac.uk). Retrieved 12 March 2019.*
[16] *Ira Chernus. "The Anabaptists". University of Colorado Boulder. Retrieved 12 May 2022.*
[17] *Walli, Koshelya: The Conception of Ahimsa in Indian Thought, Varanasi 1974, p. 113–145.*

following some of the recommended rituals got a prominence even in the Yoga Philosophy duly proposed by sage Patanjali.[18]

AHIMSA is also accommodated along with other four essential virtues; such as Satyavachanam (truthfulness), Arjavam (sincerity), Danam (charity), Tapo (penance/meditation); in Chandogya Upanishad[19], one of the oldest scripture of Indian origin developed during 8th to 7th B.C.E. AHIMSA was also considered as a spiritual doctrine which implies the total avoidance of creating harm to any creature not only by deeds, but also by words and in thoughts[20].

This publication will focus on different aspects of the doctrines of Peace and Nonviolence along with their importance in the field of socialisation and acculturation process of individuals through which their aspirations can be addressed in a progressive way.

***

---

[18] *Henk M. Bodewitz in Jan E. M. Houben, K. R. van Kooij, ed., Violence denied: violence, non-violence and the rationalisation of violence in "South Asian" cultural history. BRILL, 1999 page 30.*
[19] *Ravindra Kumar (2008), Non-violence and Its Philosophy, ISBN 978-81-7933-159-0, see page 11–14*
[20] *Kaneda, T. (2008). Shanti, peacefulness of mind. C. Eppert & H. Wang (Eds.), Cross cultural studies in curriculum: Eastern thought, educational insights, pages 171–192, ISBN 978-0-8058-5673-6, Taylor & Francis.*

Introduction

Peace is our desired level of social status and Nonviolence will be the initiative with which we want people to move on further towards the status of gaining continuation of the Peaceful resolutions in and around the state. Before considering different sources of threat to the modern society we must move through doctrines of Peace and Nonviolence along with their true nature. "Peace" is a relative term and is considered by different individuals from different view point. We can feel the peaceful situation on the basis of the mental, physical and spiritual contentment. A hungry person, for an example, cannot feel the mental and spiritual peace due to the impulse of the hunger. Similarly an individual experiencing severe pain in any of the bodily organ or system cannot experience the beauty of Meditation as some healthy person generally gains. Mahatma considered Peace as a foremost condition important for implementing Good Governance. It is also true that Peace cannot be implemented at the cost of weapons, flesh and blood; it will come through understanding of each other's need and issuing a sanction to certain extent possible for addressing wills and wishes of each other. Peace will come in its real sense for the entire community. The fulfilment of basic need of the community segments will make the initial step towards making peace process effective and result oriented. Further step will become visible in the form of regulations of need and greed of the community partners. For making our ideas more clear we should highlight different angles of consideration with which features of Truth is addressed.

We will consider distinct approaches with which "Truth" is to be addressed. True beliefs and true statements correspond to the actual state of affairs or doctrines can be considered as Truth.[21] Being a traditional model duly popularized by great thinkers and philosophers this model correlates thoughts and things in a better way. A judgement can be

---

[21] *Encyclopedia of Philosophy, Vol.2, "Correspondence Theory of Truth", auth.: Arthur N. Prior, p. 223 (Macmillan, 1969).*

considered as "True" if it correlates the external reality and facts.[22] Truth is also considered as an objective reality which is often ascribed through thoughts, words and other means.[23] Obstacle due to variations of language and dialect is considered as a limiting factor due to which any universal definition of the doctrines related to "Truth (SATYA in Sanskrit) cannot be generalised. If we put concepts into practice then the result or outcome of such practice will confirm the nature of Truth (a Pragmatic Approach)[24]. Concordance of abstract statements with the ideal limit towards which hundreds of investigations can be advanced to bring out essential ingredients of Truth is considered as a basis through which one can assess Truth.[25] True is the expedient in our way of thinking and Right is the expedient in our way of behaving.[26] Truth is a quality the value of which is confirmed by the effectiveness when applying concepts into practice.

From another angle it is confirmed that what works may or may not be considered as Truth, but what fails cannot be considered as a representation of Truth. It can be advanced only because Truth never fails.[27] We cannot confer with facts and figures that we are right during all instances, but we can easily identify instances when we are wrong.[28] Nothing considered absolutely true as some other angles of observation may consider a fact true after altering the collections of facts and figures. This is a kind of superficial examination with which nature of Truth is defined. It has limitations of approach which remained restricted to the materialistic view of facts, figures, propositions and concepts.

---

[22] *"Correspondence Theory of Truth", in Stanford Encyclopedia of Philosophy (citing De Veritate Q.1, A.1–3 and Summa Theologiae, I. Q.16).*

[23] *See, e.g., Bradley, F.H., "On Truth and Copying", in Blackburn, et al. (eds., 1999),Truth, 31–45.*

[24] *Encyclopedia of Philosophy, Vol. 5, "Pragmatic Theory of Truth", 427 (Macmillan, 1969).*

[25] *Peirce, C.S. (1901), "Truth and Falsity and Error" (in part), pp. 716–20 in James Mark Baldwin, ed., Dictionary of Philosophy and Psychology, v. 2. Peirce's section is entitled "Logical", beginning on p. 718, column 1, and ending on p. 720 with the initials "(C.S.P.)"*

[26] *James, William, The Meaning of Truth, A Sequel to 'Pragmatism', (1909).*

[27] *Sahakian, W.S. & Sahakian, M.L., Ideas of the Great Philosophers, New York: Barnes & Noble, 1966, LCCN 66--23155*

[28] *Feynman, The Character of Physical Law, New York: Random House, 1994, ISBN 0-679-60127-9.*

Deflationary theory maintains a clear view that "Truth" is an expressive predicate requiring no additional explanation.[29]

The doctrine of AHIMSA got its highest prominence during Epic Age. Both Ramayana and Mahabharata accommodated this in the process of addressing this doctrine in an integrated approach.

Mahaprasthanika Parva of Mahabharata has the following verse:

अहिंसा परमो धर्मस तथाहिंसा परो दमः।
अहिंसा परमं दानम अहिंसा परमस तपः।
अहिंसा परमो यज्ञस तथाहिस्मा परं बलम।
अहिंसा परमं मित्रम अहिंसा परमं सुखम।
अहिंसा परमं सत्यम अहिंसा परमं शरुतम॥

It literally means: "Ahimsa is the highest virtue, the highest mechanism of self-control, the greatest gift of spiritual and intellectual nature, the best suffering meant for progress of the entire community, the highest sacrifice through which through which a sinner can be isolated from the act of sins; the finest strength having perfect mental, spiritual and intellectual alignment towards Truth; is the greatest friend of an individual having affinity towards attainment of the Divine omnipresence; the greatest happiness with which eternal contentment can be advanced; the highest truth leading an individual towards the process of self actualisation; the greatest teaching."[30] Arthashastra, as compiled by Sage Chanakya, discusses why and what constitutes proportionate response and punishment.[31] In due course of time it is also advanced that war should not be an indiscriminate tool of destruction[32] , for such kind of destructive affinity of war will initiate the growth of another waves of hatred and agony which may become suffice for giving birth to another

---

[29] *Encyclopedia of Philosophy, Supp., "Truth", auth: Michael Williams, pp. 572–73 (Macmillan, 1996)*

[30] *Ahimsa: To do no harm Subramuniyaswami, What is Hinduism?, Chapter 45, Pages 359–361*

[31] *Paul F. Robinson (2003), Just War in Comparative Perspective, ISBN 0-7546-3587-2, Ashgate Publishing, see pages 114–125*

[32] *Subedi, S. P. (2003). The Concept in Hinduism of 'Just War'. Journal of Conflict and Security Law, 8(2), pages 339–361*

chances of war, for such kind of crippled effort of destroying any group or community will generate several other bands of agony and violent uprising leading ultimately towards development of globally recognisable conflicts. Vedic scriptures support use of weapons against armed attackers, or to check any other violent demonstrations.[33] The effort of AHIMSA is also not to be used to imply pacifism. The best defence mechanism is the effort where victim is protected, as well as the attacker is respected and not injures physically, mentally or spiritually if possible.[34]

Practice of Nonviolence is strategic or pragmatic.[35] Our incapabilities of distinguishing these two types of approaches may lead towards development of confusion.[36] Both types of nonviolent approaches finally move on with distinct goals, philosophies and spiritual alignments in particular.[37] Nonviolent approaches reject the use of violent operations for bringing justice for people. It also encompasses acceptance of some alternative path (popularly termed as Passive resistance) for making people aware of their rights and duties. If justice is considered as a birth right then one could claim such right in a society by adjusting their aspirations with positive waves of participation impregnated with efforts of exercising a structured claim on such rights without raising weapons.[38] Nonviolent movements also remain progressive in society without bringing any kind of fear in the minds of any of the partners of movement. It also ensures adequate spiritual and intellectual alignment of the individuals taking part in the system of

---

[33] *Subedi, S. P. (2003). The Concept in Hinduism of 'Just War'. Journal of Conflict and Security Law, 8(2), pages 339–361*

[34] *Ueshiba, Kisshōmaru (2004), The Art of Aikido: Principles and Essential Techniques, Kodansha International, ISBN 4-7700-2945-4*

[35] *A clarification of this and related terms appears in Gene Sharp, Sharp's Dictionary of Power and Struggle: Language of Civil Resistance in Conflicts, Oxford University Press, New York, 2012.*

[36] *Weber, Thomas (2003). "Nonviolence is who? Gene sharp and Gandhi". Peace & Change. 28 (2): 250.*

[37] *Nepstad, Sharon Erickson (2015). Nonviolent struggle : theories, strategies, and dynamics. New York. ISBN 978-0-19-997599-0. OCLC 903248163.*

[38] *"James L. Bevel The Strategist of the 1960s Civil Rights Movement" by Randall L. Kryn, a paper in David Garrow's 1989 book We Shall Overcome Volume II, Carlson Publishing Company*

guided movement.[39] Movement duly planned in accord to the model of Passive Resistance may continue for a longer time, but it will bring assured success without developing any kind of hatred or casualties on either side. This approach of addressing features of nonviolence ensures the linkage of nonviolence with peace.[40] Both peace and nonviolence is a pair of wheels upon which the chariot of personality is established. Simply absence of violence cannot characterize the feature of nonviolence (AHIMSA) is a better way. To trace out the real nature of the doctrine of Nonviolence we have to move back through pages of scriptures and Epics. Yoga Philosophy defined the ritual of Nonviolence in such a way that highest spiritual refinement of an individual is duly accommodated in that ritual. It defines Nonviolence (AHIMSA) as follows:

"If we say that Nonviolence (AHIMSA) is established in any context then organisms residing that context will coexist with family feelings. They even cast off their feelings of hatred and agony. They make them contented by exercising living within minimum."

If we try to restrict this doctrine of Peace and Nonviolence then also it will become evident that both nonviolence and peace got adequate importance in all schools of religion. None of the religions in this world preaches people to adopt violent means for ensuring survival and prosperity of community members. Ethical philosophy of Jainism (after Saint Mahaveera) prepared an extraordinary status for the doctrine of Peace and Nonviolence.[41] Attentiveness of the law making and law implementing agencies ensure chances of acceptance or rejection of

---

[39] *Ives, Susan (19 October 2001). "No Fear". Palo Alto College. Archived from the original on 20 July 2008. Retrieved 2009-05-17.*
[40] *Ackerman, Peter and Jack DuVall (2001) A Force More Powerful: A Century of Non-Violent Conflict (Palgrave Macmillan)*

[41] *Stephen H. Phillips & other authors (2008), in Encyclopedia of Violence, Peace, & Conflict (Second Edition), ISBN 978-0-12-373985-8, Elsevier Science, Pages 1347–1356, 701–849, 1867.*

nonviolent proposals during any of the instances as per need or as per consent of people.[42]

All rituals and customs meant for spiritual refinement are important for the spiritual ascent of the fellow aspirants, but such rituals can have some sort of limits. We will discuss few incidents from epics to reflect this proposition in detail. Emperor Bali is generally addressed Bali Chakravatri[43]. He is the grandson of Prahlaada, who in turn is the son of greatest demon king, Hiranyakashyapa, who was eliminated by Vishnu, in His Nara-simha, Man-Lion incarnation. The fellow emperor conducted a very grand Vedic ritual. While remaining as its officiator all the gods personally approached Vishnu, keeping Fire-god ahead of them to request him to ensure completion of all the rituals meant for gods. Whoever the supplicant might be and from wherever the seeker might be approaching the emperor, but if one approaches and supplicates to the fellow king he is donating that in "as is where is condition", whatever is supplicated and wherever it might be. Appeal of gods to Vishnu was to check the progression of emperor Bali in the holy path of attainment of the highest status of donor in the context. It was the result of TAPA[44] (or meditation) with which emperor Bali wanted to ascend in the path of Spirituality; such kind of ascent was supplemented considerably by the extensive charity with which the fellow king wanted to proceed. Sage Kashyapa identified presence of entire universe in lord Vishnu; even he identified himself in the Divine; a concept of Vishwaroopa[45]. Sage Kashyapa and Aditi materialised origin of Bamana (the form of lord Vishnu) for checking the ceaseless advancement of emperor Bali. Sage Baman approached the place where emperor Bali was offering charity to seekers; it was the holy conduct with which the fellow emperor wanted to gain fame and familiarity; an act which would have been enough for

---

[42] *Sharp, Gene (1973). The Politics of Nonviolent Action. Porter Sargent. p. 12. ISBN 978-0-87558-068-5.*

[43] *Bali, The Emperor, known for his grand benevolence; his courage and will power.*

[44] *The word 'tapaH'(Hindi word Tapasya) also means jnaana, gnosis, knowledge, intellect, spirit, will power, confidence factors, as such it is oriented that way; even lord Vishnu is abounding with intellect, aggregate of intellect, the only aspect of intellect, etc.*

[45] *The physique of universe which lord Krishna explained to Arjuna in The Bhagavadgita.*

gaining the status of godly characters; a conduct which would have been a suffice for claiming regulation of three realms of manifestation.

त्रीन्पदानथ भिक्षित्वा प्रतिगृह्य च मेदिनीम्। आक्रम्य लोकान् लोकार्थो सर्वलोकहिते रतः ॥ १-२९-२०
महेन्द्राय पुनः प्रादात् नियम्य बलिमोजसा। त्रैलोक्यं स महातेजाश्चक्रे शक्रवशं पुनः ॥ १-२९-२१

"Sage Vaamana begged and received a space from emperor Bali that can be covered in <u>three strides</u>[46], but strode all the three worlds in those three steps for the purpose of saving the entire manifestation, as he is interested in the welfare of all the worldly manifestations. Lord Vishnu gave the earth back to Indra restraining Emperor Bali with his vitality."[47]

We all know that Alexander invaded India main land during the ancient age when Aryan group looing after different states of India main land were not united. The fellow Greek warrior succeeded by part and considered himself as victorious. Some of the princely states were not accessible to them because of many reasons. His men finally refused to fight and Alexander preferred returning back to his native place. During one of instance when his men continued returning back some peculiar type of people were identified by them. Some of them remained engaged in preparing a yard of land to be used by them. They continued measuring that land by jumping side by side. Alexander wanted to know the exact reason because of which they were behaving in such a peculiar way. One of the saintly person admitted, "You came here to consider yourself as victorious. You want to grab all the lands. Then also you may not remain eligible for gaining ownership of all the lands. You will be entitled an access to merely a stretch of a yard of land, not more than that.'

After such conversation Alexander admitted that there are three types of people in this land: Some people work for gaining money and property, some other people work for earning fame; there is third type of people. Like these men, having no expectation from people or state. They simply work for the betterment of people without expecting anything in return. They also move through renunciation for making people and

---

[46] *Lord Vishnu is eulogised as Trivikrama, tri- vi-krama three, verily, paced - surpassing, one who surpasses all the three worlds in just three strides.*
[47] *Sri Valmiki Ramayana; Chapter 1*

states competent and stronger. If somebody wants to rule this land then they have to win the confidence of these third types of people (Third Power).

Renunciation cannot be ascribed as any escape from delivering duty to society or to escape regular economic practices for the purpose of earning a living for the community. It is also not the state during which person start gaining some additional privileges from society. Renunciation is the subject beyond the scope of religious confinement. We can expect some sort of matured approach to social subjects through which prosperity and advancement of a society can be ensured.

Renunciation is a state of approach adopted by an individual by casting off the affinity towards gaining advantages in return to services provided to society. It also ensures an intellectual and spiritual advancement of an individual needed for actualising oneself in the situation during which such individual start searching out alternative ways through which prosperity of fellow members of a community can be ensured. India has a bright history of renunciation. People from different walks of life renunciated the world for gaining prosperity meant for commons. Examples are there in plenty.

A youth from a promising farmer's family from Punjab got an assignment to go to market for selling out some farm produces for earning a profit. While moving towards the market place they were moving through a poverty struck village. They preferred feeding fellow villagers by using farm produces that they were carrying to the market. Family members of the youth came to know about the incident and were not happy because of the act. Without considering the willingness of the family members the fellow youth preferred continuing his service to poor and hungry. He also started preaching people by introducing them with noble deeds and wiser conducts. In gradual succession he preferred renunciation for the purpose of continuing his service to humanity.

State of renunciation will come after attainment of true knowledge. The term true knowledge concerns with the understanding of an individual with which omnipresence of the divine in every creation can be visualized. With such apprehension that individual start delivering society without expecting anything in return. Renunciation can be considered as a kind of intellectual .spiritual and mental enlightenment of the individual leading the person ultimately towards a state of spiritual bliss, with which special attention towards collective progress of society can be advanced. Service oriented mission developed at different places in the world exhibits several examples of renunciation. Renunciation is still going on at different places at different instances with varying objectives to work out some sort of service lines meant for ensuring collective progress of desired types.

A youth from Kolkata prepared himself for renunciation after receiving spiritual instructions of divine Teacher. During one instance the youth observed that his master performs a special type of meditation. That meditation was of a special type because of which his fellow teacher was becoming capable of gaining an instant lift from the ground. The fellow youth approached his master and wanted to learn the special type of meditation. Master was not happy after learning about the affinity of the fellow w youth towards attainment of personal advancement. The fellow master said, "I thought you will become a banyan tree , but you are trying to become a palm tree! You are nothing but a Useless fellow!" Attainment of personal advancement without considering immediate need of other people of society was not preferable by the divine master. He wanted the youth to work the progress of the entire community (collective progress). It was the way of renunciation which was preferred by Mahatma. Renunciation should be of such type which cannot imply additional burden upon society. It should have enough capability to address the issues and concerns of the adjoining society. Individual having such kinds of collective impetus can deliver services to needy and disadvantaged people. Renunciation having strict motive of individual progress is absolutely a non-desirable effort. Person who renunciated the world with such kind of restricted affinity of individual progress may not become that much effective in making the entire community that much prosperous. Third power can also have an impetus on the process of reviving human relations in a society. Saintly persons of such genre are the source of inspiration with which community segments often prefer getting involved in the process of revivals and reforms of desired types through the process of socialisation and acculturation.

Growth of spirituality went on progressive through two distinct paths: Advaita (non-duality) and Dvaita (duality).[48] Advaita emphasises practice of the Yoga of Knowledge in three distinct stages.[49] One should lead active, creative and practical life of truthfulness, fidelity, self-control and purity.[50] At certain instances the term "religion" is replaced by the term "Spirituality" to ensure expansion of the scope of spiritual ascent in modern society.[51] Further progress in this path is ascertained by accommodating scopes of human development, psychology and capacity building leading aspirants finally to realisation of the self.[52] At final instances of progress in addressing spirituality beyond the restricted scope of customs and religion brings the scope of making aspirants aware of the situation of experiencing deepest value and meanings of the soul by which regulation of senses can be materialised in day to day living.[53] Gaining spiritual experience through guided practices plays central role in modern society.[54] It has further influence on the mordernist streams of Asian traditions, making the process easily

---

[48] *Ramakrishna Puligandla (1985), Jñāna-Yoga – The Way of Knowledge (An Analytical Interpretation), University Press of America New York, ISBN 0-8191-4531-9;*
Fort, A.O. (1998), Jīvanmukti in Transformation: Embodied Liberation in Advaita and Neo-Vedanta, State University of New York Press, ISBN 0-7914-3903-8;
Richard King (1999), Indian philosophy: An introduction to Hindu and Buddhist thought, Edinburgh University Press, ISBN 0-7486-0954-7, p. 223;
Sawai, Y. (1987), The Nature of Faith in the Śaṅkaran Vedānta Tradition, Numen, 34(1), pp. 18–44
[49] *jñāna yoga in stages: samnyasa (cultivate virtues), sravana (hear, study), manana (reflect) and dhyana (nididhyasana, contemplate)*
[50] *Marwha, Sonali Bhatt (2006). Colors of Truth, Religion Self and Emotions. New Delhi: Concept Publishing Company. p. 205. ISBN 978-81-8069-268-0.*
[51] *Gorsuch, R.L.; Miller, W.R. (1999), "Assessing spirituality", in W.R. Miller (ed.), Integrating spirituality into treatment, Washington, DC: American Psychological Association, pp. 47–64*
[52] *Lockwood, Renee D. (June 2012). "Pilgrimages to the Self: Exploring the Topography of Western Consumer Spirituality through 'the Journey'". Literature and Aesthetics. 22 (1): 108. Archived from the original on 12 October 2022. Retrieved 19 September 2019. The new Western spiritual landscape, characterised by consumerism and choice abundance, is scattered with novel religious manifestations based in psychology and the Human Potential Movement, each offering participants a pathway to the Self.*
[53] *Ewert Cousins, preface to Antoine Faivre and Jacob Needleman, Modern Esoteric Spirituality, Crossroad Publishing 1992.*
[54] *Sharf, Robert H. (1995), "Buddhist Modernism and the Rhetoric of Meditative Experience" (PDF), NUMEN, 42 (3): 228–283, doi:10.1163/1568527952598549, hdl:2027.42/43810, archived from the original (PDF) on 2019-04-12, retrieved 2013-02-10*

recognisable for aspirants of west.[55] Emphasis on gaining personal experience replaced the authority of scriptures.[56] It is also becoming equally relevant for people seeking tension free life and people encountering various types of psychological and physical disorders.[57] Spiritually oriented aspirants experience higher intrinsic meaning of life, eternal peace and strength; they also extend enhanced social support to community members.[58] Application of Yoga, Meditation and Spiritual practices contemplate medical – technical approaches to ensure improvement of treatments. There exists restrictions in terms of measurement of spiritual progress at different instances of ascent because of lack any kinds of development parameters of specific types; such development is actually ensured by the Divine master; such kinds of development may be of different types and of different degrees.[59]

Our overall approach moves on towards an effort of working our the collective approaches with which human society remain engaged in forming and destroying different formats of socialisation. In certain instances we divide society in the name of religion; in some other instances it is segmented in terms of wealth, skils, compulsions, prejudices and bias. It is not the wise effort for which we are here in this world; it is also not an admissible approach with which entire society may prosper; may not lead us to move efficiently towards salvation. Our collective efforts must have a vibrant blend of initiatives marked primarily by our sincere involvement with an aspiration of working out

[55] *Sharf, Robert H. (1995), "Buddhist Modernism and the Rhetoric of Meditative Experience" (PDF), NUMEN, 42 (3): 228–283, doi:10.1163/1568527952598549, hdl:2027.42/43810, archived from the original (PDF) on 2019-04-12, retrieved 2013-02-10*

[56] *Sinari, Ramakant (2000), Advaita and Contemporary Indian Philosophy. In: Chattopadhyana (gen.ed.), "History of Science, Philosophy and Culture in Indian Civilization. Volume II Part 2: Advaita Vedanta", Delhi: Centre for Studies in Civilizations*

[57] *Joshanloo, Mohsen (4 December 2010). "Investigation of the Contribution of Spirituality and Religiousness to Hedonic and Eudaimonic Well-Being in Iranian Young Adults". Journal of Happiness Studies. 12 (6): 915–30. doi:10.1007/s10902-010-9236-4. S2CID 143848163.*

[58] *Salsman, J.M.; Brown, T.L.; Brechting, E.H.; Carlson, C.R. (2005). "The link between religion and spirituality and psychological adjustment: The mediating role of optimism and social support". Personality and Social Psychology Bulletin. 31 (4): 522–35. doi:10.1177/0146167204271563. PMID 15743986. S2CID 34780785.*

[59] *MacDonald, Douglas A.; Friedman, Harris L.; Brewczynski, Jacek; Holland, Daniel; Salagame, Kiran Kumar K.; Mohan, K. Krishna; Gubrij, Zuzana Ondriasova; Cheong, Hye Wook; Sueur, Cédric (3 March 2015). "Spirituality as a Scientific Construct: Testing Its Universality across Cultures and Languages". PLOS ONE. 10 (3): e0117701. Bibcode:2015PLoSO..1017701M. doi:10.1371/journal.pone.0117701. PMC 4348483. PMID 25734921.*

prosperity for all the segments of our society, without restricting primarily to any sort of segmentation; must not be in terms of religion, caste, culture, prejudices or bias.

Corruption, whatever may be of character or intensity, plays a role just like a blotting paper; starts draining out wealth from the main stream of local economy and makes the society crippled differently. It also impairs us artificially for accepting regulations of some other distantly located factors.

Peace and No-violence, being non-separable pair of rituals, is considered as the strong aspiration which can facilitate collectively all the individuals residing on it towards collective salvation and ultimatimate state of fufilment of principal objectives of life.

1. Context Analysis

At initial we restrict our approach of the analysis to the situation of India and some of the other adjoining states, or some other states having adequate faith on the democratic pattern of socialisation and acculturation.

Today I am completely convinced by the situation that the way India is witnessing the progression in the spheres of social and political scenario cannot be considered as the real character of our country, for the character of India is exhibited by spiritual and intellectual inclusiveness since prehistoric periods. We have also a bright side of history through which we can confer the effort of integration of spiritual ideals and doctrines time to time. Compilation of The Bhagavadgita is made primarily by Sage Veda Vyasa to integrate spiritual diversities of Vedanta, Sankhya and Yoga. Some other hybrid ideals were also configured accordingly to accommodate different units of community members remained active during Epic Age. It can be considered an effort through which unity of community segments was worked out through adopting a segment of Bhishma Parva from The Mahabharata.

Effort of Acharya Shankar (Shankaracharya) can be considered as an effective way of incorporating doctrines of Vedanta, Jainism and Buddhism in his Neo-Vedantic Initiatives. Brahma Sutra and other pioneer works of Adi Guru Shankaracharya are made through a comprehensive doctrine of Neo-Vedantic Thoughts. It was also an effort of making people united at different spheres. Hinduism or any other ism is not the real character of India. That time and after the tenure of Shankaracharya India was witnessing invasions from different parts of the world.

आ नो भद्राः क्रतवो यन्तु विश्वतोऽदब्धासो अपरितासउद्रिदः।
देवा नो यथा सदमिद् वृधे असन्नप्रायुवो रक्षितारो दिवे दिवे॥

"Ano Bhadrah Krutavo Yantu Vishwatah...", "Let Noble ideas to come to this land from rest of the world." This thought process indicates the philosophy of Universal Tolerance with which India main land started accommodating ideas and ideals from rest of the world. Message of India to the West was Spirituality. It continued with progressive motive force as saints like Kabir, Nanak, Sufis and Fakirs continued cultivating efforts of making people united.

Effort of liberating India from foreign rule became a difficult task because of the infiltration of English culture in Indian communities. Credit goes to a brilliant British officer namely Elphinstone[60]. He had drafted a forwarding letter for introducing the "English Education Plan" to be introduced in India by the British Crown. In his words, "Culture is the backbone of a society. It is confirmed that we want to make India slave for centuries. For that purpose we have to infiltrate English Culture keeping aside the fundamental human values. I admit, by introducing this English Education, India will remain slave for centuries; we may rue India even from London. Please sanction at least ten English Schools for Indian States."

Effort of the British Officer brought colour as a learned class of Indian origin moved on to support presence of British in India. Such people lost their attachment to the root of culture are continued exercising their prosperity at the disposal of British Crown. This problem of cultural divergence was perfectly identified by several Indian scholars like Raja Ram Mohan Roy, Vidyasagar, Ramakrishna, Vivekananda, Rabindranath Tagore, Rishi Aurovindo, Mahatma Gandhi and Acharya Vinoba. There are several other saintly scholars who preferred following the path of Renunciation for restoration of cultural integrity of diverged community of Indian origin.

Mahatma, along with all his fellow volunteers and freedom fighters, succeeded to certain extent in cementing the cultural and religious differences and continued addressing different problems with a clear conviction of making "Freedom" a reality. He also wanted

---

[60] *A Scottish Statesman associated with British Government and took the responsibility as Governor of Bombay Province. He has exhibited his loyalty to British Crown by working out some brilliant strategies for making British efforts effective in Indian soil.*

intellectual and cultural freedom of people of India which was lost due to brilliant conspiracy of officers and scholars like Elphinstone. Two distinct approaches developed during that time through which scholars started addressing the problem. Basic Education Plan of Mahatma, Integral Education Plan of Rishi Aurovindo and Value Education Plan of Swami Vivekananda have several approaches in common. They felt the need of Education which will ensure development of Body, Mind and Soul with simultaneous awakening of spirit. Character building was the main impetus of their plan. Just after attainment of freedom the government started searching out a balanced curriculum pattern which could address aspirations of philosophers and thinkers of Indian origin. The matter was not so simple! They had to replace all the black boards and all the whips by infusing values at different possible segments of the ladder of curriculum continuum. Plan of Basic Education duly prepared by Mahatma was on ground by part (states like Bihar and Central Province). Ultimately the plan of Basic Education kept aside as the mind-set of the upper ladder of academics was deeply inflicted with British Culture. India had to carve out ways and means of prosperity through a complicated plan of cultural and academic accommodation by acknowledging the presence of people having culture rooted to some segments of foreign land. This plan had to pay a cost by losing integrity and sovereignty of a state. Because of that reason India continued paying since day one of attainment of freedom.

Modern India, along with other prosperous states, is gaining momentum in terms of infusing human resources with better alternatives so as to equip them for the service lines with which other states are functioning. For certain products and services we have to rely upon some foreign sources; for certain stands to be taken we have to rely upon some polarised powers; for certain modifications to be adopted we had to rely upon certain foreign documentations. Days are nearby when we have to rely upon some foreign sources for learning yoga, Meditation, Veda, Scriptures, Jainism, Gandhian Thoughts, Buddhism etc. In a gradual succession we are losing our adequate hold upon the cultural, academic and intellectual enrichment which was a natural gift sanctioned by the Divine to people of India. India is still waiting for a command line to be issued by any of the polarised power.

It is true that we cannot experience the real progress without accommodating aspirations of all the segments of society. If we keep any of the segments un-attended then such under-privileged class will create problem for rest of the other community. We can examine the fact by taking examples from the subject of Tribal Development. Tribes like Birhore, Khadia, Sabar, Paharia and Mundas do not want our attention as we often approach them with food, clothing and medications. They want their right upon the forest cover which they lost during British period. Officers continued approaching them and wanted to make them fit for main-streaming. There exists a cultural gap. Tribal (as the names mentioned in this document) consider them-selves happy and contented along with the litter and canopy provided them by the Nature God. They even consider themselves rich enough in addressing issues and concerns from their specific angles which is not acknowledgeable as main-streaming. Even their worship patterns differ.

We are discussing on the relations with which human beings ensure their abled participation in their reference community for reaching up to the sources of comforts, pleasures, wills and wishes to be fulfilled. We also expect a sincere return from the couple of individuals remaining indulged in materialising success for their sensuous involvement and variously developed bonds. To understand development and continuation of this bond we may discuss the same in particular.

Human beings are godly creations with some specialties, and also with some limitations. All individuals are not competent equally in all the fields they tend to aspire for. Success in certain fields of activities and failure in some other fields make all individuals job specific. A teacher can handle the subject in which the excellence is duly attained through some formal training. Considering this context a common affair of the restructuring of skills and competence that an individual ascend with we all plan for certain human development activities and try our best to prepare an individual for the type of statehood or nationhood that one should come up with.

Ascent of the person from a local life to national and further to international life is the subject of capabilities and efforts that one put forth for gaining advancement. All individuals are not experts by born; exposure to different types of environment makes them skilled and awakened differently. Skills and competence acquired by them during the period of educational interaction and practices make them special. Fact sheet of disabilities make it clear that we are moving with some sort of limitations by all means. Both quality as well as quantity standards of human development efforts are the matters of concern. There remains some issues and concerns related to development that envisages the need of the refinement of the policy standards to regulate the functioning as well as implementation strategies that required for accommodating the skills and competence possessed by specially enabled person for the collective efforts of national economic progress. How to accommodate such skills and how to move them up through training implements will be the immediate point to be addressed.

Appropriate technologies and selected impairments envisage some of the strategic intervention that makes the human development easier through collaborative efforts of technicians, teachers and other professionals. Leaving any individual in darkness and ignoring the skills and competencies duly housed in that person will be a collective effort assisted with appropriate technologies and assistive standards. Varying impairment standards and their applicability has created a horizon of hope for specially enabled persons through which they can aspire for implementing their enhanced skills and competence for delivering their duties in more appropriate way. It is the wish factor that often makes a person more active than compared to the level duly estimated while mapping the realms of skills and competence.

Competency based curriculum design at the elementary level often points out the strength and limitations of a learner at various levels of interaction under various competencies. Such mapping will enable us to move on towards early specialization of the individual aspirant having special capabilities. For example, a person with problem of vision may be a good orator; a disabled person can have better impulse of sexual desires; a person entering the stage of teen age can be a better performer in materialising their access to newly deloped relations; a teenager may even move on perfectly towards ensuring their soft progression towards enjoying bodily relations.

Not to point out towards the limitations of any individual and to correlate the situation with skills and competence housed in the person will be the highest state of interaction that brings the individual closure to the streams of success. It will even restore the normal functioning of the specially enabled individual aiming towards incorporation of the same entity in the realm of the state level socio-economic and cultural activities. Segmentation of society on the basis of a converged dimension of working capabilities encompasses chances of the formation of close cultural groups having identical job specifications. Such close quarters often acknowledge the presence of their counterpart. Scholars maintained different views regarding addressing aspirations of individuals having enhanced capabilities in certain fields supplemented with limitations of some other degrees and extent.

Question even raised on the necessity of administering medical care if the some physical or physiological malfunctions duly diagnosed at the tender age. In order to implementing an ideal development environment at work places, certain conditions or impairments may not be considered disabilities.

These may include but must not limited to:

1.   Sexual behavior disorders of any kind proved to be against public policy;

2.   Self-imposed body adornments such as tattoos and body piercing etc.;

3.   Compulsive gambling, tendency to steal or light fires; disorders that affect a person's mental or physical state if they are caused by current use of illegal drugs or alcohol, unless the affected person is participating in a recognised programme of treatment duly prescribed by any registered medical professionals or clinics having valid registration of offering such treatments;

4. Normal deviations in height, weight and strength; and Conventional physical and mental characteristics and common personality traits.

Some of the reasonable accommodation can be of the category of best practices having adequate scope of incorporating skilled individuals for dealing with services and equipment of specific type. There is no general framework of any guideline for focusing the need of people aspiring for a suitable accommodation at service stations or work places, but some exemplar mechanism of such efforts can be placed for explaining the situation efficiently. It may vary in accord to the situation of the place and the nature of interaction with which the service line ups are accustomed with.

Selected examples of reasonable accommodation may be of following combinations by part or by whole:

1. Adopting existing facilities to make them accessible by specially enabled persons;

2. adopting existing equipment or acquiring new equipment including computer hardware and software or some other instrumentations for ensuring the smooth functioning of the individuals with certain limitations of any biological type;

3. re-organising work stations public places for ensuring safety;

4. changing training and assessment materials and systems;

5. restructuring jobs so that non-essential functions are re-assigned;

6. adjusting working time and leave calendars; providing readers, sign language interpreters, and providing specialised supervision, training and support if needed.

There are certain pre requisites and guiding principles that an employer generally receive from the state executives. Some of the general points to be considered in general may be advanced for strengthening the policy parameters specified for safeguarding the specially enabled employees at work places. When employers recruit they should: identify the inherent requirements and essential functions of the vacant position; describe clearly the necessary skills and capabilities for the job; set reasonable criteria for selection, preferably in writing, for job applicants for vacant positions. The purpose of the selection process is to assess whether or not an applicant is suitably qualified. This may require a two-stage process if an applicant has a disability: (i) Determining whether an applicant is suitably qualified; (ii) Determining whether a 'suitably qualified applicant' needs any accommodation to be able to perform the inherent requirements or essential functions of the job.

We can share one incident which took place at the foot hills of Dalma Range of Forest during British Period when the executions related to implementation of Forest Act were in progress. Gambhir Singh and Jhippa Layek of that area were known for their special skills of archery. They were capable enough in using five arrows at a time without losing any specific target. Their agitation went on progressive when the news of Forest Act reached them. They consider their access to Forest as a birth right. British Government considered Forest as their State property and prefers continuing with their ambition of draining out logs and roots collected from the richest forest base. Because of this reason regular fight in between tribal community and armed forces of British Government became a reality. Tribal leaders (as two names were mentioned earlier along with their fellow brothers and friends) took the responsibility of protecting the forest by blocking advancement of the forest officials differently. Gambhir Singh stopped the advancement by killing five guards at a time by using poisonous arrows. For the time being it stopped the advancement of the officials. Ultimately aspirations of the tribal community brought down to the ground by deploying armed forces in that area. We can take the reference of this struggle in pages of History by the name of "CHUAD Agitation." Movement led by Birsa Munda will come afterwards in pages of history. Do such tribal community consider themselves comfortable in the situation when judiciary and administration in governed by representatives of people? Do they feel that their aspirations were properly addressed?

Reality says something else. Birhore community residing the adjoining areas of Iron mines of Tatiba Region located inside Saranda Forest are not accessible completely to government officials. They usually remain non-accessible to officials as they often approach the area along with baggage of welfare schemes. Disparities in approaches and concerns of administrative wing failed to address problems because of the approach with which they continued addressing the vulnerable community segments.

We cannot confer the approach formulated by government as well as non-government agencies working in that area as an approach of Sarvodaya. Sarvodaya; as proposed and practiced by saintly crusaders like Mahatma, Kumarappa and Acharya Vinoba through their doctrines, propositions and approaches of planned activities; never kept any alternatives vacant through which aspirations of poor and marginalised individual of a state could be made less considerate. It was also a format of comprehensive development through which integrated approach of linking up people is to be ensured, for without such format of development nothing comprehensive can be achieved, for without such approach aspirations of people in common may remain off the track of the integrity of the nation, for without such approach considerations of human values may remain off the line of judiciary and administrative executions. Approach of Sarvodaya provides us a balanced impetus with which we can successfully segregate sinners from their sinful acts and conducts. It will also ensure us to address humanismic apprehension which is required for addressing the radially progressive developmental realms in a perfectly balanced system of comprehensive mechanism of acculturation.

Integrated Acculturation

European culture dominated the colonial settlement as they brought such cultural set up through promotion of state sponsored missionary as well as educational activities.[61] Acculturation can be distinguished from assimilation as the former one ensures gradual and systematic change in

---

[61] *Nutini, Hugo G. "Acculturation." In David Carrasco (ed.). The Oxford Encyclopedia of Mesoamerican Cultures. : Oxford University Press, 2001*

the cross cultural groups residing in a closed quarter through exercising convergence approaches of cultural, intellectual, spiritual as well as social dimensions.[62] It is evident from approaches duly adopted by Sarvodaya, as per the plan and approaches of Mahatma, Vinoba, Kumarappa and other Sarvodayees, (annex I) the balanced mechanism of acculturation brought some sort of comprehensive result in the form of United Democratic Republic of India. Making India united during 1947 was not an easily accomplishable task due to prevalence of cultural, religious, intellectual and social diversities.

Assimilation, as proposed by thinkers and scholars as an effective mechanism of acculturation[63], was considered as an effective format depending upon which constructive programmes of Sarvodayee[64] volunteers were planned. This approach cannot be considered as a cultural fusion[65], for the approach retains the possibility with which diverged segments of community impart themselves in the process of cross cultural exchange, for the state cannot impose any kind of sanction upon any individual or community depending merely upon the religious, social or cultural distinction, for the state cannot go one defining the judiciary or administration by any religious or cultural confinements. Total assimilation of diverged social and cultural groups[66] cannot be considered a perfect mechanism of acculturation as such mechanism will promote the monoculture by ignoring idolic, symbolic or signal related differences. Some of the community prefers worshiping idols and some other community members prefer worshiping the Divine without taking support of any recognisable forms. Stealing of idol of god will be

---

[62] *Redfield, Robert; Linton, Ralph; Herskovits, Melville J. (1936). "Memorandum for the Study of Acculturation". American Anthropologist. 38 (1): 149–152. doi:10.1525/aa.1936.38.1.02a00330. JSTOR 662563.*
[63] *Gudykunst, W. & Kim, Y. Y. Communicating with strangers: An approach to intercultural communication, 4th ed. New York: McGraw Hill.*
[64] *By the term Sarvodayee we address volunteers, freedom fighters and saints who maintained a faith in values and propositions of Mahatma Gandhi, Acharya Vinoba, Joseph Cornelius and other such leaders of same genre.*
[65] *Kramer, E. M. (in press). Dimensional accrual and dissociation: An introduction. I In J. Grace (Ed.), Comparative Cultures and Civilizations (Vol. 3). Cresskill, NJ: Hampton.*
[66] *Kramer, Eric Mark (1992). Consciousness and culture: an introduction to the thought of Jean Gebser (PDF). Contributions in sociology. Westport, Conn: Greenwood Press. pp. 1–60. ISBN 978-0313278600. Archived from the original (PDF) on 2012-04-26. Retrieved 2011-12-19.*

considered as a punishable offence by the former group[67]. Christian crucifix, on the other hand, represents a symbolic representation of the Divine. As per the recommended plan of a balanced acculturation any state should not sponsor hammering upon the emotional attachment of people by deciphering their mental, spiritual and emotional distinctions. Anekanta Philosophy of Jainism is a balanced system and also can be considered as a time tested mechanism of acculturation, for its wider dimension of acknowledging presence of diverged ideals in a community, for its ways and means of accommodating people in a society along with all sorts of spiritual as well as emotional differences, for its adaptability along with progress made by people in terms of science and technology, for its adaptability with the ideological differences maintained by an individual. Interaction potential is the mechanism with which participating segments of a community can cultivate ways and means of exploring cultural and religious unity at different levels of society. We also witness parallel development of different participants of a society by adjusting their aspirations differently time to time. It is also observed if we examine the approaches adopted by Sarvodayee leaders under the abled guidance of Mahatma (See Table 1). All the plans duly considered for India had two distinct approaches: Set of Constructive Works and Political Empowerment of People. Mahatma had successfully established a balanced coordination in between two distinct facets of freedom movement for ensuring instant progression of a neo—democratised nation. He also wanted to work out possibilities for displaying capabilities of Indian leaders and social-reformers to govern and guide a state properly.

---

[67] *Kramer, Eric Mark (1997a). Modern/postmodern: Off the Beaten Path of Antimodernism. Westport, CT: Praeger. ISBN 9780275957582.*

Table 1: Programmes and approaches adopted by Mahatma and Acharya Vinoba Bhave to promote soft acculturation process in pre-Independent India

Name of the Activity	The Objective of Acculturation to be fulfilled
All Religious Community Prayer	To minimize the cross cultural gaps developed due to differences of Religion and Worship patterns.
Basic Education Plan	Education pattern for linking up people with any economic activity or any cottage industry.
Campus Cleaning and Village Sanitation works	To liberate the specially employed group of sanitary works and to give adequate importance to campus cleaning for minimizing chances of transmission of infectious diseases.
Nature Cure	To make people aware of traditionally available methods of medication and to enhance the skills of village level, block level health workers for minimizing the effective cost which a state usually wants for providing health services to people. Community Health Service Scheme was the ambitious project adopted to address immediate need of the community.
Revival of Cottage Industry	To enhance the confidence of fellow villagers and to ensure their reliance on locally available resource base. It can be considered as a set of acculturation through which gap between resource, technology and skills of people can be adjusted.
Democratic political Will	To accommodate political will of people in general irrespective of any social, cultural, religious or caste distinctions of any type. It can be considered as a perfect way of empowering people.

Nonviolence: Tactical or Philosophical!

Thinkers tried to classify all sorts of nonviolent approaches as tactical or philosophical types. Philosophical one has an accommodation in religious preaching as a doctrine of better living. It also brings spiritual, cultural and emotional enrichment for the individual. Tactical Nonviolence, on the other hand, ensures development and implementation of nonviolent means of resistance with which social, economic and political issues are handled with adequate efficiency without harnessing any harm (physical, mechanical or emotional type) to the oppressor class. Tactically nonviolent person cannot maintain adequate faith on chances of attainment of any change in the mind-set of enemies. They simply prepare themselves mentally and tactically to resist all sorts of oppressive initiatives mounted on the community segments by the oppressive class. Application oriented nonviolence, with which people seek justice, moves on voluntarily to bring desirable change in the behavior of the opponents and oppressors.[68]

.Approaches of Convergence

Regarding doctrines of Nonviolence we must maintain our mind-set in such a way that it should not be judged from the angle of violence. From the view point of the regulation of senses Nonviolence (AHIMSA) is a state of mind which ensures the realm of our relations which distinguishes other human beings as relatives, strangers, friend, enemy or any other entity. Nonviolence will finalise the demarcation line within which our relatives gain some special treatment. Such kind of sense charged with the ritual of Nonviolence can consider a number of individuals as family members. With highest degree of such ritual filled with Nonviolence the individual start considering animals with care and respect. Animals are well treated in the family having higher state of Nonviolence as a ritual. In that context, with clear identification of the age old ritual, we can say that Nonviolence is the highest pursuit of socialisation and acculturation in a community. We cannot, even at any instance we should not, restrict the doctrine of Nonviolence to a limited quarter of any religious or social teachings. We should make it widely acceptable ritual irrespective of any social, cultural, physical or any geographical boundary. Restricting beauty of this ritual due to any reason is also a sin.

There are instances during which we gain several common resources from the nature. We are also getting equally exposed to global problems

---

[68] *Nepstad, Sharon Erickson (2015). Nonviolent struggle : theories, strategies, and dynamics. New York. ISBN 978-0-19-997599-0. OCLC 903248163.*

like pollution, depletion of ozone layers, war, cross border terrorism and many other problems. We are also getting exposed to the globally developed economic crisis due to various reasons. World Economic Forum formulated a list of most pressing points to be considered jointly to address majority of global problems (better we say it as issue).[69] These were: Food security, Inclusive growth, Future of work/unemployment, Climate change, financial crisis of 2007–2008, Future of the internet/Fourth Industrial Revolution, Gender equality, Global trade and investment and regulatory frameworks Long-term investment/Investment strategy and Future healthcare. It is also suggested that no single issue can be isolated or analysed individually at any instance. All the issues as incorporated in the list are directly or indirectly influenced by states of Peace and Nonviolence. The reason is very simple: Peace and Nonviolence signify the spiritual, mental and emotional set up of an individual. We all are, in that context, in the state of such situation where our alignment towards Peace and Nonviolence will be quantified.

.

The Core of Philosophy

From the context of Samkhya[70] Philosophy[71] it can be ascribed with utmost clarity that our entire set of mind and intellect are equally guided by the Ego. This concept, being most scientific, signifies creation of an individual due to interaction of two top most components (TATWA)

---

[69] *Hutt, Rosamond (21 January 2016). "What are the 10 biggest global challenges?". World Economic Forum. Retrieved 18 January 2018.*

[70] *The word Samkhya means empirical or relating to numbers. Philosophy got its name Samkhya due to consideration of number of elements responsible for making creations possible. 25 true principles take part to ensure manifestation of a living being.*
Reference: Apte, Vaman Shivaram (1957). The practical Sanskrit-English dictionary. Poona: Prasad Prakashan.

[71] *Systematic enumeration and rational examination of an individual on the basis of the culmination of matter and energy to ensure creation.*
Reference: Mikel Burley (2012), Classical Samkhya and Yoga - An Indian Metaphysics of Experience, Routledge, ISBN 978-0415648875, pages 47-48

namely Purusha[72] and Prakriti. Prakṛiti, being the direct participatory component of creation, includes all the cognitive, moral, psychological, emotional, sensorial and physical aspects of reality. Only Prakriti[73] acts under the orientation provided by another non-participant component namely "Purush" (it cannot be compared with electromagnetic or sub-atomic entity of driving forces or energy). Just below the sensible soul resides the pair of functional entity namely "mind" and "intellect". These paired entities are equally responsible for issuing functional command of different types for Ego (AHAM). It also signifies the quality with which the Ego will receive timely guidance. We can also bring change in the guidance issued to Ego by bringing some sort of alteration in the knowledge base and instructional mechanism. Quality parameter with which Ego works will also signify the quality of personality that the individual holds. Saints coined three different parameters with which quality of Ego can be standardized. It may be combination of best (extremely good), better (moderate) and worst (extreme bad) Ego. Combination of all the three qualities will make the personality as a unit. None of the segments will become absolute in combination and none of the quality units will be left out during formulation of the individual's consent.

Being part of an absolute consciousness, Purusha remains free from the creation unit and also remains free from any kind of quality distinction. It also remains pure and non-attributive.[74] This Ego will finalise the consent of human memory and intellect for qualifying or disqualifying any other entity of the surrounding as relative, friend or enemy. Such kind of class distinction duly made by the individual will finalise the pattern of treatment issued to different segments of society. If zone of family feeling is small then it is obvious that number of relatives will be least in number. Accordingly the human nature will be defined.

---

[72] *The creator element which influences the creation but never takes part physically in the process of creation.*

[73] *Lusthaus, Dan (2018), Samkhya, acmuller.net, Resources for East Asian Language and Thought, Musashino University*

[74] *Being non-attributive part of the creator power, Purusha remains off the quality parameters and also maintains its pure status. Reference: Sharma, C. (1997), A Critical Survey of Indian Philosophy, New Delhi: Motilal Banarsidass Publ, ISBN 81-208-0365-5*

A Strategic Alignment

We often come across doctrines of Peace and Nonviolence from different sources of academics and spiritual realms. All sections of such kinds of spiritual settings and academics maintain some sort of identical notions regarding nature of these rituals. Difference to some extent can be identified in the form of approach of seeing these things from two extreme opposite poles. One can consider nonviolence from the angles of violence. Some other person having some higher spiritual enrichment can consider nonviolence from the angle of the spiritual refinement and modification of the quality parameters of Ego.[75] Whenever we start considering "Peace" as a doctrine of community living then it always appear along with the doctrine of "Nonviolence". The master of Yoga Philosophy proposed Nonviolence as one of the ritual under the coin "Yama"[76]. Here also we are witnessing presence of Ahimsa (Nonviolence) and truth (Satya)[77] as the essential mental state with which an individual attains some sort of enhancement in terms of quality of Ego needed for regulating other actions and performances of sensory, mixed as well as motor[78] impulses. Regulation of all such impulses will signify the personality scale with which the individual may remain active in the surrounding.

Different schools of Spirituality and religion may address these rituals differently, but principle at the core remains unalterable. We must feel

---

[75] *There are three distinct parameters with which we signify quality of Ego: Extreme positive, extreme neutral and moderate types.*

[76] *Yama is the word coined by Sage Patanjali for accommodating five basic rituals (observable human activities) to make the individual fit for considering rules of spiritual living. These are AHIMSA (Nonviolence), SATYA (Truth), ASTEYA (Considering existence of Divine power as true), BRHMACHARYA (putting effort for attainment of knowledge) and APARIGRAHA (non-attachment to worldly existing things and not to store belongings in plenty).*
Reference: Yogasutras (Theory of Yoga) by Sage Patanjali.

[77] *David Kalupahana (1995), Ethics in Early Buddhism, University of Hawaii Press, ISBN 978-0824817022, page 8, Quote: The rational argument is identified with the method of Samkhya, a rationalist school, upholding the view that "nothing comes out of nothing" or that "being cannot be non-being".*

[78] *Impulse which gives motility and functional readiness to sense organs and action organs.*

the presence of divine besides us during all instances. It is the ultimate goal of a life. People start considering some of the acts and conducts according to their state of knowledge and span of information duly accommodated in mind. Along with such kind of mental and intellectual orientation an individual gains some sort of functional quality. Such individual also start searching other likeminded people having some sort of identical mental and intellectual set up of desired types. Gradual convergence of similar kind of mental and intellectually accustomed minds will form a commune. Such commune may gain an identity in the surrounding. Here takes birth a class, a community, a religious group, an organisation etc. If we aspire for attainment of unity and harmony of some wider types then it must move on through culmination of the status of mental and intellectual bases of varying types. Such kind of culmination will move on through converging approaches of the process of acculturation. It is also true that any kind of abrupt alteration may not be accepted by the members of diverged groups of community. They have some other guidelines issued from some other distant nuclear centre of socialisation and spiritual alignments.

There is another option through which spiritual convergence can be materialized. Community members should have a common core of state sponsored acculturation duly impregnated with principles of the spiritual, mental and intellectual core. In accord to the status we have, principally at the juncture of the Information age, a state sponsored acculturation which will move on smoothly and softly through participatory approaches by accommodating ideals, doctrines, rituals and principles. This approach will be populated gradually by integrating cultural differences of various stake holders of a society. Participatory approaches of different social practices will revive vibrant human to human relation, and by doing so it will diffuse different instances of human to human conflicts. Such efforts will also act as cementing enamel to let people inter-linked together differently.

Sustaining Relevance

The term Gita directly links our thinking with the conversation that took place in between Arjun, a Warrior from the side of Pandavas, and his friendly guide Krishna. It was going on amidst a critical situation in which Arjun lost his power of finalising something justifiable to have a sanction of war and killings. A series of killing of such type, in which his beloved ones were at a threshold, made him discontented. Krishna took the role of his charioteer to normalise the situation and to let Arjun understand his own status in a better way. The agitation, as described in the holy book of Mahabharata, was against the stand of his own family members having intention of grabbing all the resources by taking advantage of some conspired game-fares. The game-fare of such type with in infliction of opportunistic ideals was moved on differently and both the segments of a single family took a stand against each other.

Lord Krishna defined his stand by putting himself in the side of Pandavas with a sheer commitment of not to use his weapon at any instances. It was his stand that made him free from direct indulgence of the warfare and made it possible to guard Pandavas through delivering timely relevant instruction. In this way he has secured his position similar to that of the brain in our body. Conversation of Krishna and Arjun amidst the battle field was also an act of holy instructions duly issued for Arjun to signify his timely need. It had linked senses with duties, established correlation between rights and duties, issued bands of things to be done and things not to be done, entangled a spirit with its higher source, conferred the juxtaposition of creation and the creator and finally re-established need of knowing the self.

It will be even more perfectly balanced to contingent human efforts of ascent towards the state of the unification of conscious mind with that of masterly guide. Effort is also made to encompass the segregation of individual differences from the common philosophical knowledge to make it more people friendly and more relevant, as well as time tested one.

Gita, as a common and popularly contemplated term, indicates towards a subject related to the holy book of Gita having bands of knowledge in the form of a conversation in between Arjun and Krishna. This reality made Gita confined to a limited quarter and placed other holy efforts underneath a shadow of ignorance. We rarely talk about Ram

Gita, Sanskaar Gita and some other such efforts having a suffix Gita attached to it.

Gita, in its actual sense, stands for some sort of compilation that people can sing. It can be discussed with some beautiful rhythmic tunes. Collective recitation of Gita brings out a collective wave in the form of auditory vibrations for the purpose of cleansing the immediate surroundings. It also conferred essence of collective and community level worship for making the entire effort possible and for keeping the converged senses of cooperation and brotherhood alive.

To a compilation of prayers and songs meant for the supreme lord the World Poet coined a term "Gitanjali" for it. Linking to the practical aspects of life and mission of an individual with the specified spiritual destiny, Saint Vinoba coined the term "Katha[79] Gita (Gita through a series of stories)" and incorporated all the teachings and narratives of Gita in absolutely friendly way. Examples are in plenty. It had not diffused the glory of the original compilation of Gita, also had not conferred replacing the original poetic compilation with millions of narratives. Waves of vibrations that the chanting of Gita creates is based on the assimilation of collective vibrations of saintly senses that makes a way out through the surrounding of the place of worship and gives birth to an essence of keeping the collective vibrations of cooperation, brotherhood, divine omnipresence and inter-linkages of senses alive.

We, in the same manner, can successfully create hundreds and thousands of such narratives duly inflicted with fundamental human values to make the spark of Gita a confluous one, a vibrant one and a strategic one. It has enormous power of accommodations for incorporating all sorts of socially and culturally relevant directives within the scope of its teaching related to individual refinement impregnated with spiritual ascent. It also makes the relationship of creator and the creation a vibrant one. We can specify any of the particular effort as an initiative inflicted with divine power meant for accomplishing certain works. All such Gita, duly compiled by saintly people, are not with us. In

---

[79] Hindi term Katha means Stories. Saint Vinoba Bhave translated Shri Madbhagvadgita in Marathi and also wrote a series of books to explain teachings of Gita through simple stories which were also contextually relevant.

due course of time we have lost many of such beautiful, relevant and time tested compilations due to various reasons. Our mind kept on imbibing presence of such powers tradition by tradition through many of our rituals. Those graceful efforts played a significant role in keeping waves of community worship alive.

Wider dimensions and expanded coverage of the teachings of Gita often make people worried about what to follow and what not to follow in real life. Also in some cases it becomes difficult to think about propositions in the actual ground. Because of lack of timely relevant practical knowledge of the situation, people even keep themselves aside from following and internalising teachings of the holy book in the real life situation. Approach of such religious and cultural teaching, therefore, should have proper considerations of some practical aspects of rituals and worships.

Some people maintain a view regarding Gita is that the entire aspects depicted in this holy book are a confusing one. Saints from olden times worked differently to show that Gita is much relevant in terms of rituals and propositions presented in it. Here also we are trying to trace out a link up in between rituals, traditions and practices that we have in nature to re-establish the age old faiths of the omnipresence of divine within us at its varying formats.

We can see things as they occupy a definite shape. We cannot see energy and power due to their in capabilities of occupying space. To feel the presence of such powers in our surrounding, we often take the support of our senses and feelings. In some cases our observations are evidence based, in some other cases it may have some imaginary propositions. Here comes the act of limitations that restrict us to feel Ultraviolet and Infrared [80]radiations which remained off the band of the visible spectrum and duly restricted our sense of vision seven visible waves of light.

---

[80] Both Ultraviolet and Infrared Radiations are the parts of the invisible band of spectrum incorporated in the Solar Radiation. Our visual sense organ can feel the presence of only visible spectrum comprising seven different colours.

There arises another question related to our effort of analyzing the relevance of the teachings of The Gita in present day situation. It was the instructions delivered by Lord Krishna to Arjun during the epic age of Vedic Civilisation. That time war had its presence in the scope of royal management. That time conflicts had a final termination to war for making efforts a result oriented. Sins and sinners had their presence in olden times and are still there with us today; format and geo-locations might vary; arms and ammunitions might differ. Even from the pages of history we can see how Prince Ashoka smashed the Kingdom of Kalinga only because that kingdom had refused to hand-over the murderer of his mother to him. Later on the war and the loss of lives of many innocent people had implied a deep impression in his mind and he had decided to refuse to take part in any other battle simply meant for territorial expansion. Teachings of The Gita have worked differently during different instances of the development of conflicts and agony. Since conflicts and agony are beyond the scope of any historic time line, we can correlate teachings of any instances to prepare strategic actions of any other present day sectoral management plans. It has the impetus of the absolute knowledge of human actions, wishes, wills and conducts with absolute apprehension of delivering the needful.

The reason of discontentment, sorrow and agony of Arjun after entering the battle field was rejected instantly by Lord Krishna through implying a sanction of his indulgence in the war. Killing any individual or creating another one is not the role of any warrior. A warrior can deliver the duty in time with a clear impetus of making the wiser side victorious. Sinners will lose their lives because of their wrong – conducts only. It is the right place to mention about Upanishads, often referred as Vedantas, as they exhibit doctrines, rituals and worship patters prevalent in later Vedic Civilisation.[81] Those rituals and doctrines were duly incorporated in the great epics to make all sorts of teachings easy to understand. The Bhagavadgita along with majority of Upanishads and Brahmasutra are known as PRASTHANATRAYEE.[82] These three scriptures were studied extensively time to time to inculcate more

---

[81] Jan Gonda (1975), Vedic Literature: (Saṃhitās and Brāhmaṇas), Otto Harrassowitz Verlag, ISBN 978-3447016032
[82] Ranade, R. D. (1926), A constructive survey of Upanishadic philosophy, Bharatiya Vidya Bhavan

relevant knowledge related to Divinity and Spirituality. Out of 108 known texts of Uapnishads only a dozen from the initial collection are considered as Primary (MUKHYA).[83] Concluding parts of Brahmans and Aranyaks are also filled with Mukhya Upanishads.[84] Authorship of all the anonymous tests duly collected from the garden of Upanishads is unknown. Group of saints might have collected and represented their lessons in the form of a collection.[85] Conversation between women like Maitreyi and Gargi are also inscribed in the holy texts of Uanishads.[86] Root of all such creations is principally radiated out time to time in different forms and also in different sectorian units from Vedas.

Pluralism of world view was characterised by the Upanishadic age; gradually inclined more towards dualism by combining Sankhya and Yoga doctrines efficiently.[87] The Bhagavadgita moved on a step forward by incorporating Vedanta along with Upanishadic dcotrines with an aspirations of delivering a common pattern of rituals, social formats and political will to the youths of the olden times. Maitri Upanishad aspires for attainment of reverence and completeness by human beings with the help of the knowledge of Brahmans and repeated practices of meditation on such knowledge by the self.[88]

Further study of the Bhagavadgita reveals all such studies like the gradual unfoldment of petals of a lotus. What we think in mind that we aspire to see and experience in reality. We even plan accordingly to make things happen. If we aspire for attaining success in life and duly put our plan and efforts accordingly then the desired success must come in reality. During one of the instance emperor Ashoka, one of the powerful emperors from Maurya Dynasty who ruled during later Vedic Civilisation, invaded Kalinga for punishing the culprit (who was also the

---

[83] E Easwaran (2007), The Upanishads, ISBN 978-1586380212, pages 298-299

[84] Mahadevan, T. M. P (1956), Sarvepalli Radhakrishnan (ed.), History of Philosophy Eastern and Western, George Allen & Unwin Ltd

[85] *S Radhakrishnan, The Principal Upanishads George Allen & Co., 1951, pages 22, Reprinted as ISBN 978-8172231248*

[86] Ellison Findly (1999), Women and the Arahant Issue in Early Pali Literature, Journal of Feminist Studies in Religion, Vol. 15, No. 1, pages 57-76

[87] Glucklich, Ariel (2008), The Strides of Vishnu: Hindu Culture in Historical Perspective, Oxford University Press, ISBN 978-0-19-531405-2

[88] Hume, Robert Ernest (1921), The Thirteen Principal Upanishads, Oxford University Press, pp. 412–414

murderer of his mother). Kalinga was maintaining a voluminous army; even they had a democratic status. With only selected army Ashoka was more organised, confident and contented regarding attainment of success. Success was supplemented with proper planning and absolute positive attitude. That was the real mystery lying behind attainment of success by emperor Ashoka. What to do, how to do and when to do are some of the pre-requisites of developing a strategy for designing a strategy. For throwing out Nanda Dynasty [89] and for replacing the same by a wise king, Vishnu Gupta, popularly known as Chanakya[90] or Koutilya in History, took the support of Greeks deputed there in Indian continent by Alexander. It was the strategy of developing friendship with the enemy's enemy. Such mechanism worked perfectly and he attained success by putting his efforts in bringing change in the Indian context. The result was a long lasting success which came in the form of good government.

Although Chanakya was the most powerful person and most respected master mind of his time, then also he preferred not to put himself on the throne. He preferred maintaining his status of a king maker. Strategy of action and its importance was also perfectly narrated by Saint Valmiki in famous Epic the Ramayana. Once Sugreev, one of the warrior from the envoy of lord Rama, as described in the Ramayana, chased Ravana just after seeing him and recognising him through a window. It was absurdly planned and prematurely implemented. The result came in the form of a failure. Ravana managed to escape from the place by making the warrior entirely confused. He was the master of magical powers. With the help of his magical power he had handled the pre matured planning of Sugreev.

During another briefing on the need of planning for developing a strategy lord Rama narrated the need of gathering such a big army and seeking support of the brother of the Demon King for making things

---

⁸⁹ *Dhana Nanda was the last Emperor of Nanda dynasty. Chanakya, the Economic Advisor of Nanda Dynasty, was badly insulted by Dhana Nanda. Also oppression of Dhana Nanda became unbearable. He was not concerned about the problems faced by farmers and artisans of that territory.*
⁹⁰ *. In later period of history name of Chanakya became popular because of his contribution in the field of Economy by developing a balanced Economic Policy for a State (Arthashastra of Koutilya).*

materialised properly within least possible casualties. Every action requires a proper planning. Winning the battle against Ravana was not so easy, also it was not impossible. Proper considerations of all aspects of threat from the demon king made Rama and his warriors more prepared, more responsive and more specific. Even with more powerful army and different magical powers Ravana became the loser because of his poor planning, arrogance and over confidence. Adequate strategy was not worked out by him due to his act of the under estimation of the powers of lord Rama and his envoy.

If we start talking to a person regarding any subject matter then there will be a state of confusion in the mind of the person regarding the subject matter and related contents of the theme duly assigned to the individual. The state of confusion is only because of the prevalence of the lack of true knowledge regarding one's capabilities of doing any job with perfectness. One can even hardly confess the difficulties that the person is facing during the proposed interaction with selected groups on any selected theme. Actualisation of any kind develops in the individual because of the presence of the Self Esteem.

Self-esteem is the quality depending upon which a person organises skills and memory to prepare oneself for a right action at right time. It has no correlation with any change that intends to bring any change in the context. Self-esteem is still equally relevant in the information age. Properly organised person can materialise any action within limited resources. Even one can implement such actions with best utilisation of resources. Such kind or organised action can even bring result with an enhanced quality consideration. It can even link people with better apprehensions of collective progress. Situation that hampers our individual ascent in the path of Yoga based life is the prevalence of some negative forces within us. It has a deeper impact on senses. One can surpass all such forces with a commitment of imbibing positivity in all actions. By doing so, one can readjust all the senses for materialising the manifestation of the spirit at all instances. With the easiness of mind this process is too easy, and with the difficulties of the mental balance, one rarely capable of feeling presence of such forces.

Yoga speaks more about the strategy of actions that the actions or perfections. How to do any work is more important than the work itself. One can keep on drawing water from the well by using ropes and bucket, or it can be obtained by fitting a water lifting pump at the base of a pipe. A practice of Yoga is deeply rooted in scriptures like Rigveda.[91] The perfect meaning of the term "Yoga" is evident from another scripture namely "Katha Upanishad."[92] It continued developing as a systematic study and practice during 5th and 6th Centuries BCE.[93] The most systematic, comprehensive and effective text on Yoga developed in the form of Yoga Sutras of sage Patanjali during early centuries of the common era.[94]

The Bhagavadgita has different approaches of explaining the core concept of Yoga. It is the state which ensures detachment of individual from sufferings.[95] It is also considered as a state of mental equanimity when a person remains confident and stable during contrasting states of success and failure, happiness and sorrow etc. It is the practice of calming down the desires of mind; then seer is established in individual's fundamental nature; then arise assimilation of seer with mental and spiritual modifications with which individuals move differently.[96] The term Yoga ensures renunciation of the fellow individual (the situation attained by Lord Shiva).[97]

Variation of the principles of Yoga developed over time due incorporation of practices and thought processes of thinkers and philosophers time to time.[98]

Samkhya school of Philosophy, Hinduism and Jainism also acknowledges practices of Yoga in different ways and at different

---

[91] *Karel Werner (1977), Yoga and the Ṛg Veda: An Interpretation of the Keśin Hymn (RV 10, 136), Religious Studies, Vol. 13, No. 3, page 289–302*
[92] *Singleton, Mark (2010). Yoga Body: the origins of modern posture practice. Oxford University Press. ISBN 978-0-19-539534-1. OCLC 318191988.*
[93] *Samuel, Geoffrey (2008). The Origins of Yoga and Tantra. Cambridge University Press. ISBN 978-0-521-69534-3.*
[94] *Bryant, Edwin (2009). The Yoga Sutras of Patañjali: A New Edition, Translation, and Commentary. New York: North Point Press. ISBN 978-0-86547-736-0.*
[95] *Bhagavad Gita, 2.48, 2.50, 6.23;*
[96] *Yoga Sutras of Patanjali, 1.2–4*
[97] *Linga Purana, I.8.5a;*
[98] *White, David Gordon (2011). "Yoga, Brief History of an Idea" (PDF). Yoga in Practice. Princeton University Press. pp. 1–23.*

instances.[99] The Bhagavadgita is the only competent platform where all thought processes of epic ages, such as Yoga Sutras, Samkhya Sutras and Vedantic doctrines, are compiled efficiently with an objective to converge different thought processes to synthesise a practical approach of Yoga. Even Upanishads acknowledge influences of Yoga in different rituals and livelihood as well as social practices of community segments.[100] Mulabandhasana (a yoga state) posture of Pashupati Shiva duly excavated from Indus Valley Civilisation reveals the ancient non-Vedic origin of Yoga practices in Indian context.[101] Regulation of breath and vital energies and mechanism of doing so are mentioned in Atharvaveda and Brahmanas.[102]

We restrict our discussion around instances of the rituals, practices, traditions and thought processes inscribed in the Bhagavadgita. It has another approach with which issues discussed by saints and philosophers time to time while keeping central attention on the doctrines of The Holy Scripture where rest of the other prevalent philosophies secured a perfect accommodation.

The sole objective of The Bhagavadgita is to make people aware of their role in Nature. It also tries to diffuse all sorts of illusions from all possible angles by infusing knowledge. It also tries to link up different thought processes which were growing during Epic ages. With some sort of wider apprehension Gita wants to bring out core of the Spirituality from the limits of Religion; as such limits may not positively bring humanity, peace and prosperity in true sense.

The Holy Scripture also ensures development spirituality in multiplural society. At the beginning it speaks about performing as per the role duly assigned by the Nature; but, during last instances it instructs an aspirant to cast off all differences by resting on the one and the only

---

[99] Zimmer, Heinrich (1951). Philosophies of India. New York, New York: Princeton University Press. ISBN 0-691-01758-1.
[100] Flood, Gavin D. (1996). An Introduction to Hinduism. Cambridge University Press.
[101] Singleton, Mark (2010). Yoga Body: the origins of modern posture practice. Oxford University Press. ISBN 978-0-19-539534-1. OCLC 318191988.
[102] Whicher, Ian (1998). The Integrity of the Yoga Darśana: A Reconsideration of Classical Yoga. SUNY Press. ISBN 978-0-7914-3815-2.

one Divine.[103] The wider and noble approach with which The Bhagavadgita came in the existence amidst Bhishma Parva of the Epic MAHABHARATA to instruct a soldier from delivering duty to safeguard "DHARMA". Such kind of battle, for which the fellow soldier stood alone amidst the turmoil of right and wrong, brought a state of confusion in the mind of the fellow warrior , as he was not in a position to lift arms against relative, masters, well wishers and some elders. It was the turning point where the Divine Master wanted the soldier to recognise his duty while standing in the middle of a battle field; especially when some nobles want him to perform for safeguarding "DHARMA" by crushing sinners.

The Brahman

Yoga is a science of living, a strategy of linking up the soul with the supreme master, a process of acknowledging the Divine omnipresence, a system of reviving coordination between different organ system, a sharp impetus of integrating spiritual and intellectual segment of the individual meant primarily for gaining ascent in the path of attainment of Divinity. Science of Yoga is widely discussed at different instances in Vedic Scriptures and Epics. All the treasure of olden times are not there in our hand; even some of the scriptures are partially interpreted; even some of the sources are differently interpreted; some of the scholarly discussions like that of Sage Kapil, Sage Patanjali, Sage Shankara etc. moved on differently to enrich Central Dogma of the Science of Yoga and Meditation.

Meditation is a kind of guided practice during which spiritual enrichment, mental clearness and emotional calmness will be the desired attainable state for which aspirants remain involved in the process.[104] Although it is evident from various schools of religion, then also guided practices of meditations are prominently placed in Vedantic Schools of

---

[103] *After abandoning all varieties of religion and simply surrender unto the Divine. The supreme creator master will liberate the fellow aspirant from all sinful reactions; one shoud maintain faith and should not get inflicted with fear." Gita, Chapter 18, verse 66*
[104] *Jevning, R.; Wallace, R.K.; Beidebach, M. (September 1992). "The physiology of meditation: A review. A wakeful hypometabolic integrated response". Neuroscience & Biobehavioral Reviews. 16 (3): 415–424. doi:10.1016/s0149-7634(05)80210-6. PMID 1528528. S2CID 2650109.*

religion, Jainism and Buddhism.[105] A clear distinction between soul and mind is the special approach and uniqueness of Vedantic traditions. It also confers the possibly of advancement for all the beings: [Purnamadah Purnamidan……..][106]. Words inscribed in Veda, Upanishads and Epics are not merely words; stories are not merely stories; Verses are not merely any scholarly discourses; all such presentations convey the principal objective of making people (fellow aspirants) aware of the presence of the Divine besides their immediate context. The science of Meditation has some other applications too: it can reduce stress, anxiety, depression and pain during certain instances.[107] Exact translation of Dhyana is not exactly meditation; a limitation is there in between thought process of two extremes; contemplating upon some subject, thinking deeply, pondering upon something etc. are the scope of meditation. "Dhyana" and "Pranayaama" confer withdrawal of senses from the physical world, diverting all the senses towards the inner world of fellow aspirant, converging different sections of the wandering mind, regulation of breathing and impulse for attaining calmness of mind and diffusion of passion, regulating mind to let the illumination of soul become prominent. It is clear from the fact that we must not restrict the brightness of Dhyana and Pranayaam simply by using the term "Meditation." We also remain conscious while using "Dhyana" merely for attaining some success in terms of medical or physical means. Even aspirations of fellow individual should not be restricted to the progress of body parts and impulse transmission; it should have enough capabilities

---

[105] Dhavamony, Mariasusai (1982). *Classical Hinduism. Università Gregoriana Editrice. p. 243. ISBN 978-88-7652-482-0. Archived from the original on 2023-03-17. Retrieved 2020-10-27.*

[106] *Om Puurnnam-Adah Puurnnam-Idam Puurnnaat-Puurnnam-Udacyate |*
Puurnnasya Puurnnam-Aadaaya Puurnnam-Eva-Avashissyate ||
Om Shaantih Shaantih Shaantih ||
Meaning: Om, That (The Supreme Divine) is Purna (filled completely with Divine Consciousness); This (Inner Soul) is also Purna (filled with Divine Consciousness); Purna is manifested From Purna (From the Fullness of Divine Consciousness the complete sensible world is manifested). After taking Purna from the supreme source of Purna, Purna indeed remains (Because Divine Consciousness is Non-Dual, beyond the scope of distinctions of qualities and Infinite).

[107] *Hölzel, Britta K.; Lazar, Sara W.; Gard, Tim; Schuman-Olivier, Zev; Vago, David R.; Ott, Ulrich (November 2011). "How Does Mindfulness Meditation Work? Proposing Mechanisms of Action From a Conceptual and Neural Perspective". Perspectives on Psychological Science: A Journal of the Association for Psychological Science. 6 (6): 537–559. doi:10.1177/1745691611419671. ISSN 1745-6916. PMID 26168376. S2CID 2218023. Archived from the original on 2020-10-02. Retrieved 2020-09-30.*

to ensure enhancement of the spiritual status of the being with which omnipresence of the Divine can be acknowledged. Such acknowledgement is also not the ultimate goal of Dhyana and Pranayaam; it is the juncture during which senses are diverted from externally sensible world to internally recognisable illuminations of soul; the power which guides mind and intellect; indirectly guides senses and organ system; perfectly works to ensure manifestation of finest particles.

A child from remote area of Bengal started visiting nearby primary school to take part in formal schooling. Teacher of that school (during early decades of 19th Century) was quite friendly; even the learning environment of that school was equally friendly. The fellow learner started learning basic mathematical operations. Lessons of adding numbers developed an impression of adding living forms (Jeevatma) and Supreme master (Paramatma). That phase of learning went on continuing up to a couple of months. Finally the curriculum of subtraction was to follow during forthcoming sessions; the fellow learner refused to join that session as he was spiritually not ready to tolerate the removal of Jeevatma (living forms) from the collections of the supreme master (the Paramatma); as the fellow learner was not ready to tolerate the removal of spiritual ascent from the soul; as the fellow learner was not ready to establish a halt in his progressive trend of spiritual ascent; as he wanted to recognise the Divine omnipresence at all instances of life. Due to such kinds of spiritual orientation of the fellow aspirant during childhood he left formal school and continued joining worships of different types duly organised by villagers at different places. His affinity towards the divine and his abled narrations related to supreme master often reflected onset of Divine ascent in the fellow individual at the tender age. Similar the situation was there during stages when Sage Shankaracharya preferred renouncing the world for spreading messages of spirituality.

There are several other examples displaying stages and instances of renunciation which made aspirants famous in due course of time. Sage Shankaracharya (an 8th Century Vedic Scholar and saint) presented a harmonizing reading of the scriptures, with liberating knowledge of the self at its core, synthesizing the Advaita Vedanta[108] teachings of his time;

---

[108] *Non-duality of the Vedantic Doctrines.*

about 300 additional texts were attributed to him afterwards.[109] His contributions like Brahmasutrabhashya, commentaries on The Bhagavadgita and ten principal Upanishads.[110] Advaita Vedanta was the principal contribution duly made by sage Shankara.[111] Sage Shankara (alternatively Adi Guru Shankaracharya) was in the forefront for reviving Vedic traditions during tenure of Chandragupta II Vikramaditya).[112] Some of the stotra (poetic works), the Daksinamurti Stotra, the Bhajagovinda Stotra, the Sivanandalahari, the Carpata-panjarika, the Visnu-satpadi, the Harimide, the Dasa-shloki, and the Krishna-staka are contributed by Sage Shankaracharya during that context.[113]

Saints from Indian context always worked differently to point out spiritual enrichment of Scriptures and Epics with which ascent in the path of Spirituality can be ensured. While introducing himself to his spiritual master for the first time Sage Shankara started narrating his real nature in the form of "Nirvanashatakam: I am Consciousness, I am Bliss, I am Shiva, I am Shiva ... "[114]. Advaita Veda, which existed before the saintly scholar, was actually systematised by him.[115] Monistic spirituality reflected periodically in his works; it was a shift from realism to idealism; a doctrine which ensured chances of individual progress up to the identity of supreme master; a task of spiritual ascent which was acknowledged by the saint a possible and accomplishable destiny; a destiny which confers the regulation of senses, withdraw of senses from

---

[109] *Hacker, Paul (1995), Halbfass, Wilhelm (ed.), Philology and Confrontation: Paul Hacker on Traditional and Modern Vedanta, SUNY Press, ISBN 978-0-7914-2582-4*

[110] *Mayeda, Sengaku (2006). A thousand teachings : the Upadeśasāhasrī of Śaṅkara. Motilal Banarsidass. ISBN 978-81-208-2771-4.*

[111] *Comans, Michael (2000), The Method of Early Advaita Vedānta: A Study of Gauḍapāda, Śaṅkara, Sureśvara, and Padmapāda, Delhi: Motilal Banarsidass*

[112] *K.A. Nilakantha Sastry, A History of South India, 4th ed., Oxford University Press, Madras, 1976.*

[113] *Isaeva, Natalia (1993). Shankara and Indian Philosophy. Albany: State University of New York Press (SUNY). ISBN 978-0-7914-1281-7.*

[114] *Original Sanskrit: Nirvanashtakam Sringeri Vidya Bharati Foundation (2012);*
English Translation 1: K Parappalli and CNN Nair (2002), Saankarasaagaram, Bhartiya Vidya Bhavan, ISBN 978-81-7276-268-1, pp. 58–59;
English Translation 2: Igor Kononenko (2010), Teachers of Wisdom, ISBN 978-1-4349-9898-9, p. 148;
English Translation 3: Nirvana Shatakam Isha Foundation (2011); Includes translation, transliteration and audio.

[115] *Nakamura, Hajime (2004) [1950], A History of Early Vedanta Philosophy. Part Two, Delhi: Motilal Banarsidass Publishers*

sensible objects, attainment of Divine knowledge; a competence which will ensure Divine omnipresence at the individual level.[116]

I am other than name, form and action.
My nature is ever free!
I am Self, the supreme unconditioned Brahman.
I am pure Awareness, always non-dual.

— Adi Shankara, Upadesasahasri 11.7,

Source: Comans, Michael (2000), *The Method of Early Advaita Vedānta: A Study of Gauḍapāda, Śaṅkara, Sureśvara, and Padmapāda*, Delhi: Motilal Banarsidass

Our Basic Understanding

Brahman, a supreme indestructible entity having enough capability of ensuring all sorts of worldly manifestations, is the masterly guide of the self (Adhyatma) and also plays a role in actions pertaining to the material personality of living beings, and its development (Karma).[117] Lord of sacrifices (Adhiyajna) resides in all individuals; masterly guide of all such individuals is the universal Divine (Adhidaiva) and ever-continuing manifestations and alterations of worldly manifestations (Adhibhuta) makes the world a reality. Aspirants having capability of sustaining Dhyana to the Divine subject gains liberation; such contemplation provides them similar kinds of awareness; such kind of absolute involvement of the fellow aspirant in Divine subject by mind and intellect will undoubtedly provide them opportunities of recognising the Divine omnipresence; such awareness will facilitate the fellow individual in recognising the Divine as the Supreme creator, absolute

---

[116] *Sharma, B.N. Krishnamurti (2000). History of the Dvaita School of Vedānta and Its Literature: From the Earliest Beginnings to Our Own Times. Motilal Banarsidass Publishers. ISBN 978-81-208-1575-9.*
[117] *The Bhagavadgita VIII. 3*

source from which rest of the other manifestation become a reality; it is the omniscient(the most ancient); the possessor of an inconceivable divine form; stays beyond all darkness of ignorance; is brighter than brightness of the sun; is recognisable by fixing life –ignition (Prana) between the eyebrows and steadily remembering presence of the supreme master in all forms of creations. Great ascetics practice the vow of celibacy regularly and renounce worldly pleasures to gain the proximity to the imperishable one (the Divine). One can establish the self in steadfast yogic concentration by restraining all the gates of the body and fixing the mind in the heart region, and then drawing the life-breath to the head. While chanting "OM" (the Pranava) aspirants attain the supreme goal by overcoming bodily obstacles. Aspirants fixing on the Divine subjects with utter devotion recognises the masterly guide at all instances, and by doing so regularly they overcome the fear of turbulent cycle birth and death; as they readily attain the highest order of perfection in life. [118]

Up to the highest abode of the supreme Divine, for which we have little instances of sensible recognitions, for which we have some imaginary impetus, for which we ascribe several theories and propositions while relying upon the nature of manifestations duly accomplished, for which organisms will be subject to creation and destruction. Aspirants relying on the supreme master remain free from the fear of birth and death. One day of Brahma (kalp) lasts a thousand cycles of the four ages (Mahā Yug) and his night also extends for the same duration. One can understand the real nature of night and day in a broader spectrum; our earthly limitations of days and nights are restricted only up to the horizons of atmosphere; beyond the scope of atmosphere solar radiations start traveling ceaselessly towards the outer world. Light start travelling ceaselessly in a straight path in the Universe and start creating sense of vision by striking any non-luminous objects and bouncing off the surface of that object; in that context brightness and visibility of the Moon may change but that of the Sun remain unaltrerable for considerable time interval. Creation and destruction of the entire collection of worldly objects will indicate a day and night of

---

[118] *The Bhagavadgita VIII. 4 – 14.*

Brahman.[119] There exists another dimensions of such kinds of cycles of creation and destruction inside the individual's soul which is often persist even after disintegration of all kinds of organ and system and collapse of all the senses. Unmanifested dimension of soul (Atma) is the final attainable goal (supreme abode of the Divine master), and upon reaching the same destiny, aspirants may not return to the worldly sensible desires and passion of the world. That supreme Divine is greater than all kinds of creations which physically exist as sensible and materially recognisable; the masterly creator of all sorts of worldly manifestations; a binding force which is active inside the centrally placed mass of an atom and also active at the farthest realm of the clusters of Galaxy. Those who know the Supreme Brahman and who depart from this world, during the six months of the sun's northern course, the bright lunar fortnight, and the bright part of the solar day, attain the desired supreme destination. The practitioners of Vedic rituals, who pass away during the six months of the sun's southern course, the dark fortnight of the moon, the time of smoke, the night, attain the celestial abodes. After enjoying celestial pleasures, they again return to the worldly manifestations. These two, bright and dark paths, always exist in this world and remain restricted at the realm of the Earth; other planets have their own instances of days and nights. The way of light leads to liberation and the way of darkness leads to recycling of the Divine manifestations. [120]

Aspirants having proper knowledge of the progression through the path of spirituality never get confused of worldly manifestations and after recognising the secret of all kinds of manifestations they gain merits superior than fruits attainable because of following Vedic rituals; following performance of sacrifice; by doing austerities and charities; by following masterly instruction of the spiritual master; by analysing real nature of the non-perishable Atma (the Soul force); by acknowledging presence of the Brahman besides all kinds of worldly manifestations. [121]

Moksha, the liberation from sufferings and rebirth, is attained through illusoriness of the phenomenal world (as seems manifested

---

[119] *Discovery of Black Hole indicates the ever – continuing cycle of creation and destruction.*
[120] *The Bhagavadgita VIII. 16-26.*
[121] *The Bhagavadgita VIII. 27-28.*

because of the presence of Brahman) and disidentification from the body-mind complex and the notion of 'doership' (A creator or motivator of any of the activities duly regulated by the nature), and acquiring vidyā (knowledge) of one's true identity as Atman-Brahman (alternatively Soul force), self-luminous (svayam prakāśa[122]) awareness or consciousness which can be witnessed by the self.[123] Upanishadic statements such as <u>tat tvam asi</u> [124], destroy the ignorance or illusive intellect (avidyā) regarding one's true identity by revealing that (soul of living forms) Ātman is non-different from immortal accumulation of the supreme master (Paramatma). Adwaita Vedanta also elaborates preparatory practice on the basis of noble sayings (Mahavakyas) aiming ultimately towards attainment of liberation from confusions, sensory turbulence of contrasting feelings; such as distinction of happiness and sorrow, gains and loss, right and wrong, anger and passion; it also provides an ample scope of progress to individuals with which the fellow aspirant start recognising presence of the Divine creator besides all sorts of worldly manifestations.[125] Brahman is the true Self, consciousness, awareness, and the only Reality.[126]

Bands of Personification

Allegorical story of Nachiketa, the son of Uddalak (on Vajashravas in some other traditions), is told in Katha Upanishad.[127] There exists some back references from which conversation between Yama and a child was reported.[128]

Nachiketa observed that his father was donating only old, lame, barren or blind cows to seek Divine blessings and fame; but such

---

[122] *Illuminating oneself without relying on any of the physical factors or biochemical regulators;*

[123] *Lipner, Julius (2000), "The Self of Being and the Being of Self: Samkara on "That You Are" (Tat Tvam Asi)", in Malkovsky, Bradley J. (ed.), New Perspectives on Advaita Vedānta, BRILL*

[124] *Translated as: "that['s how] you are,"*

[125] *Barua, Ankur (2015), "Ideas of Liberation in Medieval Advaita Vedānta", Religion Compass, 9 (8): 262–271, doi:10.1111/rec3.12160*

[126] *Potter, Karl H. (2008), Encyclopedia of Indian Philosophies Vol. 3: Advaita Vedānta Up to Śaṃkara and His Pupils, Delhi: Motilal Banarsidass Publishers, ISBN 978-81-208-0310-7*

[127] *Satyamayananda, Swami (2019). Ancient Sages. Advaita Ashrama (A publication branch of Ramakrishna Math, Belur Math). p. 195. ISBN 978-81-7505-923-8.*

[128] *Rigveda (10.135), Taittiriya Brahman; Sabha Parva, Section IV of The Mahabharata.*
Reference: Radhakrishnan, S. (1994). The Principal Upanishads. New Delhi: HarperCollins Publishers India. ISBN 81-7223-124-5 p. 593.

donations, as per the understanding of the fellow boy, was not proper for fetching fame and glory for his father.[129] Nachiketa wanted his father to donate some precious belongings to obtain fame and glory for himself and for the entire territory. Nachiketa repeatedly continued requesting his father to donate his precious belongings. In a fit of anger his father said, "I give you unto Yamaraja Himself!"

Respecting words of his father Nachiketa approached Yamaraja. Yama was out of residence during that time; the fellow boy preferred waiting for Yama for three consecutive days and remained there without having food and water.

After knowing the fact that a guest was waiting at the doorstep without taking food and water, Yamaraja wanted to compensate for the type of mistake and said, "You have waited in my house for three days without hospitality; therefore ask three boons from me."

The fellow boy wanted fame, glory and spiritual contentment for his father; he also wanted to learn particulars about sacred fire sacrifices. First two demand of Nachiketa were accepted gladly by Yamaraja and their fellow boy received all such blessings and relevant knowledge.

The third one my master, "what comes after death of this body?"

Yamaraja preferred avoiding the third subject by giving excuses related to tender age of the fellow boy, "You are too young to learn about such a complicated subject, Nachiketa. Ask for something else. This subject is not clear even to gods! …", Yama said.

Yamaraja continued explaining real nature of Atman which is considered immortal and remain beyond the scope of the regulations of birth and death by elaborating following points:

1. The sound of Pranava (Om) is the syllable of the supreme Brahman which brings enlightenment in the physical existence of the living form.

---

[129] *Swami Prabhavananda and Frederick Manchester, Breath of the Eternal http://www.atmajyoti.org/up_katha_upanishad_text.asp Archived 29 April 2011 at the Wayback Machine*

2. The Atman, alternatively Pranava or symbol Om, is the same in terms of its true nature as the omnipresent Brahman. Smaller than the smallest in material manifestations and larger than the largest at the realm of universal presence, the Soul (Atman) is formless, beyond the scope of qualities and all-pervading.

3. The goal of the wise during the span of the living status is to know this Atman (Soul force) as it is the only self-illuminating source which persists even after physical death of the organism.

4. The Atman can be considered as a rider; the horses are the senses which moves frequently towards sense objects, which receives guidance through the maze of desires, wills and wishes.

5. After death, it is the immortal Atman (or Soul force) that remains in the context;

6. Mere reading of the scriptures or intellectual learning, without masterly guidance or assistance of a Divine teacher, or without addressing to the interpretations of the Divine master, one cannot realise the true nature of Atman (or Soul force).

7. One must recognise the Atman while remaining independent of the bodily manifestations, which is the seat of desire, impulses, passion and illusions.

8. The inability to realise Brahman results in one being trapped badly in the turmoil of desires, sense objects, passions and greed; only proper understanding of the Self leads to liberation.

Rights and Duties

Our definite role in immediate context is determined primarily by our aspirations, wills and wishes. Rest of the other factors are merely secondary. Gita never confers our absolute stand amidst a turmoil by altering our immediate stand to tackle a situation, or never grants us a permission to go otherwise by violating law of the nature. We have certain rights to claim; right to obtain food, right to safeguard oneself, right to arrange a shelter, right to other resources etc.; even all rights confer our some of the non-avoidable actions. On the other hand we have some duties to be delivered; duty to society, to family, to our friends, to our partners and some other such role which seeks sanction of the mental state of the doer; such delivery can make us responsible to certain extent in terms of performing in the context. It will be unlawful to claim rights without performing duties duly assigned by the Nature. Delivering duties without implying any claim upon rights is also equally unlawful. One can have aspirations of maintaining adequate balance in between rights and duties. Such a stand of an individual in society will make the society potentially vibrant. The central objective of the Gita is to make aspirants aware of their rights and duties.

Gita never instructs a Yogi to stand solely upon the point of seeking individual advancement while rejecting possibilities of collective progress of the entire society; it also never grants permission to a yogi for seeking renunciation while rejecting duties to be performed in society. Renunciation is the highest state of spiritual ascent, but it cannot pave a path of escapism by withdrawing oneself from delivering duties to the immediate context; if situation demands need of such a role to be played; if there exists any need in the context; or if all the other stakeholders of such society feel need of some collective role to be taken up. Gita also rejects need of any spiritual ascent while remaining off the main social track of collective progress; real spiritual ascent should be all inclusive and also comprehensive in nature. It would be better to examine all such instances on the basis of spirituality in absolute sense.

Consciousness Matters!

State of mental consciousness is generally classified differently by different schools of religion. It has four different states in accord to Vedic principles. State of awakened one (JAGRAT), sleeping one (SUSUPTI), Finest Consciousness (SUKSHMA) and a state of pure consciousness (Tureeya)[130] are four types of consciousness which defines the type of mental and intellectual status of an individual. This state of Consciousness is mot inwardly cognitive, nor outwardly cognitive, not even cognitive from the either sides. It cannot be identified as a

---

[130] *Turiya is discussed in Verse 7 of the Mandukya Upanishad.*

cognition-mass, not cognitive, not non-cognitive and unseen; with which there can be no dealing of any type or of any degree. It remains ungraspable, having no distinctive or recognizable marks; one cannot even think about it and also cannot be designated by any means or by any parameters. It acts as the essence of assurance, of which is the state of converged intellects and memory status implants the cessation of development, tranquil, benign and oneness. It also signifies attachment of the spirit to the admixture of the combination of other three states of consciousness and is designated as the fourth one. Consciousness possessed by the Self (Atman) is the realm of a being which confirms the personality blend with which an individual remain active in society. Such state of Atman should be discerned. It is (Tureeya state of consciousness) the state where spiritual self is properly realised, mental balance is actualized and is characterized as self-luminous, blissful, non-suffering state of mind and intellect.[131]

This consciousness will signify our approach towards life, our approach towards other beings and our bands of acceptability, or mental and spiritual sanction, with which we are going to accept some sort of doctrines and principles. Our rejection or opposition to some sort of doctrines and principles are also guided by the state of consciousness which implies an assurance of attainment of security for the individual, family unit and also for the ideals with which the unit of beings are becoming progressive.

Do all individuals gain mastery in terms of the attainment of the fourth state of mental and spiritual consciousness of desired types? Without any doubt we aspire for the progress of all individuals irrespective of any physical, psychological, spiritual or any other differences. They all are equally capable of gaining mastery to enjoy the blissful world of mental and intellectual consciousness.

---

[131] *Comans, Michael (2000). "The Method of Early Advaita Vedānta: A Study of Gauḍapāda, Śaṅkara, Sureśvara, and Padmapāda". Delhi: Motilal Banarsidass.*

Confluence of Ideals with harmony

Harmonious blend of mental and intellectual performance will be pitched in properly in the immediate surrounding during the state of the balanced consciousness of fourth type duly impregnated with all the other components of sub conscious and super-conscious states of mind and intellect. It will also signify our approaches with which we start accepting others in the realm of our different bands of activities. We accept or reject, for an example, services offered by any service professionals (doctors, teachers, engineers etc.) in the realm of our community on the ground of some sort of wills and wishes which we want to be fulfilled by the expected efforts of the service professional. We also see the world community getting divided in terms of the judicious use of Nuclear Power as duly coined by United Nations and equally being rejected by some of the war mongers. We have also witnessed, as was evident during the post war turmoil of 1941, the failure of the League of Nations and witnessed the mushrooming of violent warfare which continued up to 1945. People may say that the turmoil was terminated after bombarding Hiroshima. But the on-going facts and figures signify that the turmoil is still remaining ignited and may take the entire world in its serpentine flame at any moment. Being inflicted with such fear rest of the other nations prefers remaining engaged in mechanizing the warfare for the purpose of addressing violent warfare with much accelerated and violent retaliations.

We all know the ultimate as well as confirmed result of a war as per the format with which war mongering is continuously becoming progressive at different out pockets of society. Then also people fail to address the lumen of tension with a set of peaceful resolutions simply because of the practices of one sided efforts inflicted utterly with ambitions of superimposing wills and wishes upon some other community without indulging in safeguarding the progress and prosperity of the participant sub—groups of the referred community. We also witness the efforts and series of resolutions passed by United Nations for the purpose of retaining world peace. Then also countries prefer raising guns against each other. They prefer grabbing resources of other nations and continue violating internationally sanctioned laws. Development of group and sub-group is becoming the non-avoidable reality due to such kind of crippled apprehension of different nations.

.

Change initiated from Individual

We deserve attainment of positive approaches of life so as to ensure retention of world peace through exercising some fruitful alteration of the approaches with which global war mongers are remaining active. Such kinds of war mongers are playing the fatal game at the cost of life and prosperity of their fellow citizen. They are also bringing calamity in the form of unrest and misery. Loss of productivity is another unavoidable fate of the act of war mongering.

Since any of the government or any community is the combination of some of the empowered individuals there requires attainment of a balanced mind-set of the individual stakeholders of the community. Being charged with such kind of positive impetus they start working in a team and continue aspiring for some sort of fruitful resolutions for their reference community. Here comes the state when such community will prefer working in a team for want of a structured as well as developmental apprehension. It is fact that none of the nation states in this world are absolutely fit for exercising any of their development activities by keeping them off the track of global cooperation and mutual conducts. They are also equally exposed to all kinds of globally developing changes.

It is the role of education through which collective process of acculturation will work upon a community for enabling them to attain the desired level of mental and intellectual state of understanding collectively for all the participant members. It will also ensure the collectiveness with which the community members start working. They also start feeling the essence with which other community members and participants of extended commune are remaining active and should be allowed to remain active in the nation state. Exercises of all types (administrative, social, economic, technical or any other type) become equally configured after receiving the participatory impetus of the community members of any functional unit. Factory owner, for an example, may not remain at the work station for all the moment for implying a strong vigil upon the hands which are assigned for hammering the hot iron for the purpose of making the productivity accelerated. The participant workers should have adequate understanding of productivity cycle from which they are also sharing a benefit. Sudden halt or some other implications duly implied upon the productivity will influence their share up to a considerable mark. If all workers start working with such kind of collective apprehension then it is obvious that both productivity and the share of fellow workers on operational cycle will be secured. It is also true that the participatory effort impregnated with one sided apprehension of gaining advantage may not continue for a longer time. It will even hamper the sustainability of the entire system leading towards damage of human relations.

.

Benefit of Tolerance

Winning the heart of enemy, as duly proposed by Mahatma, is the highest spiritual bliss with which a society gains progressive momentum. It is also proposed by Vedantic as well as Biblical doctrines and is also addressed by thinkers and philosophers time to time. It is considered as the impetus with which we can kill the feeling of enemy that often gains a permanent shelter in the mind and intellect of the person working as an opponent of a group or community in a specified surrounding. Winning "hearts and minds of people" is used effectively at various instances to stop or to nullify the chances of counter insurgency in a territory having experiences of any war or any revolt.[132]

---

[132] *Russia recorded a better mechanism of tackling the situation of counter insurgency after their experiences in Afghanistan and Chechen War. Reference: Zhukov, Yuri M. (2012). "Counterinsurgency in a non- democratic state: the Russian example". The Routledge Handbook of Insurgency and Counterinsurgency. Routledge. pp. 293–307. doi:10.4324/9780203132609-32. ISBN 978-0-203-13260-9.*

People of America consider this term "winning the heart and mind of people", on the basis of the doctrine narrated by John Adams[133], to signify the radical change in the mind and approaches of people which continued during the revolution. It also signified a change in their religious sentiments and duties to the Nation State. They dramatically brought their wider bands of unity to make the birth of Democracy a reality.

Spiritual bliss with which saints and social reformers work to keep the community united is also evident from different prehistoric scriptures and ancient historical records. Upanishads also maintained practices of such doctrines for establishing good governance in a state.[134]

First and foremost question which strikes our mind instantly is the spiritual identity of a life. Life is restricted to the cycle of birth, development and death. The span between birth and death may be a prolonged one or may be followed by an immediate succession. Some fellow worshippers of knowledge understand this trend easily and consider the divine power as an immortal entity. Some other individuals remain in the clutch of confusion for a long time and fail to recognize the divine as any separate entity. Varieties of qualities in humans; such as intellect, knowledge, clarity of thought, forgiveness, truthfulness, control over the senses and mind, joy and sorrow, birth and death, fear and courage, non-violence, equanimity, contentment, austerity, charity, fame, and infamy; all develop from the supreme sense which implies a command upon memory, intellect and ego.[135] Combination of all such qualities may vary considerably. Combination of such qualities finalise the nature of an individual. Some of the combination may be wiser and some other combination may be demonic.

---

[133] *Reference: Bernard Bailyn (1992). The Ideological Origins of the American Revolution. Harvard University Press. p. 160. ISBN 9780674443020. Retrieved 20 January 2013.*

[134] *Comans, Michael (2000). "The Method of Early Advaita Vedānta: A Study of Gauḍapāda, Śaṅkara, Sureśvara, and Padmapāda". Delhi: Motilal Banarsidass.*

[135] *Bhagvadgita X – 4-5;*

The yoga of devotion makes the individual linked to the divine power and with such inclination a devotee gains the sense of divine omnipresence quite easily. Such individual considers the diversity of all the living forms as a form radiated out from the divine. All such forms even remain restricted to the divine and get merged to the source after completion of life. It is similar to the act of the formation of clouds at the ocean bed and development of streams due to down pour from the clouds. All these acts jointly ensure the cyclic movement of water from ocean to mountains and again from mountains to oceans through streams. Intermediate results may be of many types and many forms, but the real identity of water droplet remains unchanged.

Whatever we acquire in the form of knowledge will enrich the society in different ways and even it will enrich our efforts of feeling the omnipresence of the divine power. Lord describes himself as an inseparable entity of different forms and capacities which remain prevalent in the surrounding. Lord Shiva, for an example, among Rudras is divine. Every individual in this universe are capable of feeling the oneness with the divine, but they may not be capable of accommodating the source as we may not be able to accommodate the sun in our immediate surroundings. We can feel the warmth and illumination of the sun from a safest distance. Before reaching the ground such radiation is even filtered by the realm of atmosphere. We are absolutely incapable of assimilating the ultraviolet radiations at even a fraction of a percent. Such radiations are competent enough in killing any life forms. On the other hand we cannot think about birth and manifestation of any life form without the sun.

The person having true knowledge of the cycle of creation and destruction keep faith on the divine power and start exploring the existence of such power within the self. Two types of individuals see such a divine power in two different ways: one can recognize it as an inseparable part of the self and other can recognize it as a separate entity having no linkage to the self.

It is more important for an individual to realise the Divine omnipresence; that sense is the only positive impulse which is capable enough in linking up the living form to the nature with perfect band of participatory efforts; such effort will bring desired results during every instances of the functional involvement of the individual in society. Vedic rituals, medicinal herbs, worships of all types and cultivation of knowledge are nothing but different aspects of realising the omni-presence of divine power.[136]   One can recognize the role of the divine power in different realms of creation and destruction.

Person having noble conducts in society remain there in the memory of individuals for a considerable time and may secure a prominent position in the history of development. Such an individual even secure a prominent position amongst nobles because of noble deeds. They even imply a notable influence upon the social conducts. Their contribution in terms of knowledge enrichment may even become the part of the treasure of Vedas. The only lord worshipped by people is the divine power or the creation element (Purush). Common individuals do not know that they worship the supreme creation elements in varying forms. All actions, conducts, rituals and worships should be aimed ultimately towards worshiping the supreme creation element (Purush). We can even maintain our utter faith on the role of such a creation element in making the process of all the creations true.

Even sinners come out of the clutches of sin after knowing the ultimate fate of such sins and start residing in the process recognizing the presence of creator element (Purush) by the side of the holy creations. They even start recognizing the wider form of the divine manifestation and start delivering their duty in the society with an altered conducts. They quickly get the shelter of the divine and start defining their role in society.

The mighty wind blowing everywhere rests always in sky. In the same way all the organisms rest always in the divine lord and get manifested accordingly when time permits. At the end of one creation cycle all the organisms duly created will be merged into the realm of

---

[136] *Bhagvadgita IX – 15-18:*
Cultivators of knowledge worship supreme lord as an entity. They recognize the diversified forms of such divine power at different instances. Divine power is the worship, Vedic chanting, the fire , the butter and the rituals. Divine is the object of knowledge, the creator element and the Pranava (Om). It is the basis of everything that we see. It has its presence as a creator as well as destroyer element in the universe.

materials and energy and the entire collection of such kind of lump will be directed towards any of the black hole towards which the centrally located star system will feel the power of attraction. The situation of such a dramatic withdrawal of the diversity of creation may be initiated at any moment. None of the creations and destructions of any types are ever capable of binding the divine power in them. This creator power (the PURUSH element in accord to Sankhya Philosophy) remains independent of the realm of creation and destruction. It ensures the process without being involved actively in the entire process of manifestation. Buddhism adopted changes incorporated in Vedic rituals and other traditional doctrines, which remained in practice through Vedic, Sankhya and Yoga based rituals.[137]

Divine power of such a doer type may often remain non-recognisable because of the non-association of such power in the process of creation. We often recognize the intellect and soul holding such intellect as the creator element. The soul and intellect can have a reflection of the creator superconscious doer element but it cannot be ascribed directly as a doer. We also recognize the soul of an individual as a non-destroyable entity as that of the divine power. It is similar to that of a stream of water joins the other and a beam of light joins the other. All such sources lose their individual identity before joining. Similar the thing is true regarding diffusion of soul in the surrounding when any individual dies. Band of energy get absorbed in the celestial collection and may be utilized at some other instances randomly during some other phases of creations.

Because of this reason material world moves through series of changes and one change is followed by series of other changes of varying degree and intensity.

Is there any clear distinction in the process of socialisation of human beings during which we may witness activation of a Divine Power (in the form of a Prophet or AVATARA) amongst us? What kind of indications may be there depending upon which we start claiming omnipresence of

[137] *Tadeusz Skorupski (2015). Michael Witzel (ed.). Homa Variations: The Study of Ritual Change Across the Longue Durée. Oxford University Press. pp. 78–81. ISBN 978-0-19-935158-9.*

such power beside us during all instances? The Bhagavadgita highlighted it clearly during discourses in the fourth chapter.[138] Even the purpose of such manifestation is narrated by the Divine Power.[139] People, along with clear understanding of the ways and means of this divine manifestation, succeed in keeping oneself devoid of material attachment to the nature and remain contented thoroughly; by doing so they enjoy the optimum liberation.

Expectations in General

What we want from our immediate surrounding will finalise our comprehensive approach with which exploration of resources and technologies will be advanced. Our effort of linking up resources and technology will confer the effort with which we also want people to get associated with us. Our kind of will inflicted primarily with a sort of bias will generate a sort of agony in the mind of other community or ethnic group of any distant location. One sided aspiration of progress may even give birth to the sort of agony and misconduct. It may even give birth to group clashes and other oppressive conducts of varying types. We are witnessing similar kinds of unrest which are mushrooming at different out pockets of our society. We are, keeping pace with the progressive trend of conflicts, becoming bound to tackle such problems day by day.

It is also obvious that replacement of armed forces by the acts and conducts of nonviolent resolution may not bring immediate result as some of the countries are badly inflicted with an intention of grabbing resources, lands and technologies of other states without taking care of the aspirations of people settled in the state. Violation of such kinds of basic rules may bring nations back to the war front as some of the leading nations remain indulged in such kind of proxy war, cold war and armed operations. Leadership characters of those conflicting states may

---

[138] *"Whenever there is a decline in righteousness and a corresponding increase in unrighteousness, The Lord manifest and become active amongst us on earth"*
......The Bhagavadgita IV 7.
[139] *"Lord manifest and dwell amongst us to fulfill various purposes; it is not confirmed but can be proposed; to protect the righteous, to annihilate the wicked, and to re-establish the principles of dharma; the Divine Lord appear on this earth, time to time and age after age" ..... The Bhagavadgita IV 8*

also put other nations in trouble as the flow of resources, man power and currencies went on linked and interlinked day by day since last couple of decades. Bringing them out of such network will be easy to say but difficult to implement.

At some instances we may come across the situation during which some of the small and marginal stakeholders living within the jurisdiction of a state may claim that they are in the verge of extinction due to non-supportive policies of the Nation State. Lack of any kind of inclusiveness in the entire framework of development plan may give birth to such kind of separatism and unrest with which some of the states like India are suffering. Addressing all such wills and wishes while keeping the issues of National Security intact is really a matter of deep concern and is open for arranging an intensive study and scholastic interventions. We cannot go on dreaming about any rapid solution to such kinds of burning issues. Boroland of Assam, for an example, is receiving extensive in-migration of different types of Non-Boro Community and are agitating against such kind of state sponsored or some sort of illegal in-migrations. Their demand for a state to safeguard their cultural and social integrity is still a burning issue which puts even India Government in trouble.

We have examples of such kinds of unrest and agony in plenty. It also indicates that the state policy lacks some sort of inclusive efforts with which such kinds of issues would have been addressed effectively. Plans were made as a fraction of the large segments with an anticipation of gaining participation from the reference community but their faith, cultural blend and spiritual orientation utterly kept aside. It was also a plan inflicted with partial motive force of development which gained a negative response from the community members. Expectation of such type, as state planners are coining, should have some sort of comprehensive study and a kind of acculturation with which active participation of the community will be advanced. We are here to sort out such kinds of comprehensive planning process impregnated with resolutions of Peace and Nonviolence to make up our mind for comprehensive and collective progress.

To understand our expectations in a better way it would be better if we move on through an incident which was recorded during execution of a welfare activity at a village level. A farmer named Budhu received a pair of bullock from a nationalized bank. Because of certain health problem he has lost one bullock within a span of one year. Another unpaired bullock became useless. Bank wanted to recover the loan amount form him. He had two alternatives. With the help of the primary teacher of the nearby primary school he has submitted an application to the Branch Manager of the bank requesting him to provide a bullock or to take the living one back.

The application was of a peculiar type. This incident took place in a village under Nimdih Block of Saraikela, Jharkhand. Logically Budhu admitted his problem and requested a support from the financial institution. Bank had no such provision of allocating fund for a single bullock or to take the live bullock back. Because of that reason application of Budhu was kept aside. He appeal for a solution remained buried under the heap of pending applications. After a gap of five years, a new bank officer took the charge of that branch. By that time loan amount which remained in the name of Budhu became a major amount. By paying such amount one can purchase two pairs of bullock similar to those assigned to Budhu. The scheme under which Budhu received such support was under the scheme of Integrated Rural Development Scheme sanctioned by the Government. The matter went to the judiciary. Coming out of the problem and giving any adequate remedy was not in the hand of Bank, Government or even Budhu himself. The only annoying thing happening was the expenses upon the bullock which had no adequate financial return.

There was another Ashram School Teacher working in the locality. He was even popular amongst villagers because of his timely services. He came to know about the incident. The fellow teacher used to move frequently in the surrounding villages. Because of that reason he had another farmer like Budhu having only one bullock alive. He had arranged a meeting of both the farmer to sort out the problem. Both the farmer decided to work together in a condition of exchanging bullocks for alternate period of six months. Legal proceedings went in the favour of Budhu. There was adequate scope for Budhu to take another pair of bullock from the bank. But the offer was not considered fruitful by the fellow farmer because of his bitter experiences that he went through recently.

This incident tells us about the limitations of the support services of bank, government or any other welfare institutions. Coming out of the boundary for delivering timely relevant service requires flexibility. The kind of such flexibility is lacking in the present day system of support mechanism. Ultimately farmer, other socially active group and social workers came close to sort out a solution which can give immediate ease to the victim. Because of lack of certain technological input, the problem became a big one. There are instruments that can be handled efficiently even by using a single bullock. That sort of technology was absolutely unknown to both the farmers as well as to the officials. Installation of any system, monitoring of the same for a stipulated time span, giving support services to the reference group for a selected period of time and helping the person in gaining adequate pace in the production practices are some of the components which should have adequate place in the planning of extending any financial support. Loss of any kind at any place should be considered as a loss to the Nation State.

It is absolutely clear that people involved in the welfare activities rarely bring themselves perfectly in the forefront with adequate enthu; they even lose regulations upon the system due to complications of the planning and implementation process of schemes; lack of spiritual blend in the entire system of financial regulation and execution of the same is another matter of serious concern.

In the context of the Gita it can be advanced that one may not attain perfectness by merely abstaining from regular and assigned works, nor can one attain perfection of knowledge, skill and reverence by mere renunciation in terms of physical or material means.[140] It is also not possible to contemplate on the divine omnipresence simply on the basis

---

[140] *Bhagavadgita III.4*

of literal knowledge. One can rarely lead normal life and can remain active without getting involved in obligatory functions of physical as well as material means; such as taking regular meal, performing bodily functions, assigning tasks to different organ and system, performing duties duly assigned by fellow master, etc. Individuals restraining external organs of actions while continuing to dwell on sense objects in the mind, certainly delude themselves and are to be called hypocrites. Yogis remain engage along with active senses in working without attachment, are certainly superior. They retain adequate regulations upon their senses and continue inducting themselves for accepting assigned duties. One can perform Vedic duties with adequate sincerity, since action is superior to inaction. By ceasing regularised obligatory physical activity, bodily maintenance of an individual will not be possible. [141] It is too difficult to retain physical existence without performing any action even for a moment.

We must consider works as Yajna (a holy sacrifice meant for the Divine) otherwise actions of any kind may create material attachment. Such attachment, in turn, will bring miseries and sorrow; individuals are created by the Divine along with certain predetermined duties in this universe; individuals got a definite number of pulsations for ensuring their adequate span of participation in society; society ensures different bands of rights and duties for all the individuals. Such participation will ensure proper adjustment of individual and the Divine and such adjustment ensure normal confluence of collective progress in a society; such participation will grant access of individuals to all sorts of necessities meant for leading a normal life; it will also ensure feeling of the Divine omnipresence in the mind and intellect of a Yogi; a new band of positive participatory skill will be developed for ensuring practices related to collective worship.[142] Taking meal after offering the same to the Divine will gain liberation from sins; such food is cultivated by fellow farmers while taking support of the nature (rain, soil, air, sunlight, living producer community etc.); all these acts and conducts are duly incorporated in Vedas; such scriptures also instruct us to consider acts,

---

[141] *Bhagavadgita III 5-8*
[142] *The Bhagavadgita III 9-12*

conducts and discourses as Holy Sacrifice (YAJNA).[143] The term Yajna appeared in early Vedic literature during 2nd Millenium B.C.E.[144] There exists a wider meaning of Yajna in our sacred literature: Yajna is really the chaste life of the student of sacred knowledge, for only through the chaste life of a worshipper or follower of the path of knowledge; Istam (sacrificial offering) is really the chaste life of the student of sacred knowledge, on the path of such sacred life one can find the impetus of Atman.[145] Buddhism added some additional concepts and rituals in this regard and made the spiritually oriented concept of worship widely applicable.[146]

We will consider distinct approaches with which "Truth" is to be addressed. True beliefs and true statements correspond to the actual state of affairs or doctrines can be considered as Truth.[147] Being a traditional model duly popularized by great thinkers and philosophers this model correlates thoughts and things in a better way. A judgement can be considered as true if it correlates the external reality and facts.[148] Truth is also considered as an objective reality which is often ascribed through thoughts, words and other means.[149] Obstacle due to variations of language and dialect is considered as a limiting factor due to which any universal definition of the doctrines related to "Truth (SATYA in Sanskrit) cannot be generalised. If we put concepts into practice then the result or outcome of such practice will confirm the nature of Truth (a

---

[143] *Yajna has been a Vedic tradition, described in a layer of Vedic literature called Brahmanas, as well as Yajurveda.*
Reference: Laurie Patton (2005), The Hindu World (Editors: Sushil Mittal, Gene Thursby), Routledge, ISBN 978-0415772273, pages 38–39.
[144] *Monier Monier-Williams, Sanskrit English Dictionary, Oxford University Press, ISBN 978-8120831056 (Reprinted in 2011), pages 839–840*
[145] *Robert Hume, Chandogya Upanishad 8.5.1, Oxford University Press, page 266*
[146] *Tadeusz Skorupski (2015). Michael Witzel (ed.). Homa Variations: The Study of Ritual Change Across the Longue Durée. Oxford University Press. pp. 78–81. ISBN 978-0-19-935158-9.*
[147] *Encyclopedia of Philosophy, Vol.2, "Correspondence Theory of Truth", auth.: Arthur N. Prior, p. 223 (Macmillan, 1969).*
[148] *"Correspondence Theory of Truth", in Stanford Encyclopedia of Philosophy (citing De Veritate Q.1, A.1–3 and Summa Theologiae, I. Q.16).*
[149] *See, e.g., Bradley, F.H., "On Truth and Copying", in Blackburn, et al. (eds., 1999),Truth, 31–45.*

Pragmatic Approach)[150]. Concordance of abstract statements with the ideal limit towards which hundreds of investigations can be advanced to bring out essential ingredients of Truth is considered as a basis through which one can assess Truth.[151] True is the expedient in our way of thinking and Right is the expedient in our way of behaving.[152] Truth is a quality the value of which is confirmed by the effectiveness when applying concepts into practice.

From another angle it is confirmed that what works may or may not be considered as Truth, but what fails cannot be considered as a representation of Truth. It can be advanced only because Truth never fails.[153] We cannot confer with facts and figures that we are right during all instances, but we can easily identify instances when we are wrong.[154] Nothing considered absolutely true as some other angles of observation may consider a fact true after altering the collections of facts and figures. This is a kind of superficial examination with which nature of Truth is defined. It has limitations of approach which remained restricted to the materialistic view of facts, figures, propositions and concepts. Deflationary theory maintains a clear view that "Truth" is an expressive predicate requiring no additional explanation.[155]

Importance of AHIMSA (Nonviolence) and Peace in real life is rightly pointed out even at different instances of the Gita; the site where the Divine master guides a confused prince to play a definite role while standing in between two armed forces standing against each other. To trace out the real nature of the doctrine of Nonviolence we have to move back through pages of scriptures and Epics. Yoga Philosophy defined the ritual of Nonviolence in such a way that highest spiritual refinement of

---

[150] *Encyclopedia of Philosophy, Vol. 5, "Pragmatic Theory of Truth", 427 (Macmillan, 1969).*

[151] *Peirce, C.S. (1901), "Truth and Falsity and Error" (in part), pp. 716–20 in James Mark Baldwin, ed., Dictionary of Philosophy and Psychology, v. 2. Peirce's section is entitled "Logical", beginning on p. 718, column 1, and ending on p. 720 with the initials "(C.S.P.)"*

[152] *James, William, The Meaning of Truth, A Sequel to 'Pragmatism', (1909).*

[153] *Sahakian, W.S. & Sahakian, M.L., Ideas of the Great Philosophers, New York: Barnes & Noble, 1966, LCCN 66--23155*

[154] *Feynman, The Character of Physical Law, New York: Random House, 1994, ISBN 0-679-60127-9.*

[155] *Encyclopedia of Philosophy, Supp., "Truth", auth: Michael Williams, pp. 572–73 (Macmillan, 1996)*

an individual is duly accommodated in that ritual. It defines Nonviolence (AHIMSA) as follows:

"If we say that Nonviolence (AHIMSA) is established in any context then organisms residing that context will coexist with family feelings. They even cast off their feelings of hatred and agony. They make them contented by exercising living within minimum."

If we try to restrict this doctrine of Peace and Nonviolence then also it will become evident that both nonviolence and peace got adequate importance in all schools of religion. None of the religions in this world preaches people to adopt violent means for ensuring survival and prosperity of community members. Ethical philosophy of Jainism (after Saint Mahaveera) prepared an extraordinary status for the doctrine of Peace and Nonviolence.[156] Attentiveness of the law making and law implementing agencies ensure chances of acceptance or rejection of nonviolent proposals during any of the instances as per need or as per consent of people.[157]

We will elaborate different aspects related to socialisation and acculturation of an individual in the light of the knowledge confluence which is rightly materialised in the Gita.

---

[156] *Stephen H. Phillips & other authors (2008), in Encyclopedia of Violence, Peace, & Conflict (Second Edition), ISBN 978-0-12-373985-8, Elsevier Science, Pages 1347–1356, 701–849, 1867.*

[157] *Sharp, Gene (1973). The Politics of Nonviolent Action. Porter Sargent. p. 12. ISBN 978-0-87558-068-5.*

2. The Source

Do sources of knowledge trying to integrate different scriptures having explanations, instructions and basic doctrines related to Yoga equip our society efficiently for developing a comprehensive strategy of Yoga? Do we claim perfectly with absolute confidence that only Vedic Scriptures and other schools depending on Veda directly or indirectly are the only reliable sources from which doctrines of Yoga can be worked out? Strategy of integrating doctrines at different instances is made efficiently in The Bhagavadgita. Several evidences in this regard can be advanced to justify the above mentioned statement. Several other sources are there in plenty to strengthen our faith.

योग: कर्मसु कौशलम् ...   158

"Yoga Karmasu Koushalam; or   doing works skilfully; delivering duties skilfully with efficient strategy is Yoga."

It is an art of doing works skilfully; as such skilful works require enrichment the knowledge and skills of the fellow aspirant; as such efficiencies always depend upon the way fellow aspirant attends the challenging moments; as such kinds of sincere involvement of the fellow aspirant in addressing challenges requires a strategic planning. Yoga is the state of human consciousness which establishes linkages and union in between the individual and the Divine through different means of progress and spiritual practices.   Yoga confers the initiative of recognising the supreme creator power besides all sorts of worldly creations. It has the inherent incredible potential to bring enrichment, competency enhancement, stability, decision-making quality refinement, fearlessness, endurance, insight, etc. to bestow its followers.

Only a mind full of words, ideas and ideals cannot work properly, only a body with a strong physique can also make any action a

---

[158] *The Bhagavadgita II. 50;*

half dome, only skill can wait for some fretful and coordinated instructions of the mind and only intellect may indulge in some sort of arguments. That is why coordinated actions of all the parts of the individual will be the only way out.

Coordinated actions will open up horizons of the possibilities of culmination of perfectly planned actions with desired state of performance. It may not wait for the results of the previous action to come. It will indulge oneself in the vibrant process of organised actions with an aspiration of feeling one's ascent through the path of spirituality and will power. Importance of nature in our daily life is a matter beyond the questions and conflicts. For understanding such role, with a clear distinction between acts, conducts and necessity, we may go through a popular story of a beggar and King of all kings.

The conservation strategy is gaining a momentum. It is also widening the information gap between people and government. The schemes launched by government often remain off the record of people simply because of their non-participation. Due to this reason participation of people in making the schemes successful often remain off the track. We cannot put a hold on the intrusion of unauthorized hunters and poachers in the referred area of the wild habitat. We, alone on the basis of some legal frameworks, cannot put a halt on any unlawful acts and conducts of people leading to a loss of normalcy in forest biota. We simply adopt a collaborative effort by establishing proper coordination between people, government and environment through ensuring timely participation of people in the planned efforts of the government and conservators. From evidences available in nature, it has become clear that native Indians are not a threat to the wild population. They prefer living in a harmony as an ideal harvester of the forest resource. Their intended effort is meant simply for harvesting a living without implying any harm to the population residing there. Honey hunters of Sundarban and Kanha reserve forest are of such type. They rarely put a halt in the normal wandering attitude of wild animals. In Gir forest some native Indians even communicate with big cats by producing special types of sound. The fellow lion understands such dialogue and gives a way out. It is a best example of the coexistence of people and animal with an aspiration of sharing the commonly available resources.

Conflicting situation may develop any time and at any place. If we consider the modern mechanized warfare then it is becoming evident that modern wars may rarely last for a couple of days, or hardly for a couple of weeks. On the other hand, it will be so devastating that one can rarely traces out the group of warriors indulged differently in that war. This may happen only because of the extreme mechanization of the warfare.

It is also true that we cannot move on mechanizing any warfare anymore because of the involvement of a huge sanction. People, in the modern society, rarely move on for affording a war. They all imply adequate impetus on ensuring the establishment of peace, prosperity and brotherhood in our society. This effort cannot limit its expansion by any border; it can have a normal confluence through countries and states; even it can have adequate hold on the community living throughout the globe.

We all are familiar with different aspects of the holy book The Gita. It has its root deeply embedded inside the teachings of Upanishad. Upanishad, in turn, has deeply embedded roots of instructions and rituals inside Vedas. All the Vedas provide absolute knowledge to individuals having affinity of gaining prosperity in life. Remaining prosperous and ultimately imbibing the spirit of the divine is the ultimate goal of a life.

What people learn and assimilate is ensured by the cultural, social and emotional bands of the knowledge base with which participation of the person in a referred community is duly ensured. If we talk about unity in the context of Indian sub-continent then we will allocate our aspirations with the recess with which people of other continents are interacting with each other. Social and cultural bond of different communities of Indian Sub-Continent are influenced by Vedic Culture and epics. People learned to participate in social and cultural functions as per their affinities towards the social, cultural and economic bonds.

This continent has a history of invasions. But the rulers and countrymen of this region had rarely invaded any other continents simply for ensuring expansion of the territory. Invasions planned by emperor Ashoka was for the spread of the religious thought process which the fellow emperor considered a wiser and ideal one for people of all walks of life.

In the line of spiritual progress and for the cultivation of true knowledge the most interpreted creation from the Indian context was the Bhagavadgita. It is a 700-verse Hindu scripture that was developed as an inseparable part of the epic Mahabharata (chapters 23 to 40 of book 6 of the Epic called the Bhishma Parva), dated to the second half of the first millennium BCE. It was also identified as a typical of the Vedic synthesis having integration of Vedantic, Sankhyic and Yoga Philosophy of Indian origin. It is considered to be one of the Holy Scriptures for people of places developed and ruled by Aryans[159]. The philosophical issues and doubts developed in the mind of a warrior amidst a battle field were attended efficiently by lord Krishna. His discourse on various spiritual issues went on far beyond the scope of the war with which the fellow warrior was dealing[160]. Theistic scholars interpreted the term Bhagavadgita as "Rhe Words of God[161]." The Iswara Gita, Hari Gita, Ananta Gita, Vyasa Gita and some other creations are the diverged dimensions of the same creation represented by Veda Vyasa in the epic[162]. The basic creation of the integrated spiritual teachings in the form of a poetic dialogue is developed primarily by sage Veda Vyasa[163]. Different saints might have added different parts in the holy book time to time to make the creation enriched one. That is why gradual integration of Vedantic, Yogic and Sankhya philosophy went on continuing through ages[164]. Perhaps with the same effort of integration of various teachings the epic Mahabharata was also growing. Along with different evidences

---

[159] Davis, Richard H. (2014), The 'Bhagavad Gita': A Biography, Princeton University Press, ISBN 9780691139968

[160] Sargeant, Winthrop (2009), Christopher Key Chapple (ed.), The Bhagavad Gītā: Twenty-fifth Anniversary Edition, State University of New York Press, ISBN 978-1-4384-2841-3

[161] Swami Prabhavananda; Christopher Isherwood (2002). Bhagavad-Gita: The words of God. Signet Classic. ISBN 978-0-451-52844-5.

[162] Sharma, Arvind (1986). The Hindu Gītā: Ancient and Classical Interpretations of the Bhagavadgītā. London: Open Court. ISBN 978-0-8126-9013-2.

[163] Fowler, Jeaneane D (2012), The Bhagavad Gita: A Text and Commentary for Students, Eastbourne: Sussex Academy Press, ISBN 978-1-84519-520-5

[164] Upadhyaya, Kashi Nath (1998), Early Buddhism and the Bhagavadgītā, Motilal Banarsidass Publ, ISBN 978-81-208-0880-5

it is confirmed that the holy book was compiled by many authors and was also enriched time to time by many saints[165].

Second century BCE would be the probable time when the compilation of the Gita came in practice and the series of modifications went on periodically afterwards[166]. Probably the latest date of compilation of the holy book would be around the first century CE[167]. The holy book was compiled during the age when ethics of war was under a question mark and importance of renunciation was gaining popularity[168].

The Bhagavadgita principally deals with the spiritual ascent of an individual through ladders of duties and enlightenment of the self through gaining proper culmination of knowledge, devotion and services as are required for attainment of renunciation[169]. It is a great synthesis of impersonal spiritual monism with the personal god[170]. 700[171] verses of Bhagavadgita are structured in several ancient Indian poetic meters incorporated in 118 different chapters. Different chapters are interpreted differently by thinkers and philosophers time to time.

The main focus of the discussion will be on the way Acharya Vinoba developed a comprehensive thought process alongside the normal confluence of the conversation between the God and the warrior. It was judged accordingly to work out the relevance of the teachings of Gita on the basis of present day context. War like situation is still there in

---

[165] Minor 1982, p. xxxiv, Quote: "Therefore, instead of the traditional view of authorship, many scholars have argued that the Gita is not the work of one author but a composite work.".

[166] Fowler, Jeaneane D (2012), The Bhagavad Gita: A Text and Commentary for Students, Eastbourne: Sussex Academy Press, ISBN 978-1-84519-520-5

[167] Upadhyaya, Kashi Nath (1998), Early Buddhism and the Bhagavadgītā, Motilal Banarsidass Publ, ISBN 978-81-208-0880-5

[168] Arthur Llewellyn Basham (1991). The Origins and Development of Classical Hinduism. Oxford University Press. pp. 95–96. ISBN 978-0-19-507349-2.

[169] Robin Gill (2017). Moral Passion and Christian Ethics. Cambridge University Press. pp. 129–130. ISBN 978-1-107-17682-9.

[170] Raju, P.T. (1992), The Philosophical Traditions of India, Delhi: Motilal Banarsidass Publishers Private Limited

[171] Minor 1982, pp. l–li, Quote: "The current text of the Bhagavad Gita is well-preserved with relatively few variant readings and none quite serious. This is especially remarkable in the light of the numerous variants for the remainder of the Mahabharata, some of which are quite serious. Secondary insertions are found in individual manuscripts of the Gita, but these are clearly secondary. The number of stanzas in the Gita is 700, a number confirmed by Shankara, and possibly deliberately chosen in order to prevent interpolations."

and around us and us all aspire for an abled guidance from masterly instructions for overcoming the situation. The Upanishadic concept of absolute reality, a sharp deviation from the ritual driven Vedic Religion, is advanced by teachings of the Gita[172]. A focus upon a neuter principle is also advanced by this holy book at different places[173]. Atman[174] as a foundational concept is established by the principles of the Gita[175]. It also accepts Atman as a pure, unchanging and real essence of the self. An effort to combine Sankhya and Vedanta Philosophy with a clear apprehension of addressing the individual refinement through culmination of knowledge, devotion and performed actions is dealt efficiently in the holy book. It was, in that context of an effort to linking up different schools of philosophy, can be considered as an effort of reviving the spiritual faith of people during epic age.

"Atman = Brahman" as duly developed by Upanishads has maintained the central position in the Bhagavadgita[176]. The paths of knowledge, devotion or actions (performing duties) lead ultimately to renunciation. The perfect combination of the entire three paths determines the basic human nature of an individual[177]. Gita upholds the necessity of performing duties in society[178]. One should not escape or try to keep aside from the Karma or performing duties in society.

The simplicity and normal confluence with which lectures delivered by Acharya Vinoba Bhave has made the critical parts of the holy book easy to assimilate and internalise alongside the ever changing context of the society. It can be considered as an address to the world. Because of that reason the entire lecture series having combination of eighteen chatters are duly incorporated along with the recent study.

---

[172] Zaehner, R.C. (1969), The Bhagavad Gītā, Oxford University Press, ISBN 0-19-501666-1

[173] Zaehner, R.C. (1969), The Bhagavad Gītā, Oxford University Press, ISBN 0-19-501666-1

[174] Atman is a Sanskrit word which refers to the Good Self or Self extent essence of the individual.

[175] Fowler, Jeaneane D (2012), The Bhagavad Gita: A Text and Commentary for Students, Eastbourne: Sussex Academy Press, ISBN 978-1-84519-520-5

[176] Fowler, Jeaneane D (2012), The Bhagavad Gita: A Text and Commentary for Students, Eastbourne: Sussex Academy Press, ISBN 978-1-84519-520-5

[177] Franklin Edgerton (1952). The Bhagavad Gita, Part 2. Harvard University Press. pp. 44–45 with footnotes, context: pp. 30–54 (Part 2).

[178] Fowler, Jeaneane D (2012), The Bhagavad Gita: A Text and Commentary for Students, Eastbourne: Sussex Academy Press, ISBN 978-1-84519-520-5

We directly gain such a spark of the accumulation of the divine power within ourselves through cultivation of knowledge. Saints in olden time wanted to simplify the holy teachings for the purpose of making such teachings easy to assimilate for individuals of different walks of life. A state of confusion regarding duty of an individual in a society may develop at any time. It may even spoil the credential of an individual in society. Such a state of confusion may even give birth to a self-cantered apprehension of doing things. Such a state of self-cantered conduct may further lead to a state of violent ego. Person getting inflicted with such a state of violent ego may give birth to a conflict. It is also true that one can overcome the situation of the development of such a state of violent ego through cultivation of true knowledge. Bhagvadgita insists on gaining such kind of true knowledge which can ignite the mind with a feeling of the divine omnipresence.

Teachings of Bhagvadgita has its root duly converged from some prominent sources like Vedas, Upanishads, Yoga Philosophy and Sankhya Philosophy. Gita has successfully brought culmination of all the major schools of Indian philosophy for making the teachings of the Gita widely applicable and perpetually relevant. Gita also narrates the nature of conflicts and the role of knowledge, devotion and action to address such conflicts at different fronts. A warrior should attend a war for safeguarding the dependent ones; a saint should remain indulged in worshipping the holy master; a teacher should cultivate the true knowledge and also should pass on the same to the fellow students. Duty of a warrior should not be taken up with priority by any priest. Performing the duty in particular depends on the state of mind for which the intellectual sanction is ensured. Without putting oneself in a definite role in society one cannot confer about the type of duties to be accomplished at any instances. We simply put ourselves in a war front as a warrior and start delivering our duty as a perfect warrior. Swadharma (or duty of an individual in particular) is the state of mind for which the preparedness and knowledge acquisition was accomplished.

On the basis of the above discussion we can easily consider The Gita as a holy book of instructions and self-actualized guidance for which we often rely upon the Divine. We can coin any name for our

Divine master, but only name cannot alter its identity and character in particular. Our feelings pass on silently for accepting the supremacy such a guiding force having adequate hold upon our understanding and awareness. It will even facilitate us for attainment of some sort of completeness in due course of time.

the modern world we have various types of cultural and religious thought process advocating rituals, customs and traditions of different types, which are equally competent to enrich people in terms of knowledge assimilation, enhancement of devotion, courage, will power and dedication. The way we receive each of such culture to enrich our multiplurality will specify our degrees and ranges of success. Our motive force will guide accordingly to explore possibilities of working out converged cultural segments from all the rituals to move up towards vibrant as well as integrated waves of multi plurality.

India, at this juncture of the development of multiplurality, will be a best example for all of us. Here people learned a lot to live with each other tolerate each other and enrich each other differently. We cannot see light. Even we cannot see the propagation of sound through the material medium. Light strikes our eyes, reaches our brain and develops a sensation of vision through certain biochemically regulated life process of vision. With some sort of illusion, or lack of true knowledge only, we often claim that we can see light. Even all the colours radiated out from the sun are not recognisable by us. If God resides inside the individual, if all mysteries related to the ascent of a person on the path of divinity, then why any devotee search it out for gaining the blessings of any Divine power located outside the physically existing body? Why such a dwindling situation any individual face during the tenure of worship?

Lord Krishna narrated essence of feeling the Divine communion with the physically existing life through witnessing cultivation of knowledge, actualisation of the presence of any supreme power in sub conscious mind and possible ways and means to follow that power. It enables an individual to come across the feeling of the advent of some completeness in the mind through knowledge transformation. Cultivation of knowledge regarding the relationship of the divine and disciple is enrouted from the age old traditions through the turmoil of the organic evolution. That evolution brought some change in the process of exhibits, but the core remained the same. It was even more perpetual and more profound regarding the ability of harnessing the relationship of matter and energy. We cannot imagine the existence of matter without the involvement of energy, and similarly energy takes a definite visible form to occupy certain space in this universe.

3. A Noble Approach

There are millions of books and narratives with some noble initiative available for explaining and elaborating the propositions of teachings of Gita. Gita is relevant for both learners and teachers. It has something to say even to a layman having less knowledge about the mysteries hidden amidst the conversations displayed in the holy book of Gita.

The term Gita directly links our thinking with the conversation that took place in between Arjun, a Warrior from the side of Pandavas, and his friendly guide Krishna. It was going on amidst a critical situation in which Arjun lost his power of finalising something justifiable to have a sanction of war and killings. A series of killing of such type in which his beloved ones were at a threshold has made him discontented. Krishna took the role of his charioteer to normalise the situation and to let Arjun understand his own status in a better way. The agitation, as described in the holy book of Mahabharata, was against the stand of his own family members having intention of grabbing all the resources by taking advantage of some conspired game-fares. The game-fare of such type with in infliction of opportunistic ideals were moved on differently and both the segments of a single family took a stand against each other.

Lord Krishna defined his stand by putting himself in the side of Pandavas with a sheer commitment of not to use his weapon at any instances. It was his stand that made him free from direct indulgence of the warfare and made it possible to guard Pandavas through delivering timely relevant instruction. In this way he has secured his position similar to that of the brain in our body. Conversation of Krishna and Arjun amidst the battle field was also an act of holy instructions duly issued for Arjun to signify his timely need. It had linked senses with duties, established correlation between rights and duties, issued bands of things to be done and things not to be done, entangled a spirit with its higher source, conferred the juxtaposition of creation and the creator and finally re-established need of knowing the self.

It will be even more perfectly balanced to contingent human efforts of ascent towards the state of the unification of conscious mind with that of masterly guide. Effort is also made to encompass the segregation of individual differences from the common philosophical knowledge to make it more people friendly and more relevant, as well as time tested one.

Gita, as a common and popularly contemplated term, indicates towards a subject related to the holy book of Gita having bands of knowledge in the form of a conversation in between Arjun and Krishna. This reality made Gita confined to a limited quarter and placed other holy efforts underneath a shadow of ignorance. We rarely talk about Ram Gita, Sanskaar Gita and some other such efforts having a suffix Gita attached to it. Gita, in its actual sense, stands for some sort of compilation that people can sing. It can be discussed with some beautiful rhythmic tunes. Collective recitation of Gita brings out a collective wave in the form of auditory vibrations for the purpose of cleansing the immediate surroundings. It also conferred essence of collective and community level worship for making the entire effort possible and for keeping the converged senses of cooperation and brotherhood alive.

To a compilation of prayers and songs meant for the supreme lord the World Poet coined a term "Gitanjali" for it. To correlate the practical aspects of life and mission of an individual with the specified spiritual destiny, Saint Vinoba coined the term "Katha[179] Gita (Gita through a series of stories)" and incorporated all the teachings and narratives of Gita in absolutely friendly way. Examples are in plenty. It had not diffused the glory of the original compilation of Gita, also had not conferred replacing the original poetic compilation with millions of narratives. Waves of vibrations that the chanting of Gita creates is based on the assimilation of collective vibrations of saintly senses that makes a way out through the surrounding of the place of worship and gives birth to an essence of keeping the collective vibrations of cooperation, brotherhood, divine omnipresence and inter-linkages of senses alive.

---

[179] Hindi term Katha means Stories. Saint Vinoba Bhave translated Shri Madbhagvadgita in Marathi and also wrote a series of books to explain teachings of Gita through simple stories which were also contextually relevant.

We, in the same manner, can successfully create hundreds and thousands of such narratives duly inflicted with fundamental human values to make the spark of Gita a confluous one, a vibrant one and a strategic one. It has enormous power of accommodations for incorporating all sorts of socially and culturally relevant directives within the scope of its teaching related to individual refinement impregnated with spiritual ascent. It also makes the relationship of creator and the creation a vibrant one. We can specify any of the particular effort as an initiative inflicted with divine power meant for accomplishing certain works. All such Gita, duly compiled by saintly people, are not with us. In due course of time we have lost many of such beautiful, relevant and time tested compilations due to various reasons. Our mind kept on imbibing presence of such powers tradition by tradition through many of our rituals. Those graceful efforts played a significant role in keeping waves of community worship alive.

Wider dimensions and expanded coverage of the teachings of Gita often make people worried about what to follow and what not to follow in real life. Also in some cases it becomes difficult to think about propositions in the actual ground. Because of lack of timely relevant practical knowledge of the situation, people even keep themselves aside from following and internalising teachings of the holy book in the real life situation. Approach of such religious and cultural teaching, therefore, should have proper considerations of some practical aspects of rituals and worships.

Some people maintain a view regarding Gita is that the entire aspects depicted in this holy book are a confusing one. Saints from olden times worked differently to show that Gita is much relevant in terms of rituals and propositions presented in it. Here also we are trying to trace out a link up in between rituals, traditions and practices that we have in nature to re-establish the age old faiths of the omnipresence of divine within us at its varying formats. We can see things as they occupy a definite shape. We cannot see energy and power due to their in capabilities of occupying space. To feel the presence of such powers in our surrounding, we often take the support of our senses and feelings. In some cases our observations are evidence based, in some other cases it may have some imaginary propositions. Here comes the act of limitations that restrict us to feel Ultraviolet and Infrared [180]radiations which remained off the band of the visible spectrum and duly restricted our sense of vision seven visible waves of light.

There arises another question related to our effort of analyzing the relevance of the teachings of The Gita in present day situation. It was the instructions delivered by Lord Krishna to Arjun during the epic age of Vedic Civilisation. That time war had its presence in the scope of royal management. That time conflicts had a final termination to war for making efforts a result oriented. Sins and sinners had their presence in olden times and are still there with us today; format and geo-locations might vary; arms and ammunitions might differ. Even from the pages of history we can see how Prince Ashoka smashed the Kingdom of Kalinga only because that kingdom had refused to hand over the murderer of his mother to him. Later on the war and the loss of lives of many innocent people had implied a deep impression in his mind and he had decided to refuse to take part in any other battle simply meant for territorial expansion. Teachings of The Gita have worked differently during different instances of the development of conflicts and agony.

Since conflicts and agony are beyond the scope of any historic time line, we can correlate teachings of any instances to prepare strategic actions of any other present day sectoral management plans. It has the impetus of the absolute knowledge of human actions, wishes, wills and conducts with absolute apprehension of delivering the needful.

The reason of discontentment, sorrow and agony of Arjun after entering the battle field was rejected instantly by Lord Krishna through implying a sanction of his indulgence in the war. Killing any individual or creating another one is not the role of any warrior. A warrior can deliver the duty in time with a clear impetus of making the wiser side victorious. Sinners will lose their lives because of their mis-conducts only.

---

[180] Both Ultraviolet and Infrared Radiations are the parts of the invisible band of spectrum incorporated in the Solar Radiation. Our visual sense organ can feel the presence of only visible spectrum comprising seven different colours.

Here afterwards the discussion will move on to elaborate different aspects of an individual which makes them the incarnation of manifestation of the Divine. Our discussion is advanced through consideration of the acts of devotion and the state of beings in such a state of complete devotion. Will such state alone can renunciated a devoted person? Is there any instance depending upon which we can claim that the divine has extended the ultimate support to the devoted worshipper?

Once upon a time a Warrior King became famous amongst his men because of his devotion to the Master of all Masters. He had also constructed several beautiful temples in different parts of his kingdom for sheltering his masters. Temples of such types became very famous in localities. People started using such temples as their land mark signs. Not only that, some of the temples got the prominence as a market hub. Saintly persons started using these public places as their seats of religious purposes.

"Have you seen God?" one of the saint asked a youth.

Youth answered instantly, "Yes."

The kind of answer was somehow not expected.

"Where?", finally saint broke his silence.

"God is there in me. It is also there in you. The God is even speaking through you. Any customer is a God for shopkeepers. I am sure you are not getting confused", smiling face of that youth stunned all the people who were watching the conversation.

Different other instances of this type became a normal affair of the temple corridors. Things were moving softly and peacefully. All things were not in peace. All places of the kingdom ware not equally protected. Some of the places of border areas often experienced invasion of different types by different groups of bad tempered people. Most of the time the invasion of grabbers made the king worried about his ward.

He has decided to become merciless to smash all the grabbers.

Grabbers never cultivate crops. They even never take part in making instruments. They are also less interested in joining other farmers for any support. They can do only one thing. Invade a village. Put people in trouble and harvest ripe crops.

The only loser because of invasions of such grabbers in the context was farmers. The Warrior King has decided to organise a specially trained people of strong physique to tackle such grabbers and smash them instantly on the spot. The kind of firm action made all the grabbers worried. They were invading different territories of the kingdom in small groups. After the kind of firm action from the side of the kingdom all the grabbers decided to opt for joint actions. One such joint action made them victorious in a village located at the foothill of border areas. The victory was only because of delays in reaching the information to the state capita.

"We construct high altitude towers at selected places in such a way that signals of lights and flags broadcasted from one tower should be visible from other towers. In this way we can get the information instantly with a speed of light.", The kind of instruction made all the engineers of the kingdom busy in implementing the dream plan within a short span of just one year.

Farmers may remain tension free by the end of the forthcoming crop season.

Name of such towers coined by gabbers is Temple Tower. They always remain scared of matters related to temple. The turn of grabbers came. They became more united, more violent, more particular and more refined.

Instruction of direct action was already issued to villagers of border areas of the kingdom. They have a special thing, namely Temple Tower, which can link them with the state capital instantly.

During one evening, soldiers deputed at the Temple Tower observed the advancement of a large group of armed men towards their territory. The volume of such advance was so big that one can rarely finish counting properly. It was near about five thousand grabbers advancing towards the state capital.

"We grab them all, smash them all!" oppressors advancing towards the state capital were shouting in a rhyming tune.

Already it was evening time. Information system of flag cannot work properly. Other towers rarely recognise the signals. Generals decided to replace flag signals with those of fire signals. The dark side of the Temple Tower got illuminated. Luminous signal of one Temple Tower gave birth to such signals at the other. With an instantaneous speed the information of the invasion of grabbers reached the state capital and instantly made the attentive corps active.

The time was vital for the king. He was extremely busy in worshipping his King of All Kings. Even all generals were there to look after the arrangements. They all were scheduled themselves for offering services to saints, devotees, guests and people. The order came in the form of illuminated signal of keeping silence about the progression of grabbers. All the soldiers deputed at Temple Towers were not expecting such a reply from the state capital. For confirming the message of keeping silence, the signal indicating the advancement of grabbers populated for the second time. The second time also the reply was the same.

Keeping silence, means inviting massacre. They people become violent just after invading the territory.

One should not keep the law in hand without the royal concern. It was the time for generals and other men to find a hideout meant for hiding themselves. Advancement of grabbers towards the state capital made them more worried. The information was again passed on to the kingdom. Finally the team of oppressors reached the state capital by the end of the following evening.

A large camp of grabbers made the inmates of the royal court and the royal family worried about their survival. Getting feared of such intrusion, they approached the king.

"Say no to war. This time we are welcoming our God. With the same vigil we also welcome our enemy. Let us see what they want. If they want our destruction then we also want the same." The king was fixed at his stand.

The pale faces of all the inmates became more fainted after listening to their king. They were equally proud of their king because of his religious nature. The type of incident prompted all the inmates and generals of the kingdom to surrender all their worries at the disposal of the King of all Kings. The population in the royal temple courtyard increased considerably.

It was a moonlit night. It was also a special one in terms of activities and faiths.

The master mind of grabbers tossed differently to attend the royal court with their claim upon the entire kingdom. They were in a plan of throwing out the king for grabbing the entire kingdom at a single go. More alarming for them was the way they were treated on the way of their advancement. Fellow villagers and farmers offered them essentials willingly. It was more alarming that, none of the countrymen opposed the stand of their king. No war during worship of the King of all Kings was the only thing they wanted to follow to make their king wiser.

Only a peaceful mind can worship properly. All the countrymen led their worship in the same tune. They also welcomed their enemy with adequate patience and calmness of their mind.

.   The grabber master ordered his men to wait for the span of the moonlit night. The next morning will be a sunset for the king and his fellow generals. They must quit silently. If they are not moving away, then the other fate will be fatal for them all. The grabber master was in a full confidence. He was enjoying the silver markings of the moonlit night. He was also roaming around to ascertain the security of his men of actions. The echo of songs and chanting are audible from the farthest point of the forest. The grabber master was not capable of understanding the stand of king. He had no information about the peaceful stand of his opponent. That is why it was not sensible for them. He was also not confident about the policy of the king for not getting indulged in any war during any holy festival. Two riders approaching the main gate of the fort of kingdom caught the vision of the grabber master and his selected generals. "The king conspires something special for us." The grabber master said. He has issued an alert for his secret agents duly deputed at the place. "We must imply a close look upon them."

A gap of a couple of hour was the moment of the high pitched chanting and singing which was radiating out in the form of waves from the fort. That night the fort turned into a sacred temple of the King of all Kings. The Warrior King was the centre of attention. All the inmates and generals forgot about the advancement of the grabbers. They have diffused their worries. The only thing remained in front of them was the smiling face of the King of all Kings.

All on a sudden a large ball of fire smashed one of the camps of the grabbers. There was no chance of escape. The same thing happened repeatedly in the midst of the mild darkness.

"Can you see the men the king is having?" The grabber master expressed his anger. He had no preparation for putting an instant replay in action. It was so sudden and so rapid that the entire team lost their rhythm in a short span of an hour.

After coming out of the nearby hideouts, the grabber master wanted to assess the nature and extent of the damage. Only men less than five hundred were in a position to stand upon their own. They had no medications for curing wounded ones. It was also a state of utter confusion. More shameful was the act of only two men who smashed the entire team of grabbers. Finally, the grabber king changed his mind and decided to meet the king.

The onset of morning made the dream of the grabbers a matter of high risk. How to escape the territory became a challenge for them. Surrendering at the feet of king was the only way out. The Warrior King remained involved in the worship of the King of all Kings.   The grabber master came at the door step of the fort to admit his mistakes. He also expressed his desire of putting his arms down.

"I am a great failure, my king. Only the thing I want is that men. I want to see them. I've never seen such brave warriors. Once I want to see them. Please accept our humble request."

The type of request made by the grabber master was something strange for the king. It also made the king unhappy. He started searching the person who has violated his appeal.

"All the generals, please find the culprits. They should furnish reasons."

Actually there was nothing to search. All the generals and men were standing in front of their king. Who will search whom? The Warrior King ascertained the fact and answered the grabber master politely, "Actually there are nothing to search. All men are here only. So nobody used fireballs from our side. You may please find them at some other place."

The only evidence alive was the horses kept at the main gate. There were traces of fireworks lying here and there at the hinder part of the courtyard. Somebody has used canons. The question arises about the way they might have entered the main campus of the fort for taking the hold of the powerful canons. After raining fireballs on the enemy they even more silently left the place.

"The horses, your highness…" the grabber master admitted his eagerness to see those generals. The appeal remained unattended from the royal side.

Only the thing remained in the mind of grabbers was in the form of a faith upon some supreme force that saved the kingdom just before the advent of utter destruction.

Grabber master got the final lesson in the form of caring attendance of the Warrior King. He has received essential items duly required for the days they surpass inside the territory. Generals and other villagers must not put them in any trouble. It was the noble treatment to the enemy who wanted to grab the entire country. Once again the wave of green flags indicated the advent of peace in the entire territory of the Warrior King.

Devotion, in its absolute sense is a state of mind in which the fellow devotee intends to offer all sorts of success, sorrow, gain and loss at the service of the divine master. Such a masterly guiding force makes the ascent of devotee towards a state of completeness possible. There exist different states and degrees of devotion possessing equally competent capabilities suitable for an individual to work out activities meant for fulfilling wishes of the referred master.

Not only that, a devotee can even perform actions without feeling many difficulties. Devotion is the state of mind that makes the union of knowledge, intellect, courage and will power possible. It also makes the devotee fearless by means of nullifying the doubts of success. It also nullifies the feeling of supremacy which hampers the continuous progress of an individual in the path of ascent towards the state of divinity. It also makes the individual competent enough in feeling the essence of following masterly instructions before ascertaining any action as a final one.

We come across the name "Kapidhwaj", the name coined for the chariot of warrior Arjuna. Once during his stay at Rameshwaram Arjuna met the legendary character of the Indian Epic Ramayana; it was none other than the warrior Hanumana. We may not require any introduction to explain the bravery, courage, will power and devotion that Hanumana exhibited in those days. Arjuna claimed his supremacy and knowledge of Archery a unique one and indulged in a debate with the saintly warrior of courage, will power and devotion. His claim was to prove the strength of a bridge made of arrows a strong one, even stronger than the Adam's Bridge duly constructed during the period of the invasion of Sri Lanka by Rama and his group of soldiers. While demonstrating so, it was an utter failure for Arjuna. As per the previously finalised deal he had to ignite himself for sacrificing life. Arjuna indulged in such kinds of arbitrary deal with Hanumana without knowing the legendary importance and strength of the warrior and devotee of lord Rama.

Lord Krishna stopped Arjuna from sacrificing himself by claiming that there was no witness to ascertain the deal. The performance of the construction of bridge by using arrows repeated again. This time also Hanumana stepped on to it and it started collapsing. Only a new thing developed this time was some blood shed from the water started moving up. It was none other than the lord himself in the form of a turtle kept on holding the bridge in the middle with an intention of making Arjuna victorious. Hanumana identified his master in other form and agreed in helping them by all means.

Instead of getting directly involved in the struggle of Kurukshetra, Hanumana agreed to accompany them with a condition of having chances of gaining knowledge from his fellow master. That flag with a symbol of presence of Hanumana coined the term "Kapidhwaj" for the chariot of Arjuna and made it quite special amidst the war and turmoil of Kurukshetra. Gita was delivered there in the battle field for fulfilling the desire of Hanumana for having an opportunity of gaining knowledge.

Nine different forms of devotion were also described in the epic Ramayana, and duly exhibited the same through different legendary characters duly presented in it. Hanumana was at the supreme state of such devotion. His devotion to his master was not a blind one. He had a state of intellect, understanding, courage and will power. While moving towards Sri Lanka for the first time he started asking some opinion from his elders and exhibited his higher state of mental contentment. Their chances came to establish a hold upon immense potential of wealth. He has preferred bypassing such opportunity and decided to move on. Instead of having enormous power of killing the demon king and bringing Sita back then and there from the captivity of the demon king, he has decided to convey the message of presence of Sita to his master first. Only devotion made him perpetually counted and kept him free from the clutch of ego, anger and boasting attitudes.

It also signifies the essence of devotion in the process of unfolding the skilful mind and making it available for being used. Such an increased horizon of intellect can surely increase the potential of a doer. It can even equip a person with aspirations of maintaining higher state of mind for establishing a perfect balance between memory and intellect. With such a balanced state of memory and intellect one can gain desired potential in stipulated time.

Is it difficult for any ordinary person to have an experience of witnessing the holy touch of the divine master? Is divinity something special which can open up horizon for its follower after ascertaining the balanced state and enrichment of mind and intellect?

There is no such correlation between literal enrichment of mind and experiencing process of divinity. Divinity is the state of mind where people start recognising one's role in the society and all other acts and conducts of that individual are duly accorded. It cannot ascribe any state of attainment of such perfection without adhering oneself entirely in the path of worship. Divinity cannot even make a person off the track of society and cannot allow oneself to be entangled amidst any rituals and conducts. King Gopal Singh of Malla Dynasty once refused to fight against the Maratha invaders. The reason was that there was a ceremonial worship of Madan Mohan in the state capital. All the citizen of that state were also observing the week for worshipping their lord. Bhasker Pandit, the headman of the Maratha oppressors moved in easily and reached up to the state capital with an easy confluence. There occurred the miracle. That miracle has created some argument. Bhasker Pandit and his men were smashed badly by two strange and unidentified warriors. Their bravery was the exemplar ones. Some of the fellow inmates of the state capital identified one of the warriors as none other than the Madan Mohan, the divine power of the kingdom, himself. Some other fellow thinkers lost their faith on any chance of occurrence of such a miracle.

Keeping faith is, therefore with its genuine format, an individual apprehension that guides the person considerably in maintaining or rejecting any ideas and propositions. Ascent of the individual on the path of divinity is also ascertained by the state4 of mind on the ground of any intention of accepting or rejecting any ideas.

We have two different segments in our brain meant specifically for memorising things and analysing things. Both the format of brain functions are compared and maintained perfectly with an involvement of one intermediary sensory power. Perfectly balanced mind maintains adequate balance in between memory and intellect. It is also regulated considerably by our wish factor. What we wish that we often do perfectly.

Here lies the mystery, why we have so many differences in individual apprehensions and their understanding on the accommodation of such a supreme power within the junction of memory and intellect. On the basis of such balanced apprehension the success and failure of any individual is ascertained.

Intellect alone cannot fulfil the desire of the individual. Memory alone cannot graduate the effort of any individual for making efforts a fulfilled one. There should be proper and timely culmination of both memory and intellect for making the effort a successful one. Sometimes our senses move differently against our will power and, by doing so, hampers our efforts of implying adequate and timely culmination of memory with intellect. There requires a masterly guide, a way out for us having adequate capabilities of bringing success in the form of a divine ascent. It is a form of proper actualisation of our senses for making our efforts meaningful, timely relevant, graduated and human friendly. This type of effort can even intend the individual for harnessing the aspects of collective progress duly meant for some common good.

There are millions of books and narratives with some noble initiative available for explaining and elaborating the propositions of teachings of Gita. Gita is relevant for both learners and teachers. It has something to say even to a layman having less knowledge about the mysteries hidden amidst the conversations displayed in the holy book of Gita.

The term Gita directly links our thinking with the conversation that took place in between Arjun, a Warrior from the side of Pandavas, and his friendly guide Krishna. It was going on amidst a critical situation in which Arjun lost his power of finalising something justifiable to have a sanction of war and killings. A series of killings of such type in which his beloved ones were at a threshold has made him emotionally restless. Krishna took the role of his charioteer to normalise the situation and to let Arjun understand his own status in a better way. The agitation, as described in the holy book of Mahabharata, was against the stand of his own family members having intention of grabbing all the resources by taking advantage of some conspired game-fares. The game-fare of such type with in infliction of opportunistic ideals was moved on differently and both the segments of a single family took a stand against each other.

Lord Krishna defined his stand by putting himself in the side of Pandavas with a sheer commitment of not to use his weapon at any instances. It was his stand that made him free from direct indulgence of the warfare and made it possible to guard Pandavas through delivering timely relevant instruction. In this way he has secured his position similar to that of the brain in our body. Conversation of Krishna and Arjun amidst the battle field was also an act of holy instructions duly issued for Arjun to signify his timely need. It had linked senses with duties, established correlation between rights and duties, issued bands of things to be done and things not to be done, entangled a spirit with its higher source, conferred the juxtaposition of creation and the creator and finally re-established need of knowing the self.

Madbhagvad-Gita, as the complete term coined for the holy book, had also defined the role of divine power in infusing values within the intellect and senses of a fellow devotee. It has also established a perfect correlation between knowledge and devotion. None of the paired combination alone can succeed in bringing fame.

Through all the eighteen chapters of the holy book, Godly propositions were incorporated by saints and philosophers who have created it for commons. It has a perpetual compilation of various combinations of practical aspects of Yoga and Meditation. It has also narrated the true nature of Knowledge that often receive a confluence more confluous than that of a stream. Attainment of such knowledge is a subject of individual apprehension and depends solely on the purity of mind. Our discussion up to this point has made a thing clear about the nature and proposition of knowledge confluence remaining evident amongst us since centuries, with a clear impetus of facilitating its follower for gaining an ascent through divinity and perfectness. There exist narratives in different forms and in different languages meant primarily to make people aware of the eternal philosophical aspects related to teachings of Gita.

Another effort of making Gita simple, easy to understand, more confluous to attend aspirations of people, more perpetuated to incorporate aspirations of millions and more conferred to actualise role of senses. Efforts may be of varying kinds to satisfy aspirations of people in different ways possible. It may have some more relevant narratives that can efficiently link up the need of fundamental values reflected by Gita at different instances.

Perform Jointly

We will now focus on the efforts with which congress of people's aspiration can be made possible to replace all sorts of patchy repairs by incorporating desired level of linkages at the dynamics of groups, community, society and individuals. Individual may move on to fulfil basic needs of the immediate family members first. After fulfilling such needs they start considering needs of other community members of the immediate surroundings. Such kind of political, social or spiritual nexus will finally make the entire community bonded with the impetus of sharing and caring. We will gradually witness development of community level network of sharing and caring on the basis of contemplated wishes and willingness of varying degree and of varying impetus. Here comes the situation when we may witness presence or absence of some sort of mental and intellectual status of community members duly impregnated with peace and Non-violence. We will also witness development of some higher bands of spiritual union which can finally play a vital role in spreading the doctrines of peace and nonviolence at the greater degree duly aligned positively with community consciousness.

Efforts of such kind of collective execution will also raise the level of confidence of other community units and they also come up with higher aspirations of joining hands to make the development of unified human efforts of enhanced spirituality standards a reality. People start considering the doctrines of peace and nonviolence after keeping themselves free from crippled apprehension of some small purposes of life. They also start safeguarding wills and wishes of the other community members and start helping each other collectively to cast off their affinity towards acts of <u>animism</u>[181]. Animism is also considered as one of the Anthropological concept of earlier times and is not the first one.[182] It also maintains its concern with the fact related to the unit which is alive and the factors which keep the unit alive.[183] An old concept of this Animism maintains a distinct idea depending upon which animals or some other non-human living entities were considered as a living unit which cannot understand differences between matter and life.[184] Animism was finally seen as an error or mistake due to which different schools of religion grew (Edward B. Tylor). They even started maintaining some sort of distinct identity of their own.[185] We should therefore continue working on this issue until and unless the perpetual unity of desired types is properly maintained. Our awareness and mutual conduct will also start taking a definite shape after inculcating cultural, spiritual and technological apprehensions of people of immediate surroundings. Threat to humanity in and around our society is enormous. Some of the threat can be addressed simply by making community aware of their duty and rights in a society. We also confer establishment of a balance between rights and duties through which aspirations of an individual in a society is advanced.

---

[181] *It is (Animism) often considered as the faith of some Indigenous people. One can even confer the development of such acts simply for fulfilling basic needs of life without remaining inflicted with any kind of Spiritual or intellectual ascent.*
Reference: Hicks, David (2010). Ritual and Belief: Readings in the Anthropology of Religion (3 ed.). Roman Altamira. p. 359. Tylor's notion of animism—for him the first religion—included the assumption that early Homo sapiens had invested animals and plants with souls ...

[182] *Bird-David, Nurit (1999). ""Animism" Revisited: Personhood, Environment, and Relational Epistemology". Current Anthropology. 40 (S1): S67. doi:10.1086/200061.*

[183] *Harvey, Graham (2005). Animism: Respecting the Living World. London: Hurst & Co. ISBN 978-0-231-13701-0.*

[184] *Harvey, Graham (2005). Animism: Respecting the Living World. London: Hurst & Co. ISBN 978-0-231-13701-0.*

[185] *Tylor, Edward Burnett (1871). Primitive Culture: Researches into the Development of Mythology, Philosophy, Religion, Art, and Custom. Vol. 1. J. Murray. p. 260.*

Human Bonds meant for Progress

Progress of the expansion of human bonds for materializing special conducts on the basis of the doctrines of peace and nonviolence will definitely contemplate a new horizon through which Inter-cultural citizenship bands can be made possible. We also exercise the process of bringing intellectual union amongst the participant members of community with which the networked information transfer and sharing of ideals will become easy as well as confluent one. We will even contingent to certain extent for making our effort a result oriented one by letting participation of distant community member possible in the joint efforts duly planned and implemented by members of the closed user groups. One should rely perpetually on the efforts of dialogues, discussion and progressive efforts of welfare for cultivating the possibilities of making people united by all means. It is also true that this effort of linking people on the basis of peace and nonviolence may not be an initiative of one sided impetus. People working on this process will definitely exercise mechanisms of inculcating the doctrines of peace and nonviolence without becoming influenced by the prejudice and bias.

Peace and nonviolence may not be considered as any identifiable entity in nature without addressing involvement of any socially and spiritually oriented individuals residing the closed quarter under consideration duly inflicted with family feelings.

Community Experimentation

Is there any finishing line in the path of community experimentation? Do we expect some new dimensions in our community experimentations in relation to time? How do different gaps (such as gender gap, information gap, knowledge gap, gap of accessibility to resources, gap of spiritual alignments etc.) will be addressed through community experimentation?

Our understanding and approach will definitely permit us to consider all the above issues as per the convenience of approaches and resource utilisation. None of the community members should be left behind. If anyone or any group of individuals remains off the main stream then they may create a reverse current through which swiftness of collective progress will be hampered. Both Mahatma and Vinba[186] were aware of this fact and due to that reason they proposed the mechanism of ANTYODAYA (starting incorporation of the effort of addressing problems of the poorest and marginalised ones with priority). It was the impetus which coined an opportunity for Joseph Cornelius (popularly called by mahatma "Kumarappa") to design the implements of "Peace Economy". Economic plan without incorporating aspirations of poor and marginalised will not bring any collective progress. Only collective progress will ensure multi-layered unity in between closed as well as distant communities. In that context also aspirations of poorest and marginalised ones should be addressed with priority. Finally to say community experimentation is the vast area having enormous potential. It can be addressed from different angles. All such angles (more than 14 specified sectors)[187] were identified by Mahatma and his fellow associates during the period of pre-independent India. Lanza del Vasto was another associate of Mahatma who worked a lot in the field of community experimentation and successfully assimilated spiritual alignment of Mahatma and Saint Vinoba through his service lines. Lanza used to accompany Mahatma during morning walk to gain the blissful interactions with absolute and clear apprehensions. He has successfully gained a momentum in his approaches through community experimentation. We came across a long distance while discussing approaches and willingness with which successors of Mahatma worked at different instances. Still we have miles to go until and unless the World Peace in its absolute sense is properly established. Individuals who continued following doctrines of development proposed by Mahatma and his associates preferred implying adequate focus on villages. They also maintained that bright future of a nation resides in the development of villages. Collective effort of such development will definitely ensure the parallel development of other entities linked to the network of villages. It is also confirmed from the plan proposals prepared

---

[186] *Acharya Vinoba Bhave was the Spiritual successor of Mahatma who also addressed constructive work programmes duly planned by Mahatma for making the entire effort successful.*
He had also incorporated some spiritual alignment to the service lines in which fellow volunteers remained deeply linked up.
[187] *Sectors specified by Mahatma are clearly mentioned in the Constructive Work Programmes suggested by his fellow associates.*

by planners after attainment of independence that India moved off the track of the principles and proposals of Mahatma. Power continued remaining centralised without ensuring participation of the villagers in the networked planning process.

It is true that success of a government resides in the effective execution with which generals and officers engaged in the process of planning and implementation deliver their duties. Performance of individual resides in the process with which they continue delivering their duties while maintaining adequate coordination with other sectoral units of government. Executing of different units of government network resides in the knowledge base with which professionals involved in a process delivers duty.

This approach is perfectly focused on the attainment of true knowledge which will enable the individual to feel the omnipresence of the Divine. With such kind of knowledge assimilation that individual can even recognise the presence of the Divine in all other creations duly attained varying degrees and extents of manifestation. If such kind of alteration at the individual level goes on progressive then it is obvious that such kinds of individuals move forward to create extended human bonds.

Due to such kinds of enhanced awareness and structured approaches of further socialisation the value system will be protected by all means. Doctrines of Peace and Nonviolence can be addressed properly through such groups of people having affinity towards recognising the TRUTH, for such acts of recognition will actualise them all spiritually, for such acts of recognition will enable them to impart themselves in the ever continuing process of socialisation, for all such efforts designed on the basis of comprehensive doctrines of Peace and Nonviolence will be addressed perfectly. Personality development is also attains a base of social, intellectual and spiritual base upon which foundation stones of personality are laid.[188] Individuals also interpret contextual situation from different possible angles to develop an enduring pattern of personality

---

[188] *Cervone, Daniel; Shadel, William G.; Jencius, Simon (February 2001). "Social-Cognitive Theory of Personality Assessment". Personality and Social Psychology Review. 5 (1): 33–51. doi:10.1207/S15327957PSPR0501_3. ISSN 1088-8683. S2CID 16223943.*

trait.[189] Human beings continued developing cultural, spiritual, attitudinal and physiological modifications through prolonged ages of evolution.[190] Personality and individuality are also developed accordingly through ages.

---

[189] *Cervone, Daniel; Shadel, William G.; Jencius, Simon (February 2001). "Social-Cognitive Theory of Personality Assessment". Personality and Social Psychology Review. 5 (1): 33–51. doi:10.1207/S15327957PSPR0501_3. ISSN 1088-8683. S2CID 16223943.*
[190] *Bell, M. G. (2010, January 1). Consciousness: The Evolution Of The Self And Personal Individuality. Retrieved November 1, 2014, from www.agenthuman.com/product/evolution_self_personal_individuality.html#selfevol*

4. Care Management

There is no master more masterly than your own experience.

-   Author

We are moving through information age which quantifies progress in terms of speed of processing and representing services. It is confirmed from different studies of present day context that quality is a relative term. We define quality on the basis of the knowledge base of people indulged in the entire process of system design and evaluation. We also consider the fact that implementation of Zero defect system is not possible as we cannot specify absence of defect in any system from all possible angles.

The Management Model

Once Matsuhita Institute of Government and Management has organized a seminar to publish one of its ambitious management model titled Zero Defect System. It was also popular in American Industry since 1964.[191] The model was really ambitious and also was filled with doubts regarding its applicability. The reason was very simple: Defect can be pointed out in a system by some other individual having some other apprehensions of knowledge. Defectiveness of a system also depends upon the group of people having access to any segment of process, system or operations. A new dimension came in this management model in the form of quality assurance.[192] An action plan

---

[191] *A Guide to Zero Defects: Quality and Reliability Assurance Handbook. Washington, D.C.: Office of the Assistant Secretary of Defense (Manpower Installations and Logistics). 1965. p. 3. OCLC 7188673. 4155.12-H. Retrieved May 29, 2014. Early in 1964 the Assistant Secretary of Defense (Installations and Logistics) invited the attention of the Military Departments and the Defense Supply Agency to the potential of Zero Defects. This gave the program substantial impetus. Since that time Zero Defects has been adopted by numerous industrial and Department of Defense activities.*

[192] *Halpin, James F. (1966). Zero Defects: A New Dimension in Quality Assurance. New York City: McGraw-Hill. OCLC 567983091*

became popular which aimed finally towards became the organizing, motivating, and initiating elements of Zero Defects.

Absolutes of Quality Management model came in practice with a 14 point operational strategy.[193]

In due course of time four absolutes of Quality Management were identified by Crosby[194]

These absolutes were as follows:

1. Quality can be defined according to conformance to requirements.
2. Prevention is the system of quality.
3. The zero defects standardise the performance.
4. Price of nonconformance is the measurement of quality.[195]

Leading Management organizations worked out the relativity of the defectiveness of any system. Some other renowned orgnisations joined hands to work out another management model namely Total Quality Management.

Probably the term "Total Quality" was coined for the first time by the Department of Trade and Industry of United Kingdom during 1983.[196] It was implemented with certain effectiveness by Defense

---

[193] *Crosby, Philip B. (1979). "8: Quality Improvement Program". Quality Is Free: The Art of Making Quality Certain. New York City: McGraw-Hill. pp. 127–139. ISBN 9780070145122. OCLC 3843884.*

[194] *Crosby, Philip B. (1984). Quality Without Tears: The Art of Hassle-free Management. New York City: McGraw-Hill. pp. 58–86. ISBN 9780070145306. OCLC 10277859.*

[195] *Crosby, Philip B. (1979). Quality Is Free: The Art of Making Quality Certain. New York City: McGraw-Hill. pp. 85–86. ISBN 9780070145122. OCLC 3843884. Quality is free. It's not a gift, but it is free. ... Every penny you don't spend on doing things wrong, over, or instead becomes half a penny right on the bottom line.*

[196] *Martínez-Lorente, Angel R.; Dewhurst, Frank; Dale, Barrie G. (1998), "Total Quality Management: Origins and Evolution of the Term", The TQM Magazine, Bingley, United Kingdom: MCB University Publishers Ltd, vol. 10 no. 5, pp. 378–386, CiteSeerX 10.1.1.574.2414, doi:10.1108/09544789810231261, hdl:10317/441*

Department of United States.[197] It was also pointed out that the increase in quality standards will come through a continuing process of evaluation and refinement of the system implements.

In the model implement of TQM the quality was defined in accord to the requirements of the reference group. The responsibility of maintaining quality was solely considered as the subject of the higher authority engaged in the system implements.[198]

An attempt to standardize quality parameters was made by Belgium, France, Germany, Turkey, and the United Kingdom. Finally during 1990 all the quality parameters and system implements are finally superseded by ISO 9000.[199] [200]

Quality itself is a relative term that depends entirely on the quality apprehension of a limited group of people. It often implies subtle variations in between two or more quality concerns of people getting involved in delivering or accepting the services and products from the unit under consideration. What we understand as a best quality can be appreciated with some limitations to some other group of people. They may point out some of the hidden demerits of the product or services as per their level of understanding. It would be more advisable to skip and come out of the standardization of any products or services in terms of any quality parameters. More perpetually to say, one can take care of the entire system on the basis of the level of understanding a person is maintaining. Enhancing the level of knowledge and understanding and

---

[197] *United States Department of Defense (1989), Total Quality Management: A Guide for Implementation, Springfield, Virginia: National Technical Information Service, OCLC 21238720, DoD 5000.51-G*

[198] *Houston, Archester (December 1988), A Total Quality Management Process Improvement Model (PDF), San Diego, California: Navy Personnel Research and Development Center, pp. vii–viii, OCLC 21243646, AD-A202 154, retrieved 2013-10-20*
[199] *The ISO 9000 family of quality management systems (QMS) is a set of standards that helps organizations ensure they meet customer and other stakeholder needs within statutory and regulatory requirements related to a product or service.*

[200] *Hoyle, David (2007), Quality Management Essentials, Oxford, United Kingdom: Butterworth-Heinemann, p. 200, ISBN 9780750667869, OCLC 72868446, retrieved 2013-10-19*

implying the same while delivering services will be a cyclic dimension of the Care Management that remain focused upon bringing the best possible services and products from a system implement.

What one can incorporate in the system of the business cycle, and what one can keep aside for making the production and processing cycle a cheapest one, is finally reflecting a state of dilemma, with which any aspirant may remain inflicted.

Because of the aforesaid reason and some other quality standards cannot be generalised for all the service and production processes. One cannot apprehend the type, degree and extent of success on the lines of the system implement which might have brought success for some other group of individuals. Development in the refinement process for bringing an absolute standardization in any system in terms of quality is another aspect that led to the exploration of some more perfect management model impregnated with some sort of advanced system implements.

The core of System Design

These days incorporation of Information and Communication tool in the business cycle is becoming an obligatory affair. ICT is an umbrella term that incorporates a set of communication device in any system implement.[201] It often speed up the entire process, make the instrumentation process a dynamic one, keep the business cycle at proper pace and allow proper thrust upon the manual involvements. By 2014 the world's capacity to store digital information grew up to 5 zettabytes.[202] These days nearly 3 billion people register their access to internet.[203] It

---

[201] *Kondra, Imaniyal (2020). "Use of IT in Higher Education". UGC Care Journal. India: Studies in Indian Place Names. 40: 280.*

[202] *"The World's Technological Capacity to Store, Communicate, and Compute Information", Martin Hilbert and Priscila López (2011), Science, 332(6025), 60-65; see also "free access to the study" and "video animation".*

A zettabyte is a multiple of the unit byte that measures digital storage, and it is equivalent to 1,000,000,000,000,000,000,000 [10^{21}] bytes

[203] *"ITU releases annual global ICT data and ICT Development Index country rankings". www.itu.int. Retrieved 2015-09-01.*

has brought a dramatic change in the communication system through which distantly located stake holders reduced their geographical barriers and registered their presence in desired processes of the efforts related to production and services. Aspects related to Audit and Accounting, regulating human resources, designing process and instrumentation and publishing business related documents are some of the aspects duly covered up through ICT implements. It has even upgraded the entire business cycle through automation of the productivity chain.

Regarding a misconception of replacement of manual work force by the automation, it can be clarified that the entirely automated business cycle will make it more and more result oriented as well as swift and perfectly designed in terms of operational issues. It can even move the process instrumentation towards adequate success mark. Our apprehension with ICT enabled skills of workers getting involved in the entire system will keep the system implements duly involved in the business cycle a vibrant one. It can make the entire system of production and processing a competent one and also it will move up to the globally appreciable standard. The accomplishable quality enhancement may be a gain for some individual or may be meant for the gain of the entire community. Without interacting with other individual, a life process or problems related to the life process may remain un-attended. It may lead toward a chaos due to demand and supply mismatch, due to mismatch in terms of the levels of understanding. A doctor, for instance, may remain unexplored without the approach of fellow patients. Similar the case can be observed in between communications of students and teachers, advocates and clients, shop keepers and customers etc.

Communication is therefore an essential part of human society through which different entities of a system implement often comes closure to each other. It even makes the social and technological functioning appropriate as well as time tested. A farmer can communicate the entity of the immediate requirement for sorting out any problem. Reliance upon mass communication media will ensure a definite progress in time. Communication even brings people together for raising their voice jointly upon any issue. Proper and timely communication even ensures the birth of a vibrant family in the society.

Access to information will raise the level of the community consciousness that in turn will increase the levels of the understanding of people. An efficient economic process ensures the total participation of both people and the implementing agencies for enabling the soft and swift confluence of the related services and efforts. Involvement of artisans and workers in a system is primarily determined by the level of experience the referred person is maintaining.

Service Mission

We know that works of any individual is recognised in a society on the basis of the importance of the work the person associated with it. Public recognition of any individual in society indicates the importance of the person in society. Doctors and teachers generally receive higher recognition because of the importance of their services. Services of farmers and artisans are equally important in our society because of their involvement in the productivity system. A conscious society can recognize the importance of the members involved in the economy of enterprises. Only conscious members of a family can think about the well beings of a farmer in the society. Such consciousness of people, in turn, will ensure the social security of the members involved in the economy of enterprises. A life process in society, therefore, must not be standardised simply in terms of dress and wealth. It may be standardised properly in terms of efforts and knowledge. Efforts and knowledge are the two important wheels of the collective progress of a society. Standard of living of the rural society may be enhanced by ensuring some of the basic facilities like sanitation, housing, medication and access to education, access to information etc. For enhanced efforts an expanded knowledge base will play a definitive role in making a society developed and sustained one.

Another obstacle that often hampers the normal growth of any Artisan is the insecurity feeling related to the growth and development of certain components having an impact to products and services. Inability of putting forth certain new item in front of the other prevailing ones as an exemplar one often put the effort under question mark. Before placing any item for trial the fellow artisan lose all hope and come to a fixed apprehension for not contemplating upon the effort of making the productivity chain alive. Foremost reason of the sustained insecurity feeling is because of the lack of any financial stability and also lack of their direct regulation upon the market. Marketing professionals usually opt for any item that people become habituated for. They rarely agree upon putting some new item on their tray for a trial. This kind of affinity of the marketing professionals makes the marketing effort a challenging one for artisans. It can be handled properly by adopting some confidence building measures through keeping the artisan in the central focus.

Creating Artisan's group, availing community market network, making all products available at public places, availing market support to artisans by any public enterprises are some of the immediate measures which can enhance the level of confidence of fellow artisans up to a certain extent.

Demand and Supply Chain

Selection of any product or service for large scale operation is the subject of glancing upon the market for the assessment of the immediate demand of the same. There may be some of the basic questions which can be put forth for such kind of analytical study being conducted by the artisan for the purpose of the product assessment drive. Some of such questions will be as follows:

1. What type of persons gets the immediate benefit of the newly developed product or service?

2. Are there any other sources involved in the delivery of such type of services?

3. If yes, then are there any demerits remain hidden in their products and services?

4. If some demerits of available products and services are duly pointed out, then is the newly launched product and service come up in the market after resolving such demerits?

5. Is there any comparative study on the cost effectiveness of the product and service under consideration?

6. What is the immediate reference area of the product and service that bring out for the business circulation and make the entire stream operational?

7. What are the challenging aspects of the service line up related to making products and services alive?

Thinking upon all sorts of safeguards related to make the effort of productivity a successful one is the aspect that requires immediate attention of the fellow artisan. Keeping oneself aware of the advent of all sorts of difficulties is the immediate requirement of the success indication. Several issues and concerns may remain un- attentive in our way of ascertaining the global trends of peaceful resolutions and conflicts. People maintain different apprehensive thought process for making their associations and immediate concerns justifiable. They even advance their thought process to convince others regarding their stand points of rights and wrongs. It is more conspicuous to nullify the presence of some hidden currents of cross border relations duly inflicted with fulfilment of mutual desires through keeping the immediate surrounding un-attended. Such associations might bring out some worst implications for other global partners ascribed with movement of affinities of across to the same horizon of progress. Some of the nation states may claim that they are sincere enough in addressing issues and concerns related to some common good. The first blotting paper placed on the table of World Health Organisations for justifying their stand point in the context of a global pandemic. It was a serious blow and also invented a furrow in the cemented aspirations of the globally responsive character of WHO. It compelled United States of America to imply a blow upon aspirations of WHO in terms of their exit through the front door of cooperation.

We all are moving towards a society having multi-plural characteristics, where people rarely intend to ascribe themselves as a member of any specified group of extremist class in general. They may try to evolve a socialization process having multi-plural characters which will give them a wider scope of internalizing views of different segments of society. They may even start cultivating a work culture amidst a multi-plural and multifaceted human society with a constituent base of humanity and brotherhood. They also start imbibing a globally accustomed cultural base for making them fit enough for the future world order of multi-plural character. We can consider the present day turmoil as an evolutionary ascent through which people started recognising their faiths and beliefs in terms of newly implemented social, economic and religious frameworks. We simply witness the success of a community in imbibing the power of making one fit for the forthcoming days of prosperity.

The Care Apprehension

A global pandemic might bring some individuals down the track, it may even make a situation challenging for survivors, a terrific situation may be advanced for warriors and even a situation of conflict might bring inmates at the face to face conflicting calamity. The kind of pandemic having no immediate solution can issues a severe challenge for a nation state which might be addressed differently at different war fronts. One such war front is the issues and concerns related to specially enabled persons.

An efficient directives impregnated with a balanced policy framework can ensure the safety of specially enabled persons at work places. It should be adequately addressed alongside the joint consultation of the authorities implementing and monitoring the work place under consideration. It is recommended that an employer who requires a person to undergo any medical, health screening or safety test must bear the costs of the test. If an employee is frequently absent from work for reasons of illness or injury, the employer may consult the employee to assess, if the cause of the illness or injury is a disability that requires accommodation. If practicable, employers should offer alternative work, reduced work or flexible work placement, so that employees are not compelled or encouraged to apply for benefits if they could, with reasonable accommodation, continue in employment. Employers must protect the confidentiality of the information that has been disclosed and must take care to keep records of private information relating to the disability of applicants and employees confidential and separate from general personnel records. At any cost it is not advisable to reject the need of administering medical aid at the tender age in the circumstances of early diagnosis of the biological limitations of the newly introduced individuals having some special capabilities and some clinical or organizational malfunctions. For example differences between anomalies related to Tuberculosis and Leprosy are more or less having identical implications upon the health of the patients. On certain aspects Tuberculosis is more hazardous than compared of Leprosy. But social implications are more in case of Leprosy than compared to Tuberculosis. It is only because Leprosy marks the visible wounds in the form of deformities of limbs and soft body parts. Deformities inside the lungs because of Tuberculosis is not visible, that is why ex patient of tuberculosis gains an easy accommodation in society and a leper struggles a lot to return back to the native family. Deprivations that a leper has to face in society are a common affair in our country. If anyhow some of the medically certified negative patient of Leprosy gains an accommodation in family, that family will be outnumbered and all the family members suffer because of the incorporation of an ex leper in the family. The aforesaid fact raises a question on the acceptability of patient in society and exposure of a patient in society for being exploited. Social safeguards are the subjects awaiting acceptability of people for implementing the same in daily life.

Some sort of escapism prevalent amongst the associates and family members of the specially enabled person make the situation difficult for both the aspirants and aspirers. What the ways out are matters of our serious concerns. Share and Care Is it true that only parents remain concerned about their ward with some sort of physical or biological limitations?

Can we claim that a state adequately encompasses mechanism for safeguarding the aspirations of specially enabled persons having some specialties and some other limitations? Is there any self-sustained directives and guiding principles through which public service executions gain a sustained confluence of its special kind? Some of the wider dimensions of the enlightened policy standards can perpetuate our query towards attaining the refinement of the state policy standards. The entire job of accommodating people with special capabilities should be shared mutually amongst various active groups of both government as well as voluntary nature.

Some of such initiatives may be of following types:

1. State should incorporate some of the selected or all of the Enlightened Policy Standards in policy document to be streamlined for the purpose of the state level execution.
2. Voluntary organisations working in the development sector should design a comprehensive plan document for working out the mechanism of developing a strategy of safeguarding as well as promoting the aspirations of people having special capabilities.
3. Clinic centers and Health Service Agencies should allocate some of its resources for delivering Social Responsibilities in offering services to people having special capabilities.
4. Use of appropriate Language is not the only aspect that should be expected from a common citizen, but all such institutions coming in contact with specially enabled people should come across the same lines of principle for designing an ethical stand point of addressing aspirations of people in common.
5. One should not always point out limitations of the individual, but to encourage the being for the purpose of enhancing skills and competence can make a difference.
6. Keeping some seats reserved for persons having special capabilities will make them acceptable in society, then also the effort of such reservation is said to be half done without

adequate alteration in the sphere of attitudinal interactions in society.

7. Fundamental human values should be incorporated in the society for making it more vibrant in nature.

8. Attending the timely need of the people having some limitations may bring some ascribed success of considerable type. They even impart themselves in the regular process of configured activities of special standards. They even make us proud of their stand of imparting themselves in the nation building activities.

9. None of our living creatures are of any useless type. All the living partners of our society are capable enough in defining their role of percolating their service line ups.

10. Value addition to the collective progress of any nation in a standardized process can mechanise the entire system in such a way that all the members of that vibrant society become capable of exploring their service profiles in a considerable way. It can even ensure a hundred percent utilization of the human resources that is usually availed to a nation state.

The realm of Spirituality

The spiritual aspect of the service mechanism envisages the essence of considering varying differences of individuals as an opportunity of accommodating skilled individuals at various spheres of activities on the basis of the acquisition of skills and competence. Incorporation of such individualistic differences in society will pave an opportunity of establishing harmony having a prolonged continuity. The job specifications to be allocated to the specially enabled persons can make them more self-reliant and their accommodation in the main stream will become possible. "Serving Humanity means Serving God" is the highest philosophical aspiration that ties up a bond of care and being cared for a balanced social order devoid of hatred, exploitation, oppression and disparities of any kind.

The core principle which often becomes a driving force of any community is the only vibration that brings spontaneity in the referred community. It can even make the entire community participation more confluent. Success of a community regarding cultivation of a common thought process of collective progress is becoming the character of a multi-plural society, like that of India. What one can expect from any organized community is not a matter of immediate concern for some other distantly located community. Inter-relationship of different community is also developing on the basis of sharing and caring of various resource bases. People to people interaction are also becoming a rapid strand due to adherence of electronic networks.

Philosophical convergence of any type should be appreciable in all instances. They should be welcomed by all sections of society with adequate infusion of fundamental human values in regular philosophical practices. Enhancement of people to people dialogue is also of same importance. More profound stand of the vibrant community will be in a way out of solving individual difficulties through addressing issues related to skill enhancement. Socially awakened individuals always contingent to a certain extent for making people aware of their role in exploring the divine power amidst common creatures settled in the immediate surroundings.

Human beings are godly creations with some specialties, and also with some limitations. All individuals are not competent equally in all the fields they tend to aspire for. Success in certain fields of activities and failure in some other fields make all individuals job specific. A teacher can handle the subject in which the excellence is duly attained through some formal training. Considering this context a common affair of the restructuring of skills and competence that an individual ascend with we all plan for certain human development activities and try our best to prepare an individual for the type of statehood or nationhood that one should come up with.

Ascent of the person from a local life to national and further to international life is the subject of capabilities and efforts that one put forth for gaining advancement. All individuals are not experts by born. Skills and competence acquired by them during the period of educational interaction and practices make them special. Fact sheet of disabilities make it clear that we are moving with some sort of limitations by all means. Both quality as well as quantity standards of human development efforts are the matters of concern. There remain some issues and concerns related to development that envisages the need of the refinement of the policy standards to regulate the functioning as well as implementation strategies that required for accommodating the skills and competence possessed by specially enabled person for the collective efforts of national economic progress. How to accommodate such skills and how to move them up through training implements will be the immediate point to be addressed.

Appropriate technologies and selected impairments envisage some of the strategic intervention that makes the human development easier through collaborative efforts of technicians, teachers and other professionals. Leaving any individual in darkness and ignoring the skills and competencies duly housed in that person will be a collective effort assisted with appropriate technologies and assistive standards. Varying impairment standards and their applicability has created a horizon of hope for specially enabled persons with which they can aspire for implementing their enhanced skills and competence for delivering their duties in more appropriate way. It is the wish factor that often makes a person more active than compared to the level duly estimated while mapping the realms of skills and competence.

Competency based curriculum design at the elementary level often points out the strength and limitations of a learner at various levels of interaction under various competencies. Such mapping will enable us to move on towards early specialization of the individual having special capabilities. For example, a person with problem of vision may be a good orator.

Not to point out towards the limitations of any individual and to correlate the situation with skills and competence housed in the person will be the highest state of interaction that brings the individual closure to the streams of success. It will even restore the normal functioning of the specially enabled individual aiming towards incorporation of the same entity in the realm of the state level socio-economic and cultural activities. Segmentation of society on the basis of a converged dimension of working capabilities encompasses chances of the formation of close cultural groups having identical job specifications. Such close quarters often acknowledge the presence of their counterpart. Scholars maintained different views regarding addressing aspirations of individuals having enhanced capabilities in certain fields supplemented with limitations of some other degrees and extent.

Question even raised on the necessity of administering medical care if the some physical or physiological malfunctions duly diagnosed at the tender age. In order to implementing an ideal development environment at work places, certain conditions or impairments may not be considered disabilities.

These may include but must not remain limited to:

1. Sexual behavior disorders of any kind proved to be against public policy;
2. Self-imposed body adornments such as tattoos and body piercing etc.;
3. Compulsive gambling, tendency to steal or light fires; disorders that affect a person's mental or physical state if they are caused by current use of illegal drugs or alcohol, unless the affected person is participating in a recognised programme of treatment duly prescribed by any registered medical professionals or clinics having valid registration of offering such treatments;
4. Normal deviations in height, weight and strength; and Conventional physical and mental characteristics and common personality traits.

Some of the reasonable accommodation can be of the category of best practices having adequate scope of incorporating skilled individuals for dealing with services and equipment of specific type. There is no general framework of any guideline for focusing the need of people aspiring for a suitable accommodation at service stations or work places, but some exemplar mechanism of such efforts can be placed for explaining the situation efficiently. It may vary in accord to the situation of the place and the nature of interaction with which the service line ups are accustomed with.

Selected examples of reasonable accommodation may be of following combinations by part or by whole:

1. Adopting existing facilities to make them accessible by specially enabled persons;
2. adopting existing equipment or acquiring new equipment including computer hardware and software or some other instrumentations for ensuring the smooth functioning of the individuals with certain limitations of any biological type;
3. re-organising work stations public places for ensuring safety;
4. changing training and assessment materials and systems;
5. restructuring jobs so that non-essential functions are re-assigned;
6. Adjusting working time and leave calendars; providing readers, sign language interpreters, and providing specialised supervision, training and support if needed.

There are certain pre requisites and guiding principles that an employer generally receive from the state executives. Some of the general points to be considered in general may be advanced for strengthening the policy parameters **specified for safeguarding the specially enabled employees at work places**. When employers recruit they should: identify the inherent requirements and essential functions of the vacant position; describe clearly the necessary skills and capabilities for the job; set reasonable criteria for selection, preferably in writing, for job applicants for vacant positions. The purpose of the selection process is to assess whether or not an applicant is suitably qualified. This may require a two-stage process if an applicant has a disability: (i) Determining whether an applicant is suitably qualified; (ii) Determining whether a 'suitably qualified applicant' needs any accommodation to be able to perform the inherent requirements or essential functions of the job.

Tests to establish the health of an applicant or employee should be distinguished from tests that assess the ability to perform essential job functions or duties. Health testing should therefore only be carried out after an employer has established that the person is in fact competent to perform the essential job functions or duties and after a job offer has been made. The same applies to medical testing for admission to membership of an employee benefit scheme. Abilities of working with the help of tools and technologies incorporated with Information and Communication Technologies.

There are some other issues which correlates a relationship of employee and employer to which leads the entire system towards a stability in terms of prosperity and vibrant progress.

It should have a definite checklist of system implements through which the evaluation process can be advanced.

Self-Regulation

Implementation of any desirable management model from outside without ascertaining the knowledge base of fellow workers can put the entire operation under question mark. It will not ensure the proper regulation of the process in time. Rapid automation of any system implement, for an example, will destabilize the functional vibrations of the group of employee. In some cases they might agitate for the same. System automation was already delayed in countries like India, Pakistan and Bangladesh. It was only because of the lack of digital literacy among people. Some of the socio-political segments of society were also against the automation. Automation was duly accelerated afterwards because of the parallel automation process which went on speedily in countries of Europe and America. It has become an unavoidable wave.

Automation can accelerate the activity of fellow workers getting involved in a co-ordinated operation of system and service. It can also accelerate the entire process of system implement through minimizing information gap and knowledge gap. It will also make the system implement a vibrant one. Service or system check lists of any type will be handled efficiently by the automated system drives. Chances of mistakes will be nullified in some of the system implements. Operational integration of ICT in system, production cycle and services is gaining momentum day by day.

There are several things which can be avoided to make the system implement more vibrant, more result oriented and more secured.

Things to be avoided

Peace and stability of a system design is often disturbed when any of the group or community of a society start considering themselves as a deprived or disadvantaged class. Optimum care should be taken to be taken to avoid the development of such situation in which any of the group start considering themselves as a deprived class. Success index of a community or a country depends on the capability of the community to accommodate aspirations of their groups or community segments who indent to incorporate themselves in the system design.

Religion should not be the character of a nation. Any kind of extremism may prevent the normal human to human relations. It may even hamper the progression of any business cycle because of which access to a system will be disturbed or destabilised. During modern times different nations are in a networked system through which they often address some of the common objectives. It is also confirmed that the system has to confer their flexibility up to a considerable mark to ensure the effective value of their currencies in open market. Any rigid apprehension of development model will hamper their prosperity.

For want of Sustainability

Sustainable Development Goals proposed by United Nations reflects some of the recommendations duly proposed by Mahatma Gandhi. Some other measures through which a country can establish examples of efficient model of sustainable development can be adopted by taking all or majority of measures duly pointed out as follows.

Approaches of Sustainable Development on the basis of Aspirations of Mahatma:

1. Leave no one behind (ANTYODAYA).
2. Technology intervention should be simple and also can be easily accessible.
3. People to people interaction should be more to accelerate the power of executions at the level of Local Self-Government.
4. Resource based planning for accommodating cottage industries with an integrated approach of involving people in the productivity process.
5. Attainment of self-sufficiency in terms of Food, Shelter and Clothing.
6. Universality of religion (through practices of all religious prayers) is considered as most efficient measure through which class differences can be minimized considerably. It can even create a ground of multifarious co-operations and mutual conducts for accelerating productivity.
7. Agricultural practices without hampering the balance duly established by the nature.
8. Exploration of locally available resources without introducing any exotic variety for ensuring resource based planning of economic activities. Small scale productivity cycles should be interlinked through state sponsored regulations of the market and distribution system of products.
9. Promotional schemes for encouraging enterprises which are functional at the local level for gaining momentum through sequential productivity cycle under effective patronage of the State Policy during few of the initial span of growth.
10. Rather than looking for large productivity and distribution chains a state should focus on development of small scale enterprises through ensuring regulations of the industrial and agricultural development, alongside the enhancement of knowledge base of the aspirants having willingness to prosper, for ensuring sustainability of the productivity cycle.
11. Sectoral coordination should be established in between law making, planning and implementing agencies to ensure smooth and swift functioning of different agencies specified for the purpose of ensuring continuation of development.

12. Non-replaceable damage to the environment due to pollution, deforestation and other difficulties should be checked efficiently by addressing issues concerned through incorporation of the regulatory mechanism in the process of planning and implementation cycles of all sorts of development projects.

13. Resource exploitation mechanism should be replaced by resource –exploration mechanism to bring normalcy and confluence in the naturally regulated process of a system. It will also ensure the stability of the entire ecosystem alongside the economic activity of a state.

14. None of the economic activities should have any micro planning having any environmental implications.

15. Equal distribution of resources amongst people is another factor with which productivity of a state can be accelerated u to a considerable mark.

16. It is also observed that Mahatma pointed out the necessity of judicious use of resources and also wanted his fellow volunteers to consider such principles to ensure conservation of resources.

17. Mahatma never wanted to kill snakes. He had prepared instruments for capturing such snakes alive and preferred liberating those creatures in distant places.

18. Mahatma also wanted to liberate fellow workers from the sanitary –maintenance works which was previously specified for a particular untouchable class. After removal of untouchability and other curses participation of people in National Productivity will be accelerated without hampering the normal continuity of development. (A naturally accelerated format of sustainable development)

19. Technology intervention should not be of such type which moves beyond the normal understanding and knowledge base of people. It should have all inclusive mechanism to ensure effective participation of people.

20. Proper adjustment between Resource, technology and People can be established after ensuring participatory convergence of approaches and understanding of people on the basis of resource base.

21. Mahatma also wanted women to play a vital role in on farm and off farm activities by bringing them out of the boundary of kitchen and household activities. For that reason people should go for bringing simplicity in kitchen related activities. Access to money and profit should be ensured for women.

Sustainability is not any exclusive activity of a state. Role of people, government and other development organisations should be ensured to materialise effective coordination of the planning and implementing agencies getting involved in the entire national productivity cycle.

Intellectual Refinement

We are discussing at present about saints like Veda Vyasa, Maharshi Patanjali, Valmiki and many more. Their presence can be ascertained even today through their creations, acts and conducts. They had created a best possible thought process and expected people to imbibe the same for ensuring aspirations of the advancement of the society through rectifications of the individual conducts.

Rectification of such type is a continuous process. We may not be able to claim about the absolute clarity on the process of rectification as an error free system. Such kinds of thought process will remain in the atmosphere even after thousands of years for making people acquainted with such principles.

The kind of thought process will remain in the context in the form of waves. Now a day's wave theory of the propagation of energy from its origin to the seat of action has become a common point of discussion. Wave theory of the propagation of energy form place to place addresses the need of people well in advance.

Thinking and attitude of people coming out from more or less identical socio-cultural background often exhibit similarities of many types. If countries from different socio-cultural background share parts of their border then it will be obvious that they often get indulge in some locally pitched conflicts. We can take the examples of the conflict between Armenia and Azar Bizan. Some other countries also put themselves in with certain vested interests. Communities fighting with each other are not justifiable at any cost. There exists other means of communication through which people move on to express their anger and also they can imply a sanction through business confluences.

Here comes the question of work culture and sectoral coordination. We have also witnessed the attitudinal difference between Rama and Ravana, as vividly described at difference instances in the famous epic the Ramayana. Rama wanted Ravana to give Sita, his life partner, back. He had deputed his messenger twice for making Ravana, the demon king from Sri Lanka, agree upon the proposal of peace.

The proposal of peace was rejected in one hand and the power, potential and courage of lord Rama was ignored on the other. The result came in the form of a war. That war was also not meant for killing all the people of that country. It was not even meant for smashing the kingdom for grabbing resources, nor even meant for putting the name and reverence of lord Rama in the fore front. It was meant for teaching a lesson to the demon king and also for diffusing his state of ego, compulsion and desires.

The thought process that started moving along with the advancement of lord Rama was perfectly captured and imbibed by the brother of the demon king namely Bibhishan. He had managed himself to come out of the darkness of ego, compulsion and desires by harnessing the philosophy of peace, prosperity and collective progress. The result with him was also quite fruitful. He was the victorious person of that battle and duly accepted the place of his elder brother.

The Ramayana, The Mahabharata and other such scriptures always display the victory of good forces over the evil ones through inculcating waves of peace, prosperity, brotherhood, collective progress and prosperity for all. These acts also intensified at some places by linking up the bands of true and absolute knowledge with devotion to bring forth the powers of right action.

Hanumana, the warrior of lord Rama as described in the Ramayana, is the best example of such character having perfect combination of Knowledge and devotion. Once a situation developed in the middle of the journey of the envoy of Lord Rama during the moment when they had to cross a long stretch of ocean to reach Sri Lanka for obtaining information about Sita. All fellows present in the envoy started guessing about their own capabilities, only the person silent was Hanumana. His seniors wanted to know the exact reason of his silence. Hanumana said that the power possessed by him is obviously enormous, but it is not in his hand. A divine force guides the manifestation of that power. It will be implemented even at the service of the divine. Such knowledge was the exhibit of the true knowledge. Based on that knowledge one can surpass all possible obstacle whichever might come on the way. Similar thing happened with Hanumana. By crossing all the obstacles he reached the destiny and traced out Sita.

Sita noticed the presence of the messenger deputed by lord Rama. Here came the situation where Hanumana exhibited his devotion. For gaining the confidence of Sita on warriors and associates of Rama he had exhibited his enormous power in that garden where Sita was kept under observation. He even wanted to bring Sita back to Rama immediately. He was stopped by Sita by instructing him not to violate the rule of the family and tradition from which Ram is taking the lead. He was requested to follow the assignment in particular for which Rama deputed him.

Here both Sita and Hanumana exhibited their devotion to their immediate master. It was also an exhibit of their loyalty to their master. Such loyalty often culminates to give birth to enormous power with which lord Rama along with his entire envoy was advancing towards the Demon King to teach him a lesson.

The fact was developing beyond the imagination that is why it was not perceivable by persons having inflictions of ego, anger, hatred, self-centrelines and desires. Ravana perceived the development in the envoy of Rama and his advancement towards his kingdom as an impossible task. After noticing the presence of Hanumana in front of him he was not convinced by the powers of monkeys and other associates who were accompanying lord Rama. The waves of devotion of the godly presence, whom Ravana used to worship regularly, continued radiating out through the acts, conducts and attitudes of Hanumana. Then also Ravana was not in a position to accept any chance of the advancement of lord Rama towards his territory. Such standpoint of a warrior develops from the over confidence of the person about the system, implements and parts of such implements.

That over-confidence removes all possible chances of rectification of the system. Because of that reason also Ravana failed to rectify his mistakes and placed himself in the turmoil of trouble.

Whatever lessons we learn from experiences and interactions will sustain in our life for a longer time period. It can even bring sustaining happiness and contentment within us. Here lies the way in which any thought process perpetually moved from one individual to the other.

In the modern world we have various types of cultural and religious thought process possessing rituals, customs and traditions of different types , which are equally competent to enrich people in terms of knowledge, devotion, courage, will power and dedication. The way we receive each culture to enrich our multiplurality will specify our degrees and ranges of success. Our motive force will guide accordingly to explore possibilities of working out converged cultural segments from all the rituals to move up towards vibrant waves of multi plurality.

India , at this juncture of the development of multiplurality, will be a best example for all of us. Here people learned a lot to live with each other, tolerate each other and enrich each other differently.

We cannot see light. Even we cannot see the propagation of sound through the material medium. Light strikes our eye, reaches our brain and develops a sensation of vision through certain life process of vision. With some sort of illusion, or lack of true knowledge only, we often claim that we can see light. Even all the colours radiated out from the sun are not recognisable by us. If God resides inside the individual, if all mysteries related to the ascent of a person on the path of divinity, then why any devotee search it out for gaining the blessings of any Divine power located outside the physically existing body? Why such a dwindling situation any individual face during the tenure of worship?

Lord Krishna narrated essence of feeling the Divine communion with the physically existing life through witnessing cultivation of knowledge, actualisation of the presence of any supreme power in sub conscious mind and possible ways and means to follow that power. It enables an individual to come across the feeling of the advent of some completeness in the mind through knowledge transformation. Cultivation of knowledge regarding the relationship of the divine and disciple is enrouted from the age old traditions through the turmoil of the organic evolution. That evolution brought some change in the process of exhibits, but the core remained the same. It was even more perpetual and more profound regarding the ability of harnessing the relationship of matter and energy. We cannot imagine the existence of matter without the involvement of energy, and similarly energy takes a definite visible form to occupy certain space in this universe.

How do people see things and how do they correlate such unavoidable relationship of energy and matter is depend upon the level of understanding that one adheres with. A master of Physics and a master of Philosophy must have varying degree of explanations for putting forth the mystery behind the mechanism involved during inter-conversion of matter and energy. All organic combinations have certain physical and chemical sets of combinations in such a definite ways that they inculcate the abilities of interactions and abilities of giving birth to senses. Even evolution of sensory structures and related orientations became much collaborative in case of human beings. Here occurs a change which brought us near the state of explorations meant for examining the hidden mysteries behind creation and orientation of life forms in the living planet.

These days, things are known to us that earth like situation exists in the universe. Only the matter of concern is that we may not be able to reach the place even after attaining the speed as that of light in a year or two. Only we can admire the presence and orientation of such creations within our visibility. Only we can explore and examine such things with the help of optical and electronic instruments. With an understanding of such limitations human beings never arranged any voyage to explore the inner world of senses that can allow us to explore the outer orientation of time and space. Such an inner world exploration may require a little effort to culminate senses within a confinement for feeling the presence. There also resides a tremendous flux of energy accumulated within such a small space. Those mysterious combinations taking the form of life were explored differently by saints during olden times.

There developed a science of explorations of the correlations of the Creation and the Divine. Matter and energy indulged in a perfect orientation for letting senses flow through them. Arrangement and orientation of all our senses are directed outwardly. That is why we are bound to receive waves and sparks from the outside world. Our inner world remains unexplored in most of the cases. Only adherence of true knowledge and the journey of senses through inner world during meditation can pave a way out for exploring our own self. Meditation is the doorstep where orientation of senses get diverted towards the inner world and bring out mysteries associated to the fact of accommodation of the Divine power inside the living being.

Is that Divine power is restricted to the human beings only? The answer is, obviously and surely without any doubt, No. human beings has gained some sort of evolutionary supremacy in due course of time, but other beings are also of same potential and courage with a domination of animism in them. Dogs are loyal to their master, cats exhibit better vigilance power, elephants are more socialised beings having better memory power and tigers are the masters of their own territory. Taking hold upon the surrounding and defining the role according to trophic [204] level, we can easily arrange these beings and others without any difficulty.

Philosophical and Spiritual supremacy is a step forward that makes a distinction between other animals and human beings. Then also we can witness inhuman acts from human beings and humanly acts from

---

[204]. A Trophic level signifies the food habit of organisms during their representation as they exhibit in a food chain. Green Plants, for example prepares their own food with the help of sunlight and secures the first position in a food chain and basic position in the food pyramid. Second trophic level is occupied by herbivores, followed by carnivores at the third.

some inhuman animals. The orientation of sense organ and correlation of senses and sensory responses with memory and intellect is the only factor regulating such varying degrees and conducts of animismic and hunmanismic behaviours.

Presence of such a Divine power within the creation is the reason behind the maintenance of an idea of serving humanity with a correlated apprehension of serving God. Only God cannot put a direct access to the feelings of the presence of such immense power within us. It is the approach with which we offer our services to living beings can develop a way out for us to feel the difference.

Once during pre-independent period in Bombay (at present Mumbai) a youth from some semi urban place approached a saint for offering himself at the service to divine. It made the saint happy. He wanted to know the exact reason behind his stand of doing so. Saint also enquired about his capabilities and considered his offering a wise one. Actually the fellow was searching jobs in the city. He was also a normal Graduate from any sub –urban area and his financial situation was also not so good. Perhaps the sacrifice might make him temporarily happy and contented, but will become a burden in due course of time. With happiness saint suggested him for searching out a suitable job and helping the parents and inmates of the family financially. Only After gaining some wealth and knowledge the person can really enjoy the glory of sacrifice. Right now the person has nothing special to sacrifice. Such sacrifice inflicted with sorrow and agony may put both the master and the disciple in trouble.

Even divine cannot allow any individual to put oneself and families in trouble and agony. It is the only state of contentment that helps a person during movement from the physical world to the spiritual world. Offerings of any kind and in any particular form will bring happiness.

Once upon a time, a shopkeeper had a beautiful dream. The dream was so beautiful and so perfectly understandable that he feared of sharing it with others. According to his dream the God himself wanted to visit his shop. It was winter season and more special about the time that, it was raining outside. Amidst such patchy rains he preferred opening the shop. Inmates knew it better about his firmness upon any decision. He prepared some sweet dishes, some snacks and few cakes for the strange visitor of the day. Face of God was appeared in dream and was not recognisable with any clear identification marks. "The Master must introduce himself, or may give some signal so that his poor fellow can recognise", his happiness went on increasing bit by bit.

"Can I have some snacks and a cake?" An old lady was approaching the shop with a can on her hand.

"Today, actually I've not opened the shop! If you came then please, have it."

"Guest! Some special or any usual one!" Curiosity of the old lady alarmed the shopkeeper for keeping the matter a secret one.

A cowboy was approaching holding a fruit in his right hand. "That guard is chasing me. Let me come in, please."

"But, you are already inside my shop! Anyway let me see the fellow.."

Cowboy narrated the entire incident behind the reason of his hunger. That fruit was kept aside and the shopkeeper offered him a dish full of sweets, snacks and cakes.

"Don't worry my child, I'm here with you."

The matter settled in an hour. Striking of the noon time bell of the cathedral instructed the shopkeeper to finish his meal. But, what about that strange visitor! There were no traces of such visit amidst the sprinkling of droplets in the courtyard and a shower on the roads.

Evening time visitors were a cobbler, a mason, a hawker and a vagabond. Earning was not the matter of the day that is why he offered food to all the visitors with respect. It became possible because of his happiness. At last the mind refused to support him properly. Entire day and half of the night went on waiting for the master. Ultimately the time came to stop waiting for the strange visitor. His mind was still in a motive of receiving the visitor. May be the master is trying to meet him when calmness mounts the surrounding. With such anticipation he preferred keeping the door half open.

"So nice! So sweet! Really all items were tasty..", the masterly voice brought his happiness back in dream.

"I may visit you again and again."

Morning time dream mixed up profusely with chirping of birds and silver linings of the clouds.

"God came! Who was that? May be that boy! .. " Series of anticipations and guessing went on for few moments. The entire face of the shop keeper was glistening with happiness. It was the time for feeling the presence of the Master in any nearby position. It had developed a faith in his mind, "My Master must come and visit me again."

We cannot deny the role of a school in the life of any individual. The person gains a lot during school days. S(he) can learn how to impart oneself in the society by redefining ones role in society.

It is not the only aspect of life through which any individual gets an opportunity to expose oneself to the fundamental value system prevalent in society. One's choice factor plays a definitive role in this regard.

Cultural background of an individual is greatly influenced by the immediate surroundings. Human beings, for an example of an ordinary type, are vegetarian by nature, but omnivorous by intended vigil of gaining some essential proteins from the animal sources. Development of canine indicates the biologically and naturally assigned habit to human beings. If we aspire for remaining confined within the naturally sanctioned habits of our own then the acts and conducts related to the killing of animals for the sake of gaining essentials will definitely go at its minimum.

Killing of animals for obtaining food and medicine is perpetually inflicted with acts of animism. It also signifies the place of human beings at a definite trophic level. It has also exposed our relationship with other organisms and our dependency upon the source. We rarely make ourselves capable of trapping waves directly from the sun. It will always reach us through the involvement of producers (such as green plants). Maintaining green plants in nature and allowing them to prosper in our surrounding is, therefore, becoming a non-avoidable activity of the system in which we are confirming our presence. The referred system also limits our ascent and conducts. Within that limit of acts and conducts any human being can explore possibilities of registering the presence of oneself by performing the duties duly assigned to the individual perfectly, perpetually and vividly.

Escapism

One cannot escape from oneself without performing duties duly assigned by the system designed for ensuring interactions of different trophic levels. If we start claiming that tigers should not be allowed to kill deer, cats should not chase rats, snakes should not feed on frogs and owls should not puncture ripe fruits then our claims will violate the laws of nature. With certain natural instincts and for maintaining a proper balance in nature organisms ensure their definite role as per the assignments. Human beings are playing a role with some sort of exceptions. One can intend to kill deer for obtaining food, one can trap fishes, kill birds, smash snakes and chase bulls for fulfilling the need of grabbing food. With a modified vigil of registering one's presence in the cycle of energy transfer one can cultivate grains, harvest fruits and maintain mulching animals for fulfilling the requirement of food. For rest of the world the role of that human will be of a protector.

With such dual principles human beings can register the presence of oneself in between the highest and middle order of the trophic level. In another aspect we people maintain our difference from others due to our ductility, capabilities to speak, performance of exhibiting our emotions and affinity of remaining linked with others. Here comes the essence of socialisation and acculturation for the same. On the basis of such involvement in the society parents cannot escape from their duties of nourishing their children, young ones cannot escape from their duties toward elders and seniors cannot escape from their affinity of helping young ones.

Escapism of any type and any degree is the affinity of human beings for which the entire community may face sufferings, loss of trust and agony. Escapism of any type can also create individual differences, depending upon which human beings often start ascertaining one's role in society.

We cannot claim that all people make them capable enough to escape from the acts of escapism and make themselves more active, more responsible, perfectly awakened and properly adjusted. Lord Krishna instructed Arjun for gaining absolute knowledge. Yoga in action cannot work alone for giving the feeling of the presence of the Divine within the self. There requires involvement of true knowledge. Knowledge alone without any action cannot bring desired result. That is why culmination of both knowledge and action is essential for feeling the presence of a supernatural creator within the self. The state of such feeling of the culmination of knowledge and senses can make the process of renunciation of the soul possible. Aspiration of only renunciation without acquiring knowledge and without performing duty cannot work properly. It will put an individual in a state of utter confusion. The state of Self Esteem signifies the appropriate and timely correlations in between time, effort, knowledge and skills for making the role of an individual a meaningful one in the immediate surroundings.

.

Approach of Banking

In accord to the present day context the term "Conflict – Resolution' is often replaced by "Conflict- Transformation[205]" This approach encompasses the need of rebuilding lost relationships to certain extent. We can consider it as an approach of re-adjustment of issues and concerns to avoid or to minimize chances of growth of any conflict in the context. Supporting internal actors and ensuring external peace building efforts can be considered by agencies involved in the conflict transformation process. Peace and support reconciliation is ensured by promoting the moderate group residing in between two or more conflicting groups.

---

[205] *It suggests replacing the term "conflict resolution" with the term "conflict transformation" (Rupesinghe 1995).*
John Paul Lederach developed the first comprehensive and widely discussed transformation-oriented approach (Lederach 1997). (See also Lederach's article on p 7 in this issue.)

Three different level approaches of transformation which can be taken up by the agency concerned are tabulated (Table 1) to point out their relevance for three different layers of a state.

<u>Table 2: Three different levels of Conflict Transformation Approaches</u>

Levels of a State	Approaches of Transformation
Track 1: Top Leadership	Mediation at the level of State Outcome oriented approaches
Track 2: Middle Level of a State	More resolution oriented approaches
Track 3: Grassroots Level / Village Level	Problem solving workshops Community Dialogue projects Trauma Healing Technical and Academic assistance

This transformation approach is also specified by its shift from international level to regional level. This approach provide us a set of lenses through which we start addressing conflicts for the purpose of working out more sharper and effective ways out to resolve (transform) issues resulting in the growth and expansion of conflicts. Each lens has its extent with which it can imply focus on the factors related to conflict. The term lens stands for the approach which is considered for analyzing a situation. None of the lenses are capable of focusing everything of the context from which conflict is springing out. That is why complex reality of a situation requires a set of lens for ensuring effective analysis. Three lenses are fitted in the same frame to see a definite portion of reality (from close proximity, from moderate level and from a distant level). Later on these three views can be integrated to examine the reality.

Importance of lenses:

a. To see the immediate situation.
b. To see past of the immediate problems and to view the deeper relationship patterns.
c. To work out a framework that holds these aspects together for the purpose of creating a platform for addressing the context.

Conflict Transformation Framework has three distinct components through which the entire system is advanced:

a. Demonstration of the situation through prominently visible issues and concerns duly traced out through a process of the analysis of context.
b. Exploration of the horizon of preferred future.
c. The development of change process through which the analysis of context and preferred future can be made possible.

We can take an example from a grass-root level experience issue from a problem developed in a village located near Tatanagar of Jharkhand state. Statement of Problem: Budhu Sabar, a poor farmer from Nimdih Block of Singbhoom District (present name is Saraikela-Kharsawan District) received a pair of bullock financed by a Nationalised bank under IRDP[206] Scheme sponsored by Govt. of Jharkhand. Due to any fatal disease Budhu lost one of the bullocks. Another bullock became useless due to lack of effective knowledge known to Budhu. He approached the bank for seeking support. He requested bankers to get another bullock for making the pair. Bankers had no such scheme to sanction a bullock to Budhu. Bank also requested Budhu to repay the half of the amount along with interest amount. Budhu refused to pay as the source of income was not becoming effective. The loan amount went on increasing. The problem developed due to incapability of Budhu in paying back the due. Bank Manager issued a letter to Budhu for repaying the loan amount. The conflict between Budhu and Bank was addressed by A Social Worker who was working in a development Organisation. Banker requested the social worker to manage the payment of loan amount for making Budhu eligible for gaining another support as per the scheme of IRDP. The Social Worker started searching out effective technology of developing a cart to utilize the single bullock for driving a cart. He has also worked out a source to repay the loan amount through some easy instalments. Ultimately a cart is developed which can be moved by using a bullock. Budhu started earning by driving the cart and started repaying the loan.

---

[206] *Integrated Rural Development project duly implemented by State Governments in India to address problem of poverty.*

We can design the flow chart of the Conflict Transformation process as follows:

The process Design	Analysis/Steps taken
Demonstration of the situation	Budhu trapped in the problem due to loss of a bullock. Loan repayment request issued by Banker made him disturbed.
Exploration of the horizon of preferred future	Social Worker started searching effective technology and available sources of donors for addressing the issue.
The development of change process	Cart suitable for using one bullock is developed. The same is provided to Budhu. He started earning. Loan repayment process is restored. Relationship of Budhu and Banker is also restored to normal.

There are several other examples through which we can address the mechanism of Conflict Transformation process.

Culture of Speed and Body Posture

It is obvious we are moving through information which is also guided by speed with which people want a system or an instrument to work. Information system is also designed to address aspirations to increase the clock speed of a processor to make the dream of the user of technology a reality. People also prefer fast moving vehicles. It is also true that enhancement of sped and effectiveness of an instrument has some sort of reality. We cannot go on increasing the speed in a regular succession. We also cannot address a system modification simply through attaining increase in speed of processing and momentum. Another factor which drives our attention due to body focus with which mind set of youths is changing day by day. Sometimes such kind of apprehension appears absolutely irrelevant and unscientific. The way artists project themselves in movies is also changing day by day by following a format of irrelevant exhibitionism.

It is obviously admissible that we can address both the issues through Gandhian values of personality development. Let us take a simple example of a personality parameter through which essence of performing a task with adequate understanding is becoming relevant. Person A and person B are working in the same office. Person a takes more time in drafting letters as (s)he prefers preparing documents with care to minimize chances of mistakes. Person B prepares draft of documents with adequate speed and manages to finish work before time. During following day they compare their works. Person B requires extra time to resolve mistakes committed during faster speed of data entry. Person A remained effective in this regard because of negligible mistakes. We can conclude from above example that speed is essential in the information age, but speed is not the whole and sole factor with which effectiveness of a system can be ascertained. Mahatma always maintained simplicity in his daily life. He wanted other fellow workers to maintain simplicity in life. He had a deep concern regarding mental and spiritual enrichment of an individual which is also needed for enhancement of personality design. Knowledge is the actual factor which enhances personality of an individual. Body design has nothing role to play in personality enhancement. Because of that reason personality parameter is rarely influenced by anybody design. Beauty is differently explained by Mahatma. Real beauty is reflected properly through right speech, right thinking, right vision and right compassion towards creation. That is why followers of Mahatma maintained simplicity in their life and continued refining their personality formats through refinement of mind and intellect in a regular fashion through self-study and actualisation of individual characters. We cannot expect any higher order of functioning from a person badly influenced by Body Focus. It has nothing to do with personality enhancement. It has also limitations in the form of crippled apprehension which work specifically for providing intuitive alignment towards passion and fantasy leading ultimately towards falsehood. Only the way out through which an individual may effectively move is the alignment of the self towards attainment of knowledge leading the fellow finally towards personality enhancement.

5. Knowledge

Absolute knowledge cannot wait for any material set up to make it evident. It is more confluent than compared to the flow of water, faster than the speed of light and more luminous than the strong lumens like those of stars. It can make people understand things with clear apprehension of putting forth the segment of acts and conducts for the purpose of offering an understanding of facts, figures, events, mechanisms and confluence of information.

Due to lack of such absolute knowledge people often fail to understand the exact reasons behind the manifestation of the supreme power through different living forms. This supreme power resides with identical potential in all the individuals starting from tiny bacteria up to a giant whale. They all combine their own creations with the help of materials present in the real world in an absolute combination of certain format to give a prominent existence. Such individuals can move through the world with certain objectives of leading an assigned life until and unless a band of disintegration of such organic coordination breaks down due to death. In other words, energy is the only super natural power which regulates different components of nature on their way towards creation or destruction of any living form. Absolute knowledge only can make us understand the aspects related to creation and destruction. In Indian philosophy, natural components got the name Prakriti and the super natural component got the name Purush. Communion of Prakriti and Purush makes the creation possible. If such principle is true then it must be evident even at the atomic level of creation; at that level nuclear energy binds the positively charged protons along with some other uncharged particles to make the creation of nucleus possible. Electrons are bound to remain restricted around that empowered core. This mystery of creation signifies the claim of Veda regarding existence of Super Natural Power (BRAHMA)[207] in all the naturally occurring articles, "Brahma is at all places, within all particles and inside all the beings."

---

[207] Section 14, Chapter 3, Upanishad:

It is the knowledge which becomes visible through various actions of a person. It is that knowledge which differentiates a sage from a beggar; it integrates individual apprehensions to materialize each minute actions of that individual for the purpose of defining the final destiny of that person amidst the turmoil of social interactions. That knowledge becomes the guiding force behind senses and guides those senses to assimilate the signals of desired types. Desire is the state of mind which makes the individual apprehension secure within the realm of human actions. It also ensures proper coordination of all the impulses of senses to materialize the desired action. Those guiding force even acts during the process of inter –personal communication. It enables a person to go for accepting or rejecting any communication bands duly offered by some other individual. Differences of such bands of sensual communications can define the enemy and friends from amongst the group of people came in contact. Distinction of friend and enemy creates a varying matrix of inter-personal communication inflicted with protecting or smashing any individual.

Knowledge increases with corresponding increase in the experiences and mind power. In due course of time mind becomes the store house of all the information and avails them to be used by the analytical segment of the brain as per need. Here lies the mystery of success and failure of coordinated senses. It can even define the proper culmination of both the components of the intellect for making the materialization of senses possible. Person with such kind of balanced mind and intellect can speak perfectly, can listen properly, can go for smelling and tasting right things and even can feel the presence of some wealthy impulses in the surrounding.

Any sort of imbalance of mind and intellect can make the senses unfit for materializing any perfect action. The Gita points out the essence of attainment of such kind of balances of mind and intellect for regulating senses and making them fit for right and timely actions.

Sarvam khalvidam brahma, tajjalaniti santa upasita, atha khalu kratumayah puruso yatha-kratur-asmin-loke puruso bhavati tathetah pretya bhavati, sa kratum kurvita.
Meaning: Brahma is the only supreme power. Everything comes from that, sustain in that and finally returns to that, is the only power which empowers us all. People study all the aspects related to what dissolves in that, comes from that and works due to that.

Shopkeepers worship their beloved God before opening the hut, industrious people worship God just before cementing the first brick of their construction works, crafts person worship their instruments during some fixed interval of days to commemorate the supreme power. Worship of energy and efforts is the custom of universal occurrence. There occurs an emotional attachment of artisans with their instruments. They even take care of their instruments on a regular basis. Gradually they come up with an enhanced vision of putting their efforts to keep all the instruments at perfectly operational state. They even consider their instruments as their immediate focus of scheduled daily activities.

Nobody claim the direct interaction with God, but we can feel the presence of such divine power within ourselves. Manifestation of such power will put us at a state of success, where we become fearless in delivering our best possible efforts and services to our immediate reference group. That state of awakening will be the accomplishable goal for any individual including the fellow artisan.

The nature and extent of support, not only in the form of technical knowhow but also in the form of assistance to cope up with market, should be considered for making the system implement appropriate for the rural artisans and farmers. More perpetually one can plan to link up the community with the immediate availability of the resource base for ensuring greater chance of success. Proper combination of Resource, Technology and Skills can define the scope of attaining success. Development workers, since olden times through varying approaches, always worked to search out proper technology, proper mechanism to rely upon, living within minimum, and also moving out of the activities leading toward creation of best possible products and services. They also marked out the fact that technology to be adopted should be people friendly and easy to handle, even it should be compatible to the type of resource base a community relying upon. All sorts of absurdity should be removed.

Lack of confidence upon the system and its implements is the immediate set back that often brings the entire chain of productivity under question mark. One rarely prefers to wait up to the moment of the creation of any enhanced demand of the locally developed products. Better one should launch the implements on an experimental basis duly supplemented with a subtle increase in the productivity.

Financial Institutions always imply a prolonged processing of any appeal of fund. It should be made flexible in terms of availing ease of access to small and marginalised artisans. There is other side responsible for the complexity of the processing of any appeal of finance. Most of aspirants become defaulter while moving across newly implemented enterprise leading toward a severe loss because of the mismatch of resource, technology and knowledge. Yoga based actions never pass on with any blunt apprehension of such failure ultimately leading towards any mis-adjustment between resources, skills and technologies. Mis-adjustment of resources, skills and technologies often becomes so worse in some cases that can even put a crafts person or farmer to a life risk. Situation of farmers in Vidarbha because of indebtedness can be placed as an example.

Here we can take an example to exhibit the lack of proper coordination between the planning and implementing agencies duly involved in some development works. One such incident was recorded from the same area of Jharkhand during 1995. Some fellow farmers of Nimdih Block of Saraykela District of Jharkhand received Bullocks financed by a Nationalised Bank. Loss of the life of one of the bullock made another one useless, and in a gradual succession the farmer trapped in the clutch of the financial crisis because of the lack of any immediate return in terms of productivity. The marginalised farmer again trapped in the net of turmoil because of the intervention of a private source of finance for clearing the Bank Loan. The Bank was not in a situation to bring the farmer out of the previous indebtedness because of the rigidity of the financial regulations of the Development Initiatives of the government.

While planning for any industrial activity suitable for a specific rural community, one can imply the credibility of the selected products as per the global standards. Standards of such level can bring the entire system to a stream of implements having more focus upon the look and finish of the outcome to be entangled with the market system. Product should say its own purity and perfectness. It should even attend and apprehend the quality consciousness of people willing to rely upon the same. It should not even break the linkages of demand and supply for enhancing the systematized permanence. This kind of market mechanism will undoubtedly increase the market demand of the selected item.

If any business house of Europe implies stress upon manufacturing Artificial Fabrics with greater success indicators, the same can be housed in the National Economy with higher index of success supplemented with profit. Productivity should go on parallel to the demand that duly created in market. One should remain stick to the mechanism after considering the global demand. Competition alone cannot define any effort as a fruitful and time tested one. One should work to correlate acquired skills and competence of fellow workers with that of the technology available to us. Here arises the need of implementing a discussion on true knowledge.

Veda, Upanishad and other scriptures of Indian origin always describes true knowledge as a subtle confluence of streams of information and skills having adequate power of abolishing the cultural blindness and spiritual rigidness through bringing transformation in characters and will power. Knowledge is the only thing that grows on sharing. It never shrinks to its minimum. A tree of knowledge, as described by saints in Gita, spreads its leaves downwardly in the form of Vedic teachings. The upwardly spreading roots of prosperity receive continuously confluent source of knowledge from the divine and nourishes the entire creation through millions of exhibits of such knowledge. Theory of Relativity, for an example, was not there waiting in the chamber of the fellow scientist. It was there in the cultivation of his skills and ideas which, with an ultimate manifestation, enabled him to link up his observations duly required for deriving the theory. His deeper involvement in that specified faculty enabled him to weave such linkages of theories and propositions.

We always witness the manifestation of such supreme knowledge through its creations. It can even imply a guiding force for the entire creature residing in the immediate surroundings. Such a prosperous sacred fig tree (Peepal) can bring forth the absolute knowledge in the form of a normal and continuous confluence of waves of thought processes. Veda described it as an eternal one. It has a sequential expansion having a parallel pace of such considerations through knowledge transformation. Keeping oneself free from illusions and selfishness, one can realise the true nature of absolute knowledge and accordingly can put efforts to gain such knowledge at its absolute nature for making oneself contented and complete.

Down flow of senses and sensible actions become materialised through passage of such waves from the divine to the disciple with an active involvement of masterly minds. This confluence of knowledge and related mechanisms properly explained in chapter fifteen of Gita. One can get rid of the confluence of such relationships of manifestation by cutting the linkages of willingness and desire by using weapons of absolute knowledge. Desires[208] and wishes in the form of leaf grow downwardly growing tree and gains further enrichment through addition of more concepts and propositions by saints. The hidden core of all such knowledge resides only in the absolute confluence of pure knowledge through roots.

If one start moving from leaves and move gradually towards rootlets, then the enlightenment come in the form of repeated crystallization and refinement of knowledge in a regular progression. The final destiny in this way will be Divine only. Involvement of such power in all sorts of creations and actions become critical at that moment. In actual sense the source and the destiny of the confluence of energy experiences a linkage between various aspects of manifestation. Normal confluence of energy through the cycles of creation and destruction are absolutely inseparable ones. A Black Hole, for example at this critical juncture, is the seat of destruction and creation. From one side all matters and manifestations winded up for accelerating the pace of reversely directed streams and waves of creation.

---

[208] Desire is a state of mind that gives birth to a strong feeling to have something in acquisition or an affinity of wanting something to happen.
For example: I desire only to be left in the state of peaceful mind. Desire cannot kill any intellect, but in a long run, it can suppress the chances of a shift of mind towards something innovative.

This absolute knowledge empowers us adequately and facilitates us vividly during our process of identifying presence of divine in every individual with an absolute state of our contentment. Gita even facilitates us in the process of our understanding of the evolutionary trend remaining evident in the biosphere.

We can take the example of the experiences gained by a saint namely Madhavdasji [209]during his wandering days in holy places. The saint was with an absolute state of devotion and used to collect remaining food left out by saintly persons of Ashrams. From such a collection he used to offer it to the Divine first. It was his daily routine activity. One day he was late in moving out for collecting such residues from ashrams and because of forgetfulness he had taken a few without offering it to the Divine. After taking the food in mouth he has realized his mistake and started weeping like a child. He went on weeping in the same posture and the food remained in his mouth.

He was in a dilemma of his inability of taking any concrete step. He cannot take that food without offering it to his beloved god; even he could not spit it out for insulting saints who had offered him that food. With such a simplicity and contentment he had an experience of feeling the presence of his master within himself only.

Madhavdasji experienced presence of Divine power near him and got an instruction offering the same food that was there in his mouth. Such a call was even firm and absolute for conferring the presence of similar power within him. It was directing him to forget about physically evident differences. This state of mind developed in Madhavdasji because of his absolute contentment and faith on the source. He has sacrificed all his wishes worries for incorporating the impulse of Divine in the form of absolute impulse of thinking and action. His actions have correlation with mind and intellect and his intellect was developing on the basis of his repeated actions and meditations.

We cannot go blindly driven by the waves and impulses of our senses. There must remain a regulation for quantifying our relations of

---

[209] Madhavdasji |(1798-1921) was from Bengal and later on entered Vaishnavism. He learned a lot to acquire all sorts of knowledge on Hathayoga duly proposed and framed earlier by Saint Patanjali.

mind, intellect and sense organs for harnessing a success for us. Here lies the secret of the instructions inscribed in The Gita in the section of the Yoga of Knowledge (Jnan Yoga), where regulation of senses is the first step towards making the mind fit for recognizing the presence of the Divine within the bodily existence. Feeling such omnipresence of the divine is the state of mind which brings renunciation for an individual.

What we want and what we need are two different aspects present in our society and are the factor responsible for varying degree of pace in the distribution of resources in our surrounding. Some people gain a lot and keep things in reserve for future use, some other people lacks basic amenities and suffer a lot; they keep on wandering here and there in search of a living.

We never claim our absolute isolation from the immediate surrounding because of the intimate relationship we regularly exercise on a daily basis for claiming basic facilities needed for living. Entire population of human beings living in cities and villages are directly or indirectly rely upon the natural resources (Prakriti in terms of The Gita).

Resources we obtain from nature are in plenty. All such resources reach us through various mechanisms of processing. All such processing and operational activities employed a group of people differently. If nature permits some activity in common for all then we must rely upon such activities for maintaining balance in the immediate surroundings. There exist many examples to show the inter-relationship of human beings and nature. Human beings depend upon plants and other animals for food, shelter, clothing and medication. That is why our activities against the basic rules of the nature will put us in trouble.

People from tribal villages worship the Nature God in different ways. They express their happiness during their belongingness to the Nature. Different tribal leaders from olden times agitated against the Forest Act due to the intention of the law makers to break the intimate relationship of Tribal communities and forests. During British rule people from the adjoining areas of forest refused to accept the modernisation techniques duly introduced by the government. They preferred to stay adjacent to the forest biota for ensuring their sustained living.

Efforts were made to link them with the main stream of the human society. All such efforts of linking tribal communities from the main stream of society received a failure due to the gap of information, knowledge and culture that remained prevalent within the communities and the government.

Nature is the place where both living and non-living things interact in a balanced manner to make the place in this living planet a regularised one. It is better to say that the Nature moves through a self-regulating mechanism of development, creation and destruction. Several organisms developed in due course of time and several others lost their identities too. Once Dinosaurs were there in plenty and were freely roaming around in search of food. These days they are only legendary character having some place in films, fictions and parables.

The scope of this publication is to point out the propositions and concerns regarding a specified animal, namely terrestrial tiger, for its inability of coping up the changes in the habitat. Availability of the natural habitat for that animal is shrinking day by day. Human intrusions in the areas protected by law are another matter of concern. We are losing a greater segment of the population of big cats because of our inability of providing them a suitable nestling and breeding ground. They are not so adjustable like other pets and farm animals and cannot accept supremacy and command of human beings over them. This attitude made them considerably unfit for the society, and even for the wild biota.

Their violent attitude exposed them badly to the anger, agitation and violence of human beings. They even became victims of some wild games of hunting, killing and poaching. A vanity associated with killing of wild beasts made them more vulnerable. Acts and other protective measures designed by different governments have different limitations. People also learned a lot to bypass such laws and propositions for fulfilling their desires. At one place all laws and propositions are a failure. It is the law of nature, natural balance and factors of energy transfer at various trophic levels in the biosphere. The science related to such diversified mechanism of energy transfer through trophic levels made the animal absolutely linked differently to different types of energy transfer chains.

If we understand these things in a better way then all our acts and conducts should be designed in accord to the availability of resource pool without disturbing their normal linkages. Here lies the actual need of establishing perpetuated coordination between nature, economy and people. This effort moves with an insight of exploring the possible ways and means of establishing linkages in between people, ecology and economy.

What animals want and what are the things we are offering them is a matter of comparison one can come across for examining the level of sensitivity human beings have regarding the survival of our diversified biota along with their allied differences.

Some of the species have lost their identity and became extinct. Tigers are on their way towards extinction. It is not the case that we are having any shortage of forest biota or any other suitable environment for accommodating such a magnificent wild variety. It is the matter of our concern and wishes. We want them to remain confined in a small area in and around some traditionally developed forest resources. The animal concerned is not finding itself absolutely adjusted with the surrounding of such reserves.

Their wilderness put them off the mainstreaming of our society and developed a band of threat for them. Not only that, they have to face unwanted violence mounted upon them in the name of amusements and superstitions.

There are several models of conservation mechanism available for us to be practiced. Fitness of any conservation model depends entirely upon the area, the people and the biota concerned. Tiger conservation strategy developed in India was on the basis of a balanced participatory strategy having equally relevant impetus upon the government and people.

Development, Conservation and Nurturing of the Ecology should go on in a progressive way through adequate sectoral adjustment in between them. We should focus adequately on the need of conserving the biodiversity of different zones that we have in India. It is possible only through making people involved in some sort of economic activities duly promoted by the authorities concerned. We cannot force any traditional harvesters from entering the protected place simply in the name of law enforcement. We even cannot make them off the track of their traditions for keeping the biota vividly protected.

Threat to any diversified biota is not only because of the interventions of any traditional harvesters. There exist some professionally skilled groups who destabilises the situation by entering the forest biota primarily for killing and poaching animals and for gaining wealth by exporting different body parts of fellow animals to different agencies outside.

The habitat of continental tiger once extended from Siberia to the farthest corner of South Asia. In due course of time their population declined precisely as a result of habitat loss, hunting, poaching, pollution and some other unauthorised human intrusion in the protected area. The conflict between forest protector and oppressor is an issue of our concern. They even impart themselves as a supreme commander in the territory of their nestling ground.

If we understand the process of energy transfer from one trophic level to the other then the fact of conserving different trophic levels and maintaining their desired level of representation in the nature will become a must doing for us, not only for keeping our environment suitable for our living but also for preventing any naturally occurring environmental hazards. We alone cannot go on implementing our conservation strategies without imparting native Indians in our planned effort of the mechanism of conservation. Progress of social and economic importance is linked vividly with their allied importance. We may go on practicing our efforts of balancing the ecosystem at the best level of our own understanding.

Importance of nature in our daily life is a matter beyond the questions and conflicts. For understanding such role, with a clear distinction between acts, conducts and necessity, we may go through a popular story of a beggar and King of all kings.

Once upon a time, a beggar was moving through the royal path with an expectation of receiving something prosperous from the king of all kings. The poor beggar was standing by the side of a royal path with an expectation of receiving some handful of wealth. The King of all Kings often passes through that path and gives in plenty.

For making the anticipation of the poor beggar true, the band of dust with an admixture of clouds appeared at the horizon. The King of all Kings was moving in through that royal path. The very moment of prosperity and happiness would be there in the life of the fellow beggar. It might bring an end to his wandering status; it may also fulfil his desires.

The dust and cloudy appearance moved more close to the beggar and finally the moment came. A pair of empty palm was there in front of the poor beggar. The King of all Kings was begging! It made him very angry; also the act was absolutely unexpected one. With a mixture of anger and agony he had decided to offer few grains of corns to the King of all Kings.

With happiness, King of all Kings received the gift and moved on further. The day was not prosperous for the fellow beggar. His all faith and contentment on the King of all Kings duly melted. He had nothing to say but to feel, nothing to comply but to hide and nothing to offer but to gain.

Situation turned differently after returning back home. He was to sort things as per its nature and utility. Some glittering corns were of special type. His inmates identified that particular corn as costly gems. This incident made him unhappy. He understood the magical power that implied upon him by the King of all Kings. It was even more annoying to notice that the return was equally countable in terms of identical quantity of the offering. The number remained the same, but in terms of quality there was a tremendous boost. The kind of equally powered boost that he wanted to receive in life made him fully contented and compelled him to change his stand of not to offer things.

Second turn from the side of King of all Kings was about to come. This time he had prepared himself to offer his kind self at the hands of the fellow master having some sort of divine power.

He was not in a position to give up. The kind of incident made him absolutely confirmed about his stand of witnessing the magical transformation which can make him feel the action of the divine power on him. His contentment was also of absolute type because of his capabilities of witnessing the impact of such divine power on grains of corns.

The beggar symbolises a common human being bearing aspirations of progress. The King of all kings symbolises Nature. Nature is the only entity which arranges a living for all its members. Proper, timely and perfect culmination of the nature and the supernatural power (divine) can make the creation possible.

6. Citizenship: Rights and Duties

People entertain a legal safeguard duly provided by a state as per the status of birth or the status specified in the constitution of that state in accord to which the legal framework of providing citizenship to an individual is confirmed and gradually exercised along with the judiciary sanctions as duly provided for materialising the process of empowerment.

Most of the states in this world provide citizenship to an individual on the basis of family linkages and birth profiles. This question arises at this juncture as some states preferred examining the root of in-migrants to trace out their right to citizenship on the basis of the legal framework duly specified in the Citizenship charter of the constitution. In some cases, may be less in number, may become rarely traceable, people seek citizenship of a state at the cost of heavy economic investment, purchase of some property and even by paying donations.[210].

Being a western concept in general[211], providing and executing citizenship as per the legal and judiciary provisions coined in constitution is implemented and maintained by all the socially and politically recognised Nation states duly specified by the U.N. Charter.

Citizenship ideas of olden times were coined differently at different places during which some of the states (or Kingdom) was deeply influenced by slavery and injustice to women, farmers and artisans.[212] Roman execution of citizenship was a kind of inclusive effort in which

---

[210] *"Citizenship for sale: how tycoons can go shopping for a new passport". The Guardian. 2 June 2018. Retrieved 24 August 2018.*

[211] *Zarrow, Peter (1997), Fogel, Joshua A.; Zarrow, Peter G. (eds.), Imagining the People: Chinese Intellectuals and the Concept of Citizenship, 1890-1920, Armonk, NY: M. E. Sharpe, p. 3, ISBN 978-0-7656-0098-1*

[212] *Pocock, J. G. A. (1998). Shafir, Gershon (ed.). The Citizenship Debates. Chapter 2 -- The Ideal of Citizenship since Classical Times (originally published in Queen's Quarterly 99, no. 1). Minneapolis, MN: The University of Minnesota. p. 31. ISBN 978-0-8166-2880-3.*

civic participation in government was ensured.[213] . It also ensured that none of the citizen can have access to all the legally allocated sanctions for a long time. In due course of time the character of citizenship remained restricted around the physical belongings and property, whereas human relations and duty of an individual to a state became secondary. In gradual succession a basic understanding regarding enactment of citizenship is developed in which people consider it as a legal protection provided by a state to an individual which is granted free of cost and also is non-conditional.

Idea of citizenship to a nation, state or to a city was developed during middle age. It was dramatic shift of entire idea from a format of monarchy to a format of legalized system of a nation-state.[214] Being a democratic state United States of America continued overcoming the problem of slavery and caste distinction for the purpose of developing a less discriminatory citizenship system until 1965 through some provisions of legal amendments duly forwarded by the congress.[215] Sanction to curtail allowing in-migrants to gain citizenship was also under the blotting paper for ensuring a legal and natural protection to Native Americans. Soviet Federal Republic prepared a citizenship plan through which individual attaining the age of 18 years will gain citizenship of the Republic by default irrespective of their caste, colour or gender distinctions. Even they become eligible for casting votes.[216] Incorporation of the Citizenship by the place of birth also came in practice in states like Israel[217].

---

[213] *Hosking, Geoffrey (2005). Epochs of European Civilization: Antiquity to Renaissance. Lecture 5: Rome as a city-state. United Kingdom: The Modern Scholar via Recorded Books. pp. tracks 1 through 9. ISBN 978-1-4025-8360-5.*

[214] *Weber, Max (1998). Citizenship in Ancient and Medieval Cities. Chapter 3. Minneapolis, MN: The University of Minnesota. pp. 43–49. ISBN 978-0-8166-2880-3.*

[215] *"The Immigration and Nationality Act of 1952 (The McCarran-Walter Act)". The Office of the Historian. U.S. Department of State.*

[216] *"1918 Constitution of the Russian Soviet Federated Socialist Republic. Article Four: The Right to Vote".*

[217] *Safran, William (1997-07-01). "Citizenship and Nationality in Democratic Systems: Approaches to Defining and Acquiring Membership in the Political Community". International Political Science Review. SAGE Publishing. 18 (3): 313–335. doi:10.1177/019251297018003006. S2CID 145476893.*

It can be also considered as a collection of rights, primarily political participation of individual in the community, right to vote, right to access to basic facilities provided by a state and right to develop and maintain assets within the location specified by the state under a balanced jurisdiction[218].

It appears that citizenship plans developed by different states quantified the membership of an individual to a nation or state. It will also ensure the participation of an individual in the political framework. Differences may be there in accord to some sort of cultural diversities with which states are functioning. These states also exchange their cultural and political bonds while maintaining their citizenship charter as intact. Here comes the subject of dual citizenship or multiple citizenship with which some individuals mat try to explore their access to resources and political advantages from more than one states without letting states or nations to be aware of such facts and figures. How a person should behave in society often remains off the track of enactment of Citizenship Charter duly prepared under the legal framework of the constitution of a state.[219] A citizen should have legal entitlement required for maintaining human dignity.[220] State is also entitled to safeguard a citizen under the privileges of the legal framework duly coined for addressing basic as well as fundamental rights of a citizenship.[221] If any similarity in the legal framework of different states is addressing the enactment related to citizenship rights then we may move on for coining the idea of developing a global citizenship framework.

---

[218] *Leary, Virginia (2000). "Citizenship. Human rights, and Diversity". In Cairns, Alan C.; Courtney, John C.; MacKinnon, Peter; Michelmann, Hans J.; Smith, David E. (eds.). Citizenship, Diversity, and Pluralism: Canadian and Comparative Perspectives. McGill-Queen's Press - MQUP. pp. 247–264. ISBN 978-0-7735-1893-3. The concept of 'citizenship' has long acquired the connotation of a bundle of rights...*
[219] *Taylor, David (1994). Turner, Bryan; Hamilton, Peter (eds.). Citizenship: Critical Concepts. United States and Canada: Routledge. pp. 476 pages total. ISBN 978-0-415-07036-2.*
[220] *Oldfield, Adrian (1994). Turner, Bryan; Hamilton, Peter (eds.). Citizenship: Critical Concepts. United States and Canada: Routledge. pp. 476 pages total, source: The Political Quarterly, 1990 vol.61, pp. 177–187, in the book, pages 188+. ISBN 9780415102452.*
[221] *Heater, Derek (2004). A Brief History of Citizenship. NYU Press. ISBN 978-0-8147-3672-2.*

The idea of developing and maintaining global citizenship framework is proposed by different scholars.[222] Citizenship pattern declared to integrate the citizenship privileges to be gained by all the citizen of European states without losing their National citizenship can be considered as a set forward towards cultivation of the idea of Global Citizenship.[223] Development is going on towards enactment of certain legal frameworks through which member states joining the Charter of United Nations can avail their access to the Inter-nationally established law of Global Citizenship. With such enactment a state can bring easiness in their border related issues to let active people to move though their business tracks which may also enable them to serve the humanity in a better way. It is time when we prepare ourselves for accepting aspirations of others which will enable us to accelerate our social, economic as well as political activities.

---

[222] *Daniele Archibugi, "The Global Commonwealth of Citizens. Toward Cosmopolitan Democracy", Princeton University Press, Princeton, 2008*
[223] *"Consolidated versions of the Treaty on European Union"*

7. The Ultimate Gain

We all know that Alexander invaded India main land during the ancient age when Aryan group looing after different states of India main land were not united. The fellow Greek warrior succeeded by part and considered himself as victorious. Some of the princely states were not accessible to them because of many reasons. His men finally refused to fight and Alexander preferred returning back to his native place.

During one of instance when his men continued returning back some peculiar type of people were identified by them. Some of them remained engaged in preparing a yard of land to be used by them. They continued measuring that land by jumping side by side. Alexander wanted to know the exact reason because of which they were behaving in such a peculiar way. One of the saintly person admitted, "You came here to consider yourself as victorious. You want to grab all the lands. Then also you may not remain eligible for gaining ownership of all the lands. You will be entitled an access to merely a stretch of a yard of land, not more than that.'

After such conversation Alexander admitted that there are three types of people in this land: Some people work for gaining money and property, some other people work for earning fame; there is third type of people. Like these men, having no expectation from people or state. They simply work for the betterment of people without expecting anything in return. They also move through renunciation for making people and states competent and stronger. If somebody wants to rule this land then they have to win the confidence of these third types of people (Third Power).

Renunciation cannot be ascribed as any escape from delivering duty to society or to escape regular economic practices for the purpose of earning a living for the community. It is also not the state during which person start gaining some additional privileges from society. Renunciation is the subject beyond the scope of religious confinement.

We can expect some sort of matured approach to social subjects through which prosperity and advancement of a society can be ensured.

Renunciation is a state of approach adopted by an individual by casting off the affinity towards gaining advantages in return to services provided to society. It also ensures an intellectual and spiritual advancement of an individual needed for actualising oneself in the situation during which such individual start searching out alternative ways through which prosperity of fellow members of a community can be ensured. India has a bright history of renunciation. People from different walks of life renunciated the world for gaining prosperity meant for commons. Examples are there in plenty.

A youth from a promising farmer's family from Punjab got an assignment to go to market for selling out some farm produces for earning a profit. While moving towards the market place they were moving through a poverty struck village. They preferred feeding fellow villagers by using farm produces that they were carrying to the market. Family members of the youth came to know about the incident and were not happy because of the act. Without considering the willingness of the family members the fellow youth preferred continuing his service to poor and hungry. He also started preaching people by introducing them with noble deeds and wiser conducts. In gradual succession he preferred renunciation for the purpose of continuing his service to humanity.

State of renunciation will come after attainment of true knowledge. The term true knowledge concerns with the understanding of an individual with which omnipresence of the divine in every creation can be visualized. With such apprehension that individual start delivering society without expecting anything in return. Renunciation can be considered as a kind of intellectual .spiritual and mental enlightenment of the individual leading the person ultimately towards a state of spiritual bliss, with which special attention towards collective progress of society can be advanced. Service oriented mission developed at different places in the world exhibits several examples of renunciation. Renunciation is still going on at different places at different instances with varying objectives to work out some sort of service lines meant for ensuring collective progress of desired types.

A youth from Kolkata prepared himself for renunciation after receiving spiritual instructions of divine Teacher. During one instance the youth observed that his master performs a special type of meditation. That meditation was of a special type because of which his fellow teacher was becoming capable of gaining an instant lift from the ground. The fellow youth approached his master and wanted to learn the special type of meditation. Master was not happy after learning about the affinity of the fellow w youth towards attainment of personal advancement. The fellow master said, "I thought you will become a banyan tree , but you are trying to become a palm tree! You are nothing but a Useless fellow!"

Attainment of personal advancement without considering immediate need of other people of society was not preferable by the divine master. He wanted the youth to work the progress of the entire community (collective progress). It was the way of renunciation which was preferred by Mahatma. Renunciation should be of such type which cannot imply additional burden upon society. It should have enough capability to address the issues and concerns of the adjoining society. Individual having such kinds of collective impetus can deliver services to needy and disadvantaged people. Renunciation having strict motive of individual progress is absolutely a non-desirable effort. Person who renunciated the world with such kind of restricted affinity of individual progress may not become that much effective in making the entire community that much prosperous. Third power can also have an impetus on the process of reviving human relations in a society. Saintly persons of such genre are the source of inspiration with which community segments often prefer getting involved in the process of revivals and reforms of desired types through the process of socialisation and acculturation.

8. Meditation

Meditation is the juncture when aspirants start withdrawing senses from the immediate context and start contemplating upon the inner world.

-   Chandan Sukumar Sengupta

There exist some instances during which we expect some basic advancement in the thought process and practices of an individual before moving towards states of Yoga and Meditation. Consideration of Peace and Nonviolence is one such instance. We can consider Pilgrimage as a journey where an individual goes in search of some expanded meaning about their good self, about others, divine, or to explore some higher meaning of life through gaining experiences.[224] It often involves a journey primarily meant for searching moral or spiritual significance of life. The person associated to such kind of focused movement is called a pilgrim. Pilgrimage is also associated to biological, social, spiritual and psychological therapeutic benefits,[225] for it provides a spiritual enrichment to a pilgrim, for it ensures the advancement of the knowledge base of a pilgrim by exposing the individual to some higher order of attainment of experiences, for it becomes helpful for an individual in the path of spiritual, social and psychological actualisation of the soul. Pilgrimage to Peace and Nonviolence always contains faith expectancy and search for wholeness. Because of that reason this type of pilgrimage does not require any tourism. It does not mean that we restrict ourselves from visiting sacred places and hermitage of saints[226]. We also move through some experience sharing to make ourselves enriched.

---

[224] *Plate, S. Brent (September 2009). "The Varieties of Contemporary Pilgrimage". Cross Currents. 59 (3): 260–267. doi:10.1111/j.1939-3881.2009.00078.x*

[225] *Warfield, Heather A.; Baker, Stanley B.; Foxx, Sejal B. Parikh (14 September 2014). "The therapeutic value of pilgrimage: a grounded theory study". Mental Health, Religion & Culture. 17 (8): 860–875. doi:10.1080/13674676.2014.936845. ISSN 1367-4676. S2CID 143623445.*

[226] *Werner, Karel (1994). A popular dictionary of Hinduism. Richmond, Surrey: Curzon. ISBN 0700702792. Retrieved 30 October 2016.*

After incorporating justice in larger concept of peace, a theory of "Active Peace" is proposed.[227] An idea of restoration of peace is advanced according to which the involvement of local community and locally active administrative units are considered as an important component to be considered as unavoidable conditions.[228] Pilgrimage of Peace and Nonviolence confers the journey of an individual from ground level of understanding of concepts and propositions related to Peace and Nonviolence to a higher level of self actualisation, for such kind of spiritual and intellectual advancement will ensure the capability of a person with which omnipresence of the Divine can be felt, for a better understanding of the conceptual and practical nature of the doctrines related to Peace and Nonviolence can be felt with better understanding. We consider this work as a pilgrimage as it ensures our spiritual, intellectual and psychological understanding of the doctrines of Peace and Nonviolence. It will also confer our adequate alignment towards the rituals associated to the doctrines of Peace and Nonviolence.

Upanishadic source got its prominence in The Bhagavadgita at different places with which the entire discussion moved on towards attainment of ascent through enhancement of consciousness; this enhancement is considered as a key to spiritual advancement.[229] Different ladders of advancement, such as breath control, introspective withdrawal of the senses, meditation (dhyana), mental concentration, logic and reasoning, and spiritual union, are coined by sage Patanjali to point out linkages and importance of all the stages in the path of spiritual ascent. Another objective of Yoga, as described in The Bhagavadgita, is to unite to Soul with the universal Brahman.[230]

Those who perform prescribed duties without desiring the results of actions being performed are actual stage of renunciation and individuals who have merely ceased performing sacrifices, rejected

---

[227] *"The Theory of Active Peace". internationalpeaceandconflict.org. Archived from the original on 25 July 2015.*
[228] *Jyot Hosagrahar: Culture: at the heart of SDGs. UNESCO-Kurier, April-Juni 2017; Rick Szostak: The Causes of Economic Growth: Interdisciplinary Perspectives. Springer Science & Business Media, 2009, ISBN 9783540922827.*
[229] *Jacobsen, Knut A., ed. (2011). Yoga Powers. Leiden: Brill. ISBN 978-9-0042-1214-5.*
[230] *Jacobsen, Knut A., ed. (2011). Yoga Powers. Leiden: Brill. ISBN 978-9-0042-1214-5.*

moments of enjoyments, abandoned bodily activities and rejected objects of attainment of physical pleasure may not be considered as a Yogi. [231] Identification of a true Yogi is really a difficult task. This initiative requires a perfect vision with which people start recognising different levels of Yoga and Meditation. All instances of living forms are residing at any of the specified ladders leading an individual towards the horizon of complete renunciation.

Yoga has a wider meaning through which we can recognise its wider spiritual perspective. The word "Yoga" does not exist in the Sanskrit scriptures, epics or commentaries of saints. The actual word is "Yoga," which means "union."; which refers to the union of the consciousness of an individual with the divine omnipresence. Mind of Yogi is fully involved in God. Such an awakened mind and intellect is naturally remaining ignorant of the physical and material world. A true yogi is also a person moving towards renunciation.

Renunciation is not different from Yoga, as rarely aspirants become yogis without renouncing worldly desires; for none gain the moments of feeling the divine omnipresence without regulating senses, without rejecting worldly desires and without attaining true knowledge.[232] Renunciation is the stage of life which encourages an individual to link up senses to the higher order of divinity which is possible only when the mind and intellect start withdrawing from worldly attachments and physical attainable means of living. It also encompasses a new set of objectives of life with which the fellow yogi

---

[231] *Gita Chapter 6 , Verse 1: The Supreme Lord said; anāśhritaḥ—not desiring; karma-phalam—results of actions; kāryam—obligatory; karma—work; karoti—perform; yaḥ—one who; saḥ—that person; sanyāsī—in the renounced order; cha—and; yogī—yogi; cha—and; na—not; niḥ—without; agniḥ—fire; na—not; cha—also; akriyaḥ—without activity;*

[232] *yaṁ sannyāsam iti prāhur yogaṁ taṁ viddhi pāṇḍava*
na hyasannyasta-saṅkalpo yogī bhavati kaśhchana

yam—what; sanyāsam—renunciation; iti—thus; prāhuḥ—they say; yogam—yog; tam—that; viddhi—know; pāṇḍava—Arjun, the son of Pandu; na—not; hi—certainly; asannyasta—without giving up; saṅkalpaḥ—desire; yogī—a yogi; bhavati—becomes; kaśhchana—anyone

continues identifying the real objective of remaining alive and becoming intellectually active.

To the soul, having affinity to prosper in the paths of Yoga, work without attachment consider steps of Yogic practices as means; to the sage who is already elevated in paths of Yoga accept tranquillity in meditation as means of progress and prosperity. [233] In that way it can be considered as an ever-continuing process of self-actualisation and self – advancement.

Regulation of senses and affinity to withdraw from sensible objects is another important step to be followed by an individual. After attainment of such a situation a sage continues reject desires of seeking access to fruits of actions. [234] Without degrading the self, one should have adequate hold on the mental state; for mind is the best friend as well as an enemy; for friendship of mind will pave the path of prosperity for the scholar; for such regulations with positive apprehension will link up senses to the higher state of consciousness; for such an enhanced mind cannot accommodate any states of confusions; for such kind of awakened mind will develop networked ladders with intellects. [235] Our mind operates at four different levels.[236]

Mind becomes friend for those who have conquered it by regulating senses and desires of implying any hold upon worldly sensible things. Having no regulation on mind will develop the mental entity as an enemy. The yogis who have conquered the mind rise above the dualities; such as cold and heat, happiness and sorrow, honor and dishonour, praise and criticism etc. Such individuals remain peaceful, undisturbed and steadfast in their affinity and practices of devotion to the divine. They also remain undisturbed in all circumstances; for their

---

[233] *The Bhagavadgita 6.3;*
[234] *The Bhagavadgita VI.4;*
[235] *The Bhagavadgita VI.5;*
[236] *Mind: When it creates thoughts, we call it mana, or the mind.*
Intellect: When it analyses and decides, we call it buddhi, or intellect.
Chitta: When it gets attached to an object or person, we call it chitta.
Ego: When it identifies with the bodily identifications and becomes proud of things like wealth, status, beauty, and learning, we call it ahankār, or ego.

regulated senses will provide them a perfect hold on the balanced actions of knowledge driven actions; for such kinds of balanced mental, intellectual and spiritual efforts help them to feel the divine omnipresence at all instances. They start recognising the divine in all kinds of worldly objects. Their intellect provides them actual impetus of recognising things as godly creations and start treating objects accordingly. [237]

Awakened Yogis start recognising friends, enemies and relatives with identical feelings and ensure kindness to all the beings while maintaining equal impetus of delivering duties without considering any attainable results. Their social and intellectual actions will be regulated accordingly by their enhanced state of mind to ensure prosperity of all. It is also a state of mind and intellect where leadership qualities develop in an individual with which the individual start delivering duties with higher perspectives of socialisation.

Those who seek the state of Yoga and Meditation should reside in seclusion, constantly engaged in meditation with adequate regulation of intellect, mind and body; should remain free from feelings of desires and affinity of gaining enjoyment. One should make a seat in a sanctified place for practicing different postures of Asanas (Bodily positions along with stability of mind and body). One should place some insulators of heat on ground for preventing bodily loss of heat; it should be neither too high nor too low. Seated firmly on it, the fellow individual should strive to gain perfectness of mind and intellect by focusing it in meditation along with focussed concentration; by regulating all thoughts and activities, by linking up different aspects of thought process to actualise the self; by preventing development of negative thought processes in mind and by enhancing steps of self-esteem. There exists some pre-defined mechanisms of practicing Asanas (Physical postures) while keeping senses, mind, intellect and body under control. A Yogi should practice Asanas with enhanced serene, fearless and unwavering mind; [238] while doing so the vigilant scholar should meditate on the supreme

---

[237] *The Bhagavadgita VI. 6-8;*
[238] *such individual remain staunch in the vow of celibacy;*

master, having divine alone as the supreme attainable goal. Constantly keeping the mind absorbed in divine, the fellow scholar of disciplined mind attains renunciation, and abides in the state of consciousness through recognising the divine omnipresence. While doing so the fellow Yogi will gain contentment and remain in absolute peace.[239]

There exist some limitations due to which preachers often fail in gaining the state of renunciation; those who eat too much or too little, sleep too much or too little, cannot attain success in the paths of Yoga; as the matters related to attainment of renunciation is the subject of adequate freedom of mind from the worldly desires; as the instance related to attainment of renunciation is the aspect which requires adequate enrichment of the intellect; as such attainment of divine driven renunciation requires intellectual maturity with which individuals seek completeness of the alignment of regulation of senses and breath. It is the state when a Yogi ascends to the state of Renunciation.[240]

Person having ability to regulate affinity to sensible objects can gain enrichment of adequate levels of stability; even they learn to withdraw the mind from selfish cravings and mobilise the same on the unsurpassable welfare of the self.[241] The mind, being restrained from material gains and physical activities, becomes steady by the practice of Yoga and Meditation; a converging juncture of mind, body and intellect which ensures the accommodation of awakened mind; a stage when contentment of mind and intellect become filled with rejoice and happiness; such happiness is absolutely different from sense driven states of pleasure; a state which is often called Samadhi (a steadfast spiritual enrichment when individual recognises objectives of remaining alive). At this state of supreme boundless divine bliss, individual never deviates from the recognition of Eternal Truth ; the state at which individuals

---

[239] *The Bhagavadgita VI. 10-15*
[240] *The Bhagavadgita VI. 16*
[241] *Such persons can be considered at the states of Yoga and they remain free from all yearning of the senses; Just as a lamp in a windless place does not flicker, so the disciplined mind of a yogi remains steady in meditation on the Divine. They even recognise the presence of divine in every elementary parts of creations; they also understand the cyclic processes involved in the rogression of creation and destruction.*

never consider any other attainable to be higher; the state of balanced mind when the fellow individual never becomes inflicted with any kinds of sensible difficulties or conflicts; they even become efficient in tackling conflicts. Even individuals feel the state of Yoga at different instances of acculturation of socialisation.[242]   This Yoga should be resolutely practiced with utter determination and utmost care while remaining free from prejudices and bias. They rarely restrict themselves merely up to the worldly sensible desires and wishes.[243]

सङ्कल्पप्रभवान्कामांस्त्यक्त्वा सर्वानशेषतः |
मनसैवेन्द्रियग्रामं विनियम्य समन्ततः || 24||
शनैः शनैरुपरमेद्बुद्ध्या धृतिगृहीतया |
आत्मसंस्थं मनः कृत्वा न किञ्चिदपि चिन्तयेत् || 25||
यतो यतो निश्चरति मनश्चञ्चलमस्थिरम् |
ततस्ततो नियम्यैतदात्मन्येव वशं नयेत् || 26||
प्रशान्तमनसं ह्येनं योगिनं सुखमुत्तमम् |
उपैति शान्तरजसं ब्रह्मभूतमकल्मषम् || 27||

Renouncing all desires is essential aspect before feeling presence of the Divine. By doing so one should bring the restless and wandering mind to the subject of the Divine. With such steadiness aspirants start recognising the universal Divine without remaining restricted to attending sensible objects and without remaining deprived of feeling happiness and contentment.

They also become free from material contaminations and with the blessings of the Divine start experiencing the higher states of happiness and contentment. They also start recognising everything as the real manifestations of the Divine.[244]

---

[242] *That state of severance from union with misery is known as Yoga; this Yoga also ensures union of the soul and the divine; it establishes a balance between entities like mind, body, spirit and intellect; a state at which bodily functional units provide adequate support to the emotional and intellectual states of the being.*
[243] *The Bhagavadgita VI. 17-23.*
[244] *The Bhagavadgita VI. 28-29.*

यो मां पश्यति सर्वत्र सर्वं च मयि पश्यति |
तस्याहं न प्रणश्यामि स च मे न प्रणश्यति || 30||
सर्वभूतस्थितं यो मां भजत्येकत्वमास्थितः |
सर्वथा वर्तमानोऽपि स योगी मयि वर्तते || 31||

One can recognise the Divine omnipresence with utmost easiness whenever such aspirant starts recognising the Divine in every worldly manifested object. The seeker and worshipper of the universal Divine always dwells in the realm of the supreme master and remain involved all kinds of activity without remaining inflicted with desires of seeking any result or waiting for results to come.[245]

Such aspirants are true Yogis who can recognise the Divine in all living beings and respond to the joys and sorrows of other organisms as if they were their own. It is true that the mind is very difficult to restrain; as it continues moving towards different sources of sensible objects and sensory impulses; as it repeatedly shifts from one theme to the other; as it rarely retains any aspect of knowledge and skill up to any prolonged span without experiencing any halt. But by practice and detachment, it can be regulated perfectly with ever continuing impulses of perfectness and vigil.[246]

असंयतात्मना योगो दुष्प्राप इति मे मतिः |
वश्यात्मना तु यतता शक्योऽवाप्तुमुपायतः || 36||

"Aspirants succeed easily in the path of Yoga while maintaining mental steadiness; for, such steadiness will ensure perfect regulations of senses; for, such steadfast nature ensures stability of knowledge. "[247]

Worshipper of Yoga succeeds in overcoming all sorts of difficulties and continuously moves towards the ascent in the path of spirituality.[248] Such kinds of successive move will quantify the process of withdrawing senses from sensible objects to minimise states of illusion.

---

[245] *The Bhagavadgita VI. 30-31*
[246] *The Bhagavadgita VI. 32,35*
[247] *The Bhagavadgita VI 36*
[248] *Bhagavad Gita VI.40*

Divine wisdom, in certain cases will go on continuing through generations in some families, and is of very rare occurrence in the context as such fortunate families are very less in number. In certain instances people rarely become successful in retaining rituals and traditions through un-interrupted practices. Aspirants of such traditions will practice harder to bring perfectness in their aspirations of Yoga. In gradual succession they also feel the Divine omnipresence; it ensures a natural ascent of the aspirant towards the Divine. [249]

As evident from the Bhagavadgita attainment of the feeling of the Divine omnipresence is not a difficult or non-attainable state of conscious mental and spiritual status as such kinds of capabilities are there dormant in the competence ladders of the fellow aspirant. A true master can make it possible by issuing timely relevant instructions to the fellow aspirant as the kind of timely relevant instructions enlightened a warrior amidst a battlefield. It is clearly mentioned in The Bhagavadgita the regular practice of Yoga brings perfectness in an aspirant. With such kind of aspiration the fellow worshipper reaches up to the highest state of Yoga.

"Of all yogis, those whose minds are always contented in the Divine, and who keeps oneself faithfully in the Divine, will be considered as the highest of all Yogis."[250] It is the highest state of devotion, the highest pursuit of knowledge and the highest pursuit of self-sacrifice where the fellow worshipper feels the utter integration of the soul with that of the supreme master. It is the state which brings absolute regulation of senses and makes the effort of all senses possible to recognise the Divine omnipresence; a state of being where men may not appeared merely men, animals may not appear merely animals, flies may not appear flies and stones may not appear merely stones, but the fellow worshiper start searching out impulses of the supreme master (the Divine) in all worldly sensible objects. It is the state which removes all sorts of anger, agony, and falsehood from the good self and will make the individual a true enunciator. Such enunciator will link up the sensible

---

[249] *The Bhagavadgita VI 41-44*
[250] *The Bhagavadgita VI.47*

impulses with the supreme master and start encouraging other fellow partners for doing the same. It was the state which brought noble thoughts of Acharya Shankar in the form of some glittering coins:

1: AHAM BRHMASMI. (I am Brahman.)

2: BRAHMA SATYA JAGAT MITHYA. (Only Brahman is True, rest of the other worldly objects are merely illusions.)

3: TATWAMASI. (Elements are there in and around us.)

4: SARVAM KHALVIDAM BRAHMA. (Whatever we see around us is nothing but different manifestations of the Brahman.)

The Brahman was identified as the creation force and regulation force which ensures manifestation of the Divine by part. Human beings are also a part of such manifestations; they are a part of the whole; a part of the entire creation which is growing differently under the sincere regulations of the Divine.

One should strive to a Yogi (Worshipper of the Divine); as such state is superior to a worker, superior to a seeker of merely knowledge, superior to ritualistic performer and even superior to a saint (ascetic).[251]

---

[251] *The Bhagavadgita VI. 46*

9. Learning form Experience

What brought The Gita in Context?

Teachings of Veda and Epics are in continuation from age old traditions. After the Epic Age we have passed on a span of thousands of years. Are such age old teachings becoming irrelevant day by day? Is the discussion on such teachings becoming useless in present day context?

If we start searching proper answer to these questions then we have to rely on the fact of the exact relationship with which the time and philosophy move on. Actually Philosophy and Religion never take the support of the confluence of time. Time can even repeat itself through predetermined actions. Philosophy never intends to influence the normal cycle of the confluence of time. Therefore, both of these aspects of our daily life are independent of each other and reflect themselves independently.

Yoga stands for a way of living that often satisfies a person through exposing the individual to the guiding forces of the supreme master and enabling the person to feel omnipresence of related divine. It also links an individual with all such forces which can play a defining role on the way of experiencing such kind of divine omnipresence.

There exist different literary and ritual sources having enough potential to correlate the human practices and related philosophical beliefs. We cannot simply deny the existence of any supreme power only on the ground of its non-visibility. In some cases such supreme power may remain off the limit of our senses. If we try to sum up all such teachings duly proposed by thinkers and philosophers of olden times, then the collected instructions having integration of all the divine thought processes will become enriched one. It will address all sorts of propositions and concerns related to various aspects of our daily life. We also know another fact related to holy books that most interpreted literature among all available scriptures and publications is The Bhagvadgita. Different saints considered it differently and also tried to work out its relevance in our daily life as per their levels of understanding. Relevance of the teachings of Gita has an everlasting impression in the minds of thinkers and philosophers. Most commonly discussed part of all such propositions is the considerations related to the essence of Jnan Yoga (Yoga of Knowledge and intellect) and Karma Yoga (the Yoga of Performance, Actions and Perfections). We cannot translate the Sanskrit term "Karma" directly as "Actions" in English. The term Karma has a wide range of considerations. It correlates skill acquisition, mental preparedness for getting indulge in activities, establishment of correlations in between different aspects of life and remaning attached to the implications of actions and perfections.

It is also true that we cannot segregate any living being from its external world. We can even assign a definite task to that individual on the basis of the skills and competence possessed by the person. Our expectation from that individual will be centralised on the basis of such considerations. We consider that individual successful only after ascertaining the meaningful and fruitful participation of the same in the proposed action. A knowledge base empowers an individual to define its role in society, or to work in the extended environment. It can even ascertain its own horizon of activities. That individual can even surpass trying days with the help of the organised framework of knowledge.

We acquire skills in life through series of interactions and training, gain competence through guided practices, confine ourselves to certain segments of duties and concerns as per wishes, mechanise our welfare and warfare for fulfilling individual as well as collective concerns and claim our status on the basis of our role in the community. Through all such efforts, carrying types of skill acquisition and knowledge confluence, we feel the presence of a masterly power having affinity of guiding the self. It even intends to make an individual a special one by providing scope of ascent in terms of spirituality. Spirituality of specific type and its expansion by all means is the subject where mind, body, skills and competence culminate properly to ascertain the refinement of an individual.

While talking about absolute knowledge with its super confluous characters we may feel some sort of difficulties due to limitations of our senses. We want to see some relevant things, but our senses may not equip us properly in doing so. Similar will be the situation is regarding all other senses. Such kinds of sensuous limitations compelled us to imagine about the presence and propagation of some super natural things having extra ordinary characters. We cannot segregate matter and energy in our surrounding by any means or by any mechanism as the involvement of nuclear energy enables the binding of different sub-atomic particles housed inside the centrally placed nucleus of an atom. Energy involvement is there even at the stage of certain sub atomic state of bindings. In the same way we cannot segregate the God or divine power from its creations. We can feel its presence but may not be able to describe it by furnishing evidences. We can talk upon it the way a blind person talks to other visually impaired ones, or like a physically challenged one with another person having similar limitations.

Our present effort is a continuation of all such previously organised efforts of making the divine confluous through our senses, making an individual feel its presence within the sub conscious mind. An earthen candle cannot describe its glory. It is the subject of other individuals having an opportunity of getting enlightened amidst darkness by placing oneself juxtaposed to the earthen candle with an affinity of getting illuminated. The Sun cannot describe itself by any means; it is solar radiation and the act of Nuclear Reaction taking place at the surface of the sun which describes the power game of the ignited giant. We also cannot put us in a move to reach the surface of any star to examine the mechanism duly involved in its affinity towards act of availing radiations, we can feel it and gain it with its graceful vitality to enrich ourselves. There are many other instances available in our nature that describes vividly the presence of such divine power with its empowered vigil of creations and destructions. We can simply feel them, and in certain instances correlate them with our acts of creations and destructions. We can even make some of our efforts a prolonged one through designing participatory efforts of specific type for enlightening the phenomenon of the divine omnipresence. It is the realm where all individuals in this planet can feel the essence of exercising the global communion and can impart themselves in making the nature more confluous, more vibrant, more and more habitable and more prosperous.

Spirituality brings lives closure, makes people awakened, provides a scope of feeling the presence of divine power within the scope of living beings and intensifies our senses and makes us more contented for gaining the power of our effort of assimilating knowledge. In this publication we limit our discussion on and around the relevance of Knowledge Confluence, Enhancement of Wisdom and Karma Yoga in present day context. Yoga of Action, Perfectness and Performance has a close link with the knowledge base of a performer. Because of that reason we can point out some aspects of the confluence of knowledge to enlighten the core principle of Yoga in an integrated fashion. It will become an exemplar effort for people to ensure its practical utility. Things already mentioned in Upanishadas were pitched in again in Madbhagvadgita to make people aware of the practical utility of acts and conducts of a Yoga based life. A Yoga based life can have a sense of completeness for ensuring complete unfoldment of petals of skills and competences. It will even make people aware of the on-going situation. Because of that reason also Yoga comes in the fore front of discussion time to time with a clear apprehension of individual as well as collective progress.

Our tendency to add a prefix with the term Yoga by using different terms like Karma (action, perfection, skills and competence), Jnan (knowledge), etc. is a common one. All such ideals related to Yoga ultimately points out towards the accumulation of some positive waves for experiencing presence of a link with the Divine and, at some higher states of practice, to feel the presence of such Divine in every creation. When any confluence of such positive waves comes on surface through experiences and practices we rarely become capable of bifurcate them from one another. It is also a state of feeling the presence of all such waves with a band of stress on some other aspects of Yoga. Confluence of action, perfection or skill, for an example, without adequate support of knowledge may not be a desired result of Yoga. Here becomes the concept of Integral Yoga alive and Bhgvadgita is the ideal place where we can experience the integration of various streams of knowledge for bringing out the waves of knowledge, prosperity and wisdom.

As we have pointed out earlier, there developed a conflict between youths of the same royal family during the epic age. Kouravs and Pandavas indulged in a severe battle for establishing their territorial dominance. Was that conflict developed all on a sudden? Was there any other issue which compelled them to fight for claiming lives of each other?

Obviously, the answer to all such question related to find out the root cause of war is, No. there developed a conflicting situation during the Epic Age because of some mis –conduct of some members of the royal family. They raised their weapons to kill each other. The conflict has a back reference of the time when eight Basus from heaven allegedly indulged in taking away the holy cow, namely Kama Dhenu, with them to the heaven without giving any message to Saint Vashishtha. That time Vashishtha was not there in the hermitage. Whenever he came to know about the incident he had angrily cursed them that they would have to come to the earth for leading a life like those of normal human beings. All the Basus started appealing for the relief from the curse. With a little bit empathy Saint Vashishtha told them to find out such mother who can liberate them from the life immediately after birth. They moved on searching for the same and recognized Ganga as the mother having such power. On the other hand Shantanu, the member of the Royal family, was travelling by the sideline of the river Ganga. King Shantanu recognized a beautiful lady there at the river bank. She was none other than Ganga. Shantanu approached the lady for developing a marital bond and wanted to make her a life partner. The lady agreed upon a condition. The condition was that after marriage she can do with her kids whatever she wishes to, Shantanu cannot stop her from doing so. The condition was accepted gladly by the royal king and the infused deeply in the bond of marriage. As per the previously expressed wishes she started bringing all her kids to death immediately after the birth and her own river currents received all her sacrifices. The king remained merely as spectator; he had nothing to say as per the agreement. Lastly King Shantanu stopped her from sacrificing her eighth kid. It was protected by the King. The name coined for that holy boy was Devbrat. After that incident Ganga left Shantanu alone and moved on her own courses.

Deep sorrow mounted on the king. He again started remaining off his normal duties and day to day royal practices. During another instances he met another beautiful daughter of a fisherman. She was also beautiful and attractive. But she refused to develop any marital relations with the king by saying that his elder son will be the only prince and future king. She might have no chance of making her own son a king. It was a failure of the king. He had no scope of developing any permanent bond with Satyawati. Devbrat came to know about the incident and finalized to keep himself off the crown for convincing Satyawati for joining the royal family as a queen. Ultimately the happiest moments came in the life of Shantanu at the cost of the sacrifice of his beloved son. Satyawati became the mother of Chitrangad and Vichitrbirya. Devbrat became Bhishma because of his stand of remaining off the crown.

In due course of time both the sons of Satyawati remained issue less. That time she requested Bhishma to marry for keeping the family tree of the royal family evergreen. Bhishma remained stick to his oath and started working out a strategy to bring issues in the lives of both the daughter in law. Ultimately Dhritarashtra and Pandu took birth. In due course of time Dhritarashtra became the father of a hundred sons including Duyodhan; Pandu became the father of five sons, Arjun was one of them. After the untimely death of Pandu, Dhritarashtra ascended the throne. He was blind by birth. Jealous Duryodhan once planned to smash Pandavas by burning them alive in a house made of wax; although the plan was a failure due to some brilliant efforts of some of the warriors of that family. They, along with their mother Kunti, escaped the situation and reached another place safely. Duryodhan took it for granted that Pandavas along with their mother must have lost their lives. Pandavas remained wandering for few months and finally reached the place where king Drupad arranged a ceremony for selecting abled one for his daughter Draupadi. The person should marry his daughter only after hitting the eye of a fish by arrow only by seeing the image of that fish in water. It was a critical task to be accomplished, but Arjun was the abled warrior who has accomplished the task for accepting Draupadi as his wife. After reaching home they said to their mother about their victory. Mother instructed them to share the thing they received by becoming victorious. Accordingly all the five brothers jointly married Draupadi.

By that time Dhritarashtra, Bhishma and Bidur, the elder members of the royal family, came to know about Pandavas and finally they planned to bring them back in the family. Pandavas got the territories of Indraprashtha and started governing the state happily. Duryodhan with his uncle Shakuni planned to invade Pandava bothers to play chess with him. The game was not a fare one because of the involvement of Shakuni. Pandavas started losing their lands, territories, money, wealth and many other things including themselves. Ultimately they brought Draupadi in the royal court and started insulting her by snatching her dresses. It was none other than Lord Krishna who saved Draupadi from getting insulted and molested. The final agreement was made on the condition of 13 years of exile including a yearlong incognito (remaining non recognizable hide outs) for Pandavas. If anybody identify them during their last year then they have to go back for another round of such exile. If they complete the tenure successfully then only they will get all their wealth back.

During the last year Pandavas remained in the palace of King Virat by accepting duties of cooks and helpers. That time Duryodhan invaded the kingdom of King Virat. During that encounter Duryodhan and Arjun came face to face in the battle field and remained victorious. That time the tenure of their exile was over. Pandava brothers prepared a proposal for King Dhritarashtra and said that they would make them contented even with a gift of five villages. That too was not accepted by Duryodhan. Even Lord Krishna himself visited the royal court to make them convinced for the deal. That time also Duryodhan insulted Lord Krishna badly. It was the critical juncture where a war became unavoidable. All the godly efforts of diffusing the tension remained in vein because of the adamant nature of the elder son of Gandhari. That day the happiest person in the royal court was Shakuni; his plan was working perfectly with all minute incarnations. He patted Duryodhan and committed him for giving all possible support.

Lord Krishna was approached by both the rival brothers, Arjun and Duryodhan for making his stands in the battle field clear. He had decided to help both the brothers by part. His armed forces would join a side and he himself would join the other side. There developed a situation when Duryodhan claimed the support of his Army. Lord Krishna joined the battle field as a chariot driver along with Arjun. It was the first point where Arjun remained victorious by recognizing the hidden power of the Divine for having its ability of issuing timely instructions and guide, which the army could not have. He had even identified the importance of strategy and planning as more important factors than compared to numbers. Ultimately both the families entered the battle field along with their supporters and well-wishers.

Despondence of Arjun, as narrated in the first chapter of The Gita, was the only reason Lord Krishna started reminding him his duties. He had also started narrating religious and noble acts which could make a person wise and contented. The Gita got its reference at this critical juncuture for diffusing the war and on the other hand it was also a strict instruction for Arjuna for delivering his duties as a warrior and an avenger. Lord Krishna marked the starting of the situation as an unavoidable one because of the series of sins committed by Kauravas. That is why it is the duty of Arjun to make the wiser side victorious by smashing all the culprits who have joined the side and even supported the sinners.

Teachings of Veda and Epics are from age old traditions. After the Epic Age we have passed on a span of thousands of years. Are such age old teachings becoming irrelevant day by day? Is the discussion on such teachings becoming useless in present day context?
If we start searching proper answer to these questions then we have to rely on the fact of the exact relationship with which the time and philosophy move on. Actually Philosophy and Religion never take the support of the confluence of time. Time can even repeat itself through predetermined actions. Philosophy never intends to influence the normal cycle of the confluence of time. Therefore, both of these aspects of our daily life are independent of each other and reflect themselves independently. What happened in Epic Age and the way Lord Rama

handled the situation during that time had a deeper impact in the society during that time. It has exhibited the value system with which a State and a family can define their role in society. Those values are still relevant. Advent of any change in the material world has no power of influencing the fundamental value system with which a community leader should work. There are millions of books and narratives with some noble initiative available for explaining and elaborating the propositions of teachings of Gita. Gita is relevant for both learners and teachers. It has something to say even to a layman having less knowledge about the mysteries hidden amidst the conversations displayed in the holy book of Gita.   The term Gita directly links our thinking with the conversation that took place in between Arjuna, a Warrior from the side of Pandavas, and his friendly guide Krishna. It was going on amidst a critical situation in which Arjuna lost his power of finalising something justifiable to have a sanction of war and killings. A series of killing of such type in which his beloved ones were at a threshold made Pandavas discontented and disturbed. Krishna took the role of his charioteer to normalise the situation and to let Arjuna understand his own status in a better way. The agitation, as described in the holy book of Mahabharata, was against the stand of his own family members having intention of grabbing all the resources by taking advantage of some conspired game-fares. The game-fare of such type with in infliction of opportunistic ideals was moved on differently and both the segments of a single family took a stand against each other.

Lord Krishna defined his stand by putting himself in the side of Pandavas with a sheer commitment of not to use his weapon at any instances. It was his stand that made him free from direct indulgence of the warfare and made it possible to guard Pandavas through delivering timely relevant instruction. In this way he has secured his position similar to that of the brain in our body. Conversation of Krishna and Arjuna amidst the battle field was also an act of holy instructions duly issued for Arjuna to signify his timely need. It had linked senses with duties, established correlation between rights and duties, issued bands of things to be done and things not to be done, entangled a spirit with its higher source, conferred the juxtaposition of creation and the creator and finally re-established need of knowing the self.

Madbhagvad-Gita, as the complete term coined for the holy book, had also defined the role of divine power in infusing values within the intellect and senses of a fellow devotee. It has also established a perfect correlation between knowledge and devotion. None of the paired combination alone can succeed in bringing fame. Through all the eighteen chapters of the holy book, Godly propositions were incorporated by saints and philosophers who have created it for commons. It has a perpetual compilation of various combinations of practical aspects of Yoga and Meditation. It has also narrated the true nature of Knowledge that often receive a confluence more confluous than that of a stream. Attainment of such knowledge is a subject of individual apprehension and resides solely on the purity of mind.

Our discussion up to this point has made a point clear about the nature and proposition of knowledge confluence remaining evident amongst us since centuries with a clear impetus of facilitating its follower for gaining an ascent through divinity and perfectness. There exist narratives in different forms and in different languages meant primarily to make people aware of the eternal philosophical aspects related to teachings of Gita.
Another effort of making Gita simple, easy to understand, more confluous to attend aspirations of people, more perpetuated to incorporate aspirations of millions and more conferred to actualise role of senses. Efforts may be of varying kinds to satisfy aspirations of people in different ways out. It may have some more relevant narratives that can efficiently link up the need of fundamental values reflected by Gita at different instances.

Effort is also made to curtail unwanted explanations for maintaining the flow of the vibration of thought process intact. Discussion on any philosophical aspects should not go in a hurry and also it should not be too slow. It should have adequate stress of combined segments of knowledge and information to keep things enlightened and actualised. It will be even more perfectly balanced to contingent human efforts of ascent towards the state of the unification of conscious mind with that of masterly guide. Effort is also made to encompass the segregation of individual differences from the common philosophical knowledge to make it more people friendly and more relevant, as well as time tested one.

Gita, in its actual sense, stands for some sort of compilation that people can sing. It can be discussed with some beautiful rhythmic tunes. Collective recitation of Gita brings out a collective wave in the form of auditory vibrations for the purpose of cleansing the immediate surroundings. It also conferred essence of collective and community level worship for making the entire effort possible and for keeping the converged senses of cooperation and brotherhood alive. To a compilation of prayers and songs meant for the supreme lord the World Poet coined a term "Gitanjali" for it. To align the practical aspects of life and mission of an individual with the specified spiritual destiny, Saint Vinoba coined the term "Katha Gita (Gita through a series of stories)" and incorporated all the teachings and narratives of Gita in absolutely friendly way. Examples are in plenty. It had not diffused the glory of the original compilation of Gita, also had not conferred replacing the original poetic compilation with millions of narratives. Waves of vibrations that the chanting of Gita creates is based on the assimilation of collective vibrations of saintly senses that makes a way out through the surrounding of the place of worship and gives birth to an essence of keeping the collective vibrations of cooperation, brotherhood, divine omnipresence and interlinkages of senses alive.

We, in the same manner, can successfully create hundreds and thousands of such narratives duly inflicted with fundamental human values to make the spark of Gita a confluous one, a vibrant one and a strategic one. It has enormous power of accommodations for incorporating all sorts of socially and culturally relevant directives within the scope of its teaching related to individual refinement impregnated with spiritual ascent. It also makes the relationship of creator and the creation a vibrant one. We can specify any of the particular effort as an initiative inflicted with divine power meant for accomplishing certain works. All such Gita, duly compiled by saintly people, are not with us. In due course of time we have lost many of such beautiful, relevant and time tested compilations due to various reasons. Our mind kept on imbibing presence of such powers tradition by tradition through many of our rituals. Those graceful efforts played a significant role in keeping waves of community worship alive.

Gita was interpreted differently by different saints since olden times. Still we have a lot to explore from it in the true sense. The teachings and discourses duly incorporated by Saint Veda Vyasa reflect the teachings of Upanishads put together. Saint Vyasa wanted to incorporate all the fundamental value system and yoga based life in a compact compilation to provide people an ease of access to the divine knowledge. If we correlate different scriptures and Epics side by side then the value system duly reflected through all the propositions of saints will reflect each other's presence in common. We can better understand this aspect by taking an example of idol making. We use clay for shaping it differently to reflect our imagination and art, similarly the case is there with Philosophy of Yoga. We can correlate Yoga with all aspects of our life. In that sense we can even say that, "All Life is Yoga."

This extended philosophy and belief cannot cripple our mind and intellect. We can even, for an example, consider the life of a beggar as a manifestation on the basis of Yoga. The beggar prepares the mind for begging something from any individual. In failing to get anything the fellow beggar prefers to move on further to gain a living. Ultimately the fellow beggar surrenders himself/herself at the disposal of the almighty. Time cannot permit us to move as per our own wishes and willingness, but philosophy can do so. We can even adhere to certain principles and propositions to express our wishes and willingness to move through such doctrines. People maintain faith on certain principles and rituals in which they feel themselves properly secured. Such security feelings will give birth to a communion having identical wishes and willingness. They even come across certain rituals to accomplish the jointly with an affinity of exhibiting a community feelings.

Conflicting Intellects

It will be even more perfectly balanced to contingent human efforts of ascent towards the state of the unification of conscious mind with that of masterly guide. Effort is also made to encompass the segregation of individual differences from the common philosophical knowledge to make it more people friendly and more relevant, as well as time tested one.

Gita, as a common and popularly contemplated term, indicates towards a subject related to the holy book of Gita having bands of knowledge in the form of a conversation in between Arjun and Krishna. This reality made Gita confined to a limited quarter and placed other holy efforts underneath a shadow of ignorance. We rarely talk about Ram Gita, Sanskaar Gita and some other such efforts having a suffix Gita attached to it.

Gita, in its actual sense, stands for some sort of compilation that people can sing. It can be discussed with some beautiful rhythmic tunes. Collective recitation of Gita brings out a collective wave in the form of auditory vibrations for the purpose of cleansing the immediate surroundings. It also conferred essence of collective and community level worship for making the entire effort possible and for keeping the converged senses of cooperation and brotherhood alive.

To a compilation of prayers and songs meant for the supreme lord the World Poet coined a term "Gitanjali" for it. To correlate the practical aspects of life and mission of an individual with the specified spiritual destiny, Saint Vinoba coined the term "Katha Gita (Gita through a series of stories)" and incorporated all the teachings and narratives of Gita in absolutely friendly way. Examples are in plenty. It had not diffused the glory of the original compilation of Gita, also had not conferred replacing the original poetic compilation with millions of narratives. Waves of vibrations that the chanting of Gita creates is based on the assimilation of collective vibrations of saintly senses that makes a way out through the surrounding of the place of worship and gives birth to an essence of keeping the collective vibrations of cooperation, brotherhood, divine omnipresence and inter-linkages of senses alive.

We, in the same manner, can successfully create hundreds and thousands of such narratives duly inflicted with fundamental human values to make the spark of Gita a confluous one, a vibrant one and a strategic one. It has enormous power of accommodations for incorporating all sorts of socially and culturally relevant directives within the scope of its teaching related to individual refinement impregnated with spiritual ascent. It also makes the relationship of creator and the creation a vibrant one. We can specify any of the particular effort as an initiative inflicted with divine power meant for accomplishing certain works. All such Gita, duly compiled by saintly people, are not with us. In due course of time we have lost many of such beautiful, relevant and time tested compilations due to various reasons. Our mind kept on imbibing presence of such powers tradition by tradition through many of our rituals. Those graceful efforts played a significant role in keeping waves of community worship alive.

Wider dimensions and expanded coverage of the teachings of Gita often make people worried about what to follow and what not to follow in real life. Also in some cases it becomes difficult to think about propositions in the actual ground. Because of lack of timely relevant practical knowledge of the situation, people even keep themselves aside from following and internalising teachings of the holy book in the real life situation. Approach of such religious and cultural teaching, therefore, should have proper considerations of some practical aspects of rituals and worships.

Some people maintain a view regarding Gita is that the entire aspects depicted in this holy book are a confusing one. Saints from olden times worked differently to show that Gita is much relevant in terms of rituals and propositions presented in it. Here also we are trying to trace out a link up in between rituals, traditions and practices that we have in nature to re-establish the age old faiths of the omnipresence of divine within us at its varying formats.

We can see things as they occupy a definite shape. We cannot see energy and power due to their in capabilities of occupying space. To feel the presence of such powers in our surrounding, we often take the support of our senses and feelings. In some cases our observations are evidence based, in some other cases it may have some imaginary propositions. Here comes the act of limitations that restrict us to feel Ultraviolet and Infrared radiations which remained off the band of the visible spectrum and duly restricted our sense of vision seven visible waves of light.

A Divine Inclination

We are discussing at present about saints like Veda Vyasa, Maharshi Patanjali, Valmiki and many more. Their presence can be ascertained even today through their creations, acts and conducts. They had created a best possible thought process and expected people to imbibe the same for ensuring aspirations of the advancement of the society through rectifications of the individual conducts.

Rectification of such type is a continuous process. We may not be able to claim about the absolute clarity on the process of rectification as an error free system. Such kinds of thought process will remain in the atmosphere even after thousands of years for making people acquainted with such principles.

The kind of thought process will remain in the context in the form of waves. Now a day's wave theory of the propagation of energy from its origin to the seat of action has become a common point of discussion. Wave theory of the propagation of energy form place to place addresses the need of people well in advance.

Thinking and attitude of people coming out from more or less identical socio-cultural background often exhibit similarities of many types. If countries from different socio-cultural background share parts of their border then it will be obvious that they often get indulge in some locally pitched conflicts. We can take the examples of the conflict between Armenia and Azar Bizan. Some other countries also put themselves in with certain vested interests. Communities fighting with each other are not justifiable at any cost. There exists other means of communication through which people move on to express their anger and also they can imply a sanction through business confluences.

Here comes the question of work culture and sectoral coordination. We have also witnessed the attitudinal difference between Rama and Ravana, as vividly described at difference instances in the famous epic the Ramayana. Rama wanted Ravana to give Sita, his life partner, back. He had deputed his messenger twice for making Ravana, the demon king from Sri Lanka; agree upon the proposal of peace. The proposal of peace was rejected in one hand and the power, potential and courage of lord Rama was ignored on the other. The result came in the form of a war. That war was also not meant for killing all the people of that country. It was not even meant for smashing the kingdom for grabbing resources, nor even meant for putting the name and reverence of lord Rama in the fore front. It was meant for teaching a lesson to the demon king and also for diffusing his state of ego, compulsion and desires.

The thought process that started moving along with the advancement of lord Rama was perfectly captured and imbibed by the brother of the demon king namely Bibhishan. He had managed himself to come out of the darkness of ego, compulsion and desires by harnessing the philosophy of peace, prosperity and collective progress. The result with him was also quite fruitful. He was the victorious person of that battle and duly accepted the place of his elder brother.

The Ramayana, the Mahabharata and other such scriptures always display the victory of good forces over the evil ones through inculcating waves of peace, prosperity, brotherhood, collective progress and prosperity for all. These acts also intensified at some places by linking up the bands of true and absolute knowledge with devotion to bring forth the powers of right action.

Hanumana, the warrior of lord Rama as described in the Ramayana, is the best example of such character having perfect combination of Knowledge and devotion. A critical situation developed in the middle of the journey of the envoy of Lord Rama when they had to cross a long stretch of ocean to reach Srilanka for obtaining information about Sita. All fellows present in the envoy started guessing about their own potential; only the person silent was Hanumana. His seniors wanted to know the exact reason of his silence. Hanumana said that the power possessed by him is obviously enormous, but it is not in his hand. A divine force guides the manifestation of that power. It will be implemented even at the service of the divine. Such knowledge was the exhibit of the true knowledge. Based on that knowledge one can surpass all possible obstacle whichever might come on the way. Similar thing happened with Hanumana. By crossing all the obstacles he reached the destiny and traced out Sita.

Sita noticed the presence of the messenger deputed by lord Rama. Here came the situation where Hanumana exhibited his devotion. For gaining the confidence of Sita on warriors and associates of Rama he had exhibited his enormous power in that garden where Sita was kept under observation. He even wanted to bring Sita back to Rama immediately. He was stopped by Sita by instructing him not to violate the rule of the family and tradition from which Ram is taking the lead.

He was requested to follow the assignment in particular for which Rama deputed him.

Here both Sita and Hanumana exhibited their devotion to their immediate master. It was also an exhibit of their loyalty to their master. Such loyalty often culminates to give birth to enormous power with which lord Rama along with his entire envoy was advancing towards the Demon King to teach him a lesson.

The fact was developing beyond the imagination that is why it was not perceivable by persons having inflictions of ego, anger, hatred, self-centrelines and desires. Ravana perceived the development in the envoy of Rama and his advancement towards his kingdom as an impossible task. After noticing the presence of Hanumana in front of him he was not convinced by the powers of monkeys and other associates who were accompanying lord Rama. The waves of devotion offered to the god, whom Ravana worshipping, was radiating out through the acts, conducts and attitudes of Hanumana. Then also Ravana was not in a position to accept any chance of the advancement of lord Rama towards his territory. Such standpoint of a warrior develops from the over confidence of the person about the system, implements and parts of such implements. That over-confidence removes all possible chances of rectification of the system. Because of that reason also Ravana failed to rectify his mistakes and placed himself in the turmoil of trouble. Whatever lessons we learn from experiences and interactions will sustain in our life for a longer time period. It can even bring sustaining happiness and contentment within us. Here lies the way in which any thought process perpetually move from one individual to the other.

In the modern world we have various types of cultural and religious thought process possessing rituals, customs and traditions of different types, which are equally competent to enrich people in terms of knowledge, devotion, courage, will power and dedication. The way we receive each culture to enrich our multiplurality will specify our degrees and ranges of success. Our motive force will guide accordingly to explore possibilities of working out converged cultural segments from all the rituals to move up towards vibrant waves of multi plurality. India, at this juncture of the development of multiplurality, will be a best example for all of us. Here people learned a lot to live with each other tolerate each other and enrich each other differently.

We cannot see light. Even we cannot see the propagation of sound through the material medium. Light strikes our eye, reaches our brain and develops a sensation of vision through certain life process of vision. With some sort of illusion, or lack of true knowledge only, we often claim that we can see light. Even all the colours radiated out from the sun are not recognisable by us. If God resides inside the individual, if all mysteries related to the ascent of a person on the path of divinity, then why any devotee search it out for gaining the blessings of any Divine power located outside the physically existing body? Why such a dwindling situation any individual face during the tenure of worship?

Lord Krishna narrated essence of feeling the Divine communion with the physically existing life through witnessing cultivation of knowledge, actualisation of the presence of any supreme power in sub conscious mind and possible ways and means to follow that power. It enables an individual to come across the feeling of the advent of some completeness in the mind through knowledge transformation. Cultivation of knowledge regarding the relationship of the divine and disciple is enrouted from the age old traditions through the turmoils of the organic evolution. That evolution brought some change in the process of exhibits, but the core remained the same. It was even more perpetual and more profound regarding the ability of harnessing the relationship of matter and energy. We cannot imagine the existence of matter without the involvement of energy, and similarly energy takes a definite visible form to occupy certain space in this universe.

How do people see things and how do they correlate such unavoidable relationship of energy and matter is depend upon the level of understanding that one adhares with. A master of Physics and a master of Philosophy must have varying degree of explanations for putting forth the mystery behind the mechanism involved during inter-conversion of matter and energy. All organic combinations have certain physical and chemical sets of combinations in such a definite ways that they inculcate the abilities of interactions and abilities of giving birth to senses. Even evolution of sensory structures and related orientations became much collaborative in case of human beings. Here occurs a change which brought us near the state of explorations meant for examining the hidden mysteries behind creation and orientation of life forms in the living planet.

These days, things are known to us that earth like situation exists in the universe. Only the matter of concern is that we may not be able to reach the place even after attaining the speed as that of light in a year or two. Only we can admire the presence and orientation of such creations within our visibility. Only we can explore and examine such things with the help of optical and electronic instruments. With an understanding of such limitations human beings never arranged any voyage to explore the inner world of senses that can allow us to explore the outer orientation of time and space. Such an inner world exploration may require a little effort to culminate senses within a confinement for feeling the presence. There also resides a tremendous flux of energy accumulated within such a small space. That mysterious combination taking the form of life was explored differently by saints during olden times.

There developed a science of explorations of the correlations of the Creation and the Divine. Matter and energy indulged in a perfect orientation for letting senses flow through them. Arrangement and orientation of all our senses are directed outwardly. That is why we are bound to receive waves and sparks from the outside world. Our inner world remains unexplored in most of the cases. Only adherence of true knowledge and the journey of senses through inner world during meditation can pave a way out for exploring our own self. Meditation is the doorstep where orientation of senses get diverted towards the inner world and bring out mysteries associated to the fact of accommodation of the Divine power inside the living being.

Is that Divine power is restricted to the human beings only? The answer is, obviously and surely without any doubt, No. human beings have gained some sort of evolutionary supremacy in due course of time. But other beings are also of same potential and courage with a domination of animism in them. Dogs are loyal to their master, cats exhibit better vigilance power, elephants are more socialised beings having better memory power and tigers are the masters of their own territory. Taking hold upon the surrounding and defining the role according to trophic   level, we can easily arrange these beings and others without any difficulty.

Philosophical and Spiritual supremacy is a step forward that makes a distinction between other animals and human beings. Then also we can witness inhuman acts from human beings and humanly acts from some inhuman animals. The orientation of sense organ and correlation of senses and sensory responses with memory and intellect is the only factor regulating such varying degrees and conducts of animismic and humanismic behaviours. Presence of such a Divine power within the creation is the reason behind the maintenance of an idea of serving humanity with a correlated apprehension of serving God. Only God cannot put a direct access to the feelings of the presence of such immense power within us. It is the approach with which we offer our services to living beings can develop a way out for us to feel the difference.

A youth from Mumbai approached a saint for offering himself at the service to divine. It made the saint happy. He wanted to know the exact reason behind his stand of doing so. Saint also enquired about his capabilities and considered his offering a wise one. Actually the fellow was searching jobs in the city. He was also a normal Graduate from any sub –urban area and his financial situation was also not so good. Perhaps the sacrifice might make him temporarily happy and contented, but will become a burden in due course of time. With happiness saint suggested him for searching out a suitable job and helping the parents and inmates of the family financially. Only after gaining some wealth and knowledge the person can really enjoy the glory of sacrifice. Right now the person has nothing special to sacrifice. Such sacrifice inflicted with sorrow and agony may put both the master and the disciple in trouble.

Even divine cannot allow any individual to put oneself and families in trouble and agony. It is the only state of contentment that helps a person during movement from the physical world to the spiritual world. Offerings of any kind and in any particular form will bring happiness.

What happened in Epic Age and the way Lord Rama handled the situation during that time had a deeper impact in the society during that time. It has exhibited the value system with which a State and a family can define their role in society. Those values are still relevant. Advent of any change in the material world has no power of influencing the fundamental value system with which a community leader should work.

There are millions of books and narratives with some noble initiative available for explaining and elaborating the propositions of teachings of Gita. Gita is relevant for both learners and teachers. It has something to say even to a layman having less knowledge about the mysteries hidden amidst the conversations displayed in the holy book of Gita. The term Gita directly links our thinking with the conversation that took place in between Arjuna, a Warrior from the side of Pandavas, and his friendly guide Krishna. It was going on amidst a critical situation in which Arjuna lost his power of finalising something justifiable to have a sanction of war and killings. A series of killing of such type in which his beloved ones were at a threshold was not acceptable to Arjun. Krishna took the role of his charioteer to normalise the situation and to let Arjuna understand his own status in a better way. The agitation, as described in the holy book of Mahabharata, was against the stand of his own family members having intention of grabbing all the resources by taking advantage of some conspired game-fares. The game-fare of such type with an infliction of opportunistic ideals was moved on differently and both the segments of a single family took a stand against each other. Lord Krishna defined his stand by putting himself in the side of Pandavas with a sheer commitment of not to use his weapon at any instances. It was his stand that made him free from direct indulgence of the warfare and made it possible to guard Pandavas through delivering timely relevant instruction. In this way he has secured his position similar to that of the brain in our body. Conversation of Krishna and Arjuna amidst the battle field was also an act of holy instructions duly issued for Arjuna to signify his timely need. It had linked senses with duties, established correlation between rights and duties, issued bands of things to be done and things not to be done, entangled a spirit with its higher source, conferred the juxtaposition of creation and the creator and finally re-established need of knowing the self.

Madbhagvad-Gita, as the complete term coined for the holy book, had also defined the role of divine power in infusing values within the intellect and senses of a fellow devotee. It has also established a perfect correlation between knowledge and devotion. None of the paired combination alone can succeed in bringing fame. Through all the eighteen chapters of the holy book, Godly propositions were incorporated by saints and philosophers who have created it for commons. It has a perpetual compilation of various combinations of practical aspects of Yoga and Meditation. It has also narrated the true nature of Knowledge that often receive a confluence more confluous than that of a stream. Attainment of such knowledge is a subject of individual apprehension and resides solely on the purity of mind. Our discussion up to this point has made a point clear about the nature and proposition of knowledge confluence remaining evident amongst us since centuries with a clear impetus of facilitating its follower for gaining an ascent through divinity and perfectness. There exist narratives in different forms and in different languages meant primarily to make people aware of the eternal philosophical aspects related to teachings of Gita.

Another effort of making Gita simple, easy to understand, more confluous to attend aspirations of people, more perpetuated to incorporate aspirations of millions and more conferred to actualise role of senses. Efforts may be of varying kinds to satisfy aspirations of people in different ways out. It may have some more relevant narratives that can efficiently link up the need of fundamental values reflected by Gita at different instances. Effort is also made to curtail unwanted explanations for maintaining the flow of the vibration of thought process intact. Discussion on any philosophical aspects should not go in a hurry and also it should not be too slow. It should have adequate stress of combined segments of knowledge and information to keep things enlightened and actualised. It will be even more perfectly balanced to contingent human efforts of ascent towards the state of the unification of conscious mind with that of masterly guide. Effort is also made to encompass the segregation of individual differences from the common philosophical segments of knowledge to make it more people friendly and more relevant, as well as time tested one.

Gita, in its actual sense, stands for some sort of compilation that people can sing. It can be discussed with some beautiful rhythmic tunes. Collective recitation of Gita brings out a collective wave in the form of auditory vibrations for the purpose of cleansing the immediate surroundings. It also conferred essence of collective and community level worship for making the entire effort possible and for keeping the converged senses of cooperation and brotherhood alive.

To a compilation of prayers and songs meant for the supreme lord the World Poet coined a term "Gitanjali" for it. To align the practical aspects of life and mission of an individual with the specified spiritual destiny, Saint Vinoba coined the term "Katha Gita (Gita through a series of stories)" and incorporated all the teachings and narratives of Gita in absolutely friendly way. Examples are in plenty. It had not diffused the glory of the original compilation of Gita, also had not conferred replacing the original poetic compilation with millions of narratives. Waves of vibrations that the chanting of Gita creates is based on the assimilation of collective vibrations of saintly senses that makes a way out through the surrounding of the place of worship and gives birth to an essence of keeping the collective vibrations of cooperation, brotherhood, divine omnipresence and interlinkages of senses alive.

We, in the same manner, can successfully create hundreds and thousands of such narratives duly inflicted with fundamental human values to make the spark of Gita a confluous one, a vibrant one and a strategic one. It has enormous power of accommodations for incorporating all sorts of socially and culturally relevant directives within the scope of its teaching related to individual refinement impregnated with spiritual ascent. It also makes the relationship of creator and the creation a vibrant one. We can specify any of the particular effort as an initiative inflicted with divine power meant for accomplishing certain works. All such Gita, duly compiled by saintly people, are not with us. In due course of time we have lost many of such beautiful, relevant and time tested compilations due to various reasons. Our mind kept on imbibing presence of such powers tradition by tradition through many of our rituals. Those graceful efforts played a significant role in keeping waves of community worship alive.

Gita was interpreted differently by different saints since olden times. Still we have a lot to explore from it in the true sense. The teachings and discourses duly incorporated by Saint Veda Vyasa reflect the teachings of Upanishads put together. Saint Vyasa wanted to incorporate all the fundamental value system and yoga based life in a compact compilation to provide people an ease of access to the divine knowledge. If we correlate different scriptures and Epics side by side then the value system duly reflected through all the propositions of saints will reflect each other's presence in common. We can better understand this aspect by taking an example of idol making. We use clay for shaping it differently to reflect our imagination and art, similarly the case is there with Philosophy of Yoga. We can correlate Yoga with all aspects of our life. In that sense we can even say that, "All Life is Yoga."

This extended philosophy and belief cannot cripple our mind and intellect. We can even, for an example, consider the life of a beggar as a manifestation on the basis of Yoga. The beggar prepares the mind for begging something from any individual. In failing to get anything the fellow beggar prefers to move on further to gain a living. Ultimately the fellow beggar surrenders himself/herself at the disposal of the almighty. Time cannot permit us to move as per our own wishes and willingness, but philosophy can do so. We can even adhere to certain principles and propositions to express our wishes and willingness to move through such doctrines.

People maintain faith on certain principles and rituals in which they feel themselves properly secured. Such security feelings will give birth to a communion having identical wishes and willingness. They even come across certain rituals to accomplish the jointly with an affinity of exhibiting a community feelings.

We have considerations of science which encompasses a restricted scope depending upon which all kinds of elements and energy play a vital role jointly in making this universe a reality. Matter does not include any massless particles such as photons, or any other electro-magnetic waves such as light or heat or magnetic impulses.[252] Dual nature of matter (particle nature and wave nature) is acknowledged by Dr. Louis De. Broglie (1924): Particles are bundles of waves which move with a group

---

[252] *"Matter (physics)". McGraw-Hill's Access Science: Encyclopedia of Science and Technology Online. Archived from the original on 17 June 2011. Retrieved 24 May 2009.*

velocity and possess an effective mass.[253] Detail discussion in this field is not our principal objective. Quantum electrons, as well as electrons under the regulation of atoms and large molecules, behave like wave and particle at different instances.[254] Even light waves, although having some electromagnetic characteristics, can have angular momentum during formation of vortex.[255] Science confers the properties of matter and energy alongside their duality. Propositions have limitations up to different dimensions duly exhibited by a galaxy. It is estimated that Milky Way Galaxy[256], the parental segment of our Solar System, accommodates near about 100 to 400 billion stars. One can easily estimate the vast expansion with which this galaxy confers its status in space. There are other galaxies having more volume that compared to the collective volume of several other galaxies. The Solar System is located at near about 27,000 light years from the Galactic Centre.[257] Whatever be the volume and whatever the content is, all kinds of celestial collections represent four different dimensions (such as length, breadth, height and time).

Being special member of Solar System, the Earth is the place which got the name Living Planet due to presence and evolution of life in it. All living forms got some sort of similarities in terms of combination of atoms to form large and complex molecules; combination of carbon, hydrogen, oxygen and nitrogen manufactured different types of proteins; such proteins took the role of shaping bodily constructions; several other molecules took part secondarily to bring variations. Nucleic acids took the role of encoding and transmitting template of protein molecules to

---

[253] *de Broglie, Louis Victor. "On the Theory of Quanta" (PDF). Foundation of Louis de Broglie (English translation by A.F. Kracklauer, 2004. ed.). Retrieved 25 February 2023.*
[254] *Arndt, Markus; Hornberger, Klaus (2014). "Testing the limits of quantum mechanical superpositions". Nature Physics. 10 (4): 271–277. arXiv:1410.0270v1. doi:10.1038/nphys2863. ISSN 1745-2473.*
[255] *Allen, L.; Beijersbergen, M. W.; Spreeuw, R. J. C.; Woerdman, J. P. (1992). "Orbital angular momentum of light and the transformation of Laguerre-Gaussian laser modes". Physical Review A. 45 (11): 8185–8189. doi:10.1103/PhysRevA.45.8185.*
[256] *"How Many Stars in the Milky Way?". NASA Blueshift. Archived from the original on January 25, 2016.*
[257] *Gillessen, Stefan; Plewa, Philipp; Eisenhauer, Frank; Sari, Re'em; Waisberg, Idel; Habibi, Maryam; Pfuhl, Oliver; George, Elizabeth; Dexter, Jason; von Fellenberg, Sebastiano; Ott, Thomas; Genzel, Reinhard (November 28, 2016). "An Update on Monitoring Stellar Orbits in the Galactic Center". The Astrophysical Journal. 837 (1): 30. arXiv:1611.09144. Bibcode:2017ApJ...837...30G. doi:10.3847/1538-4357/aa5c41. S2CID 119087402*

ensure continuation of generations. Through a prolonged span of organic evolution the living planet reached up to the evolution of human beings.

Our discussion will move on towards convergence of principles of Knowledge and Science, which is also a pre-requisite for understanding different aspects of spirituality. Question often arises about the purpose of organic evolution which went on progressive towards the evolution of human beings; increase of cranial capacity, attainment of grip of arms, development of bipedalism, erect posture are some of the physical and anatomical development; intellect, mind, ego, senses and bodily organ system are some of the functional development which ensured refinement of development in human beings.

Scope of our discussion regarding spiritual ascent depends entirely on the ways and means of functioning of senses, ego, intellect, mind, spirit and the soul. Science rarely confers manifestation of the living body under a balanced regulation and support of the soul; but spiritual orientation of saintly persons contributed a lot to ensure progress of fellow individual and aspirants in this line to ensure spiritual ascent of the fellow aspirant. The evolutionary track leading towards origin of hominids deviated from that of apes near about 4 to 8 million years ago.[258] *Homo habialis*, the earliest form of hominids evolved around 2.8 million years ago.[259] Rapid encephalization[260], a process leading towards enlargement of brain capacity and volume, occurred in due course of time; it was just doubled in *Homo erectus*.[261] Scholars often indulge in debates regarding exact site of the origin of modern man. The forerunner of modern man Home sapiens evolved in between 400,000 to 250,000 years ago.[262] Men moved on towards development of lithic technology

---

[258] *Clark, G.; Henneberg, M. (June 2015). "The life history of Ardipithecus ramidus: a heterochronic model of sexual and social maturation". Anthropological Review. 78 (2): 109–132. doi:10.1515/anre-2015-0009. S2CID 54900467.*

[259] *Ghosh, Pallab (March 4, 2015). "'First human' discovered in Ethiopia". BBC News. London. Archived from the original on April 18, 2015. Retrieved April 19, 2015.*

[260] *Such an increase in human brain size is equivalent to each generation having 125,000 more neurons than their parents.*

[261] *Swisher, Carl C. III; Curtis, Garniss H.; Lewin, Roger (2001) [Originally published 2000]. Java Man: How Two Geologists Changed Our Understanding of Human Evolution. Chicago: University of Chicago Press. ISBN 978-0-226-78734-3. LCCN 2001037337. OCLC 48066180.*

[262] *O'Neil, Dennis. "Early Modern Homo sapiens". Evolution of Modern Humans: A Survey of the Biological and Cultural Evolution of Archaic and Modern Homo sapiens (Tutorial). San Marcos, CA: Palomar College. Archived from the original on April 30, 2015. Retrieved April 20, 2015.*

just 50,000 years ago.[263] Evidences suggest that social and cultural attitude of human beings continued changing gradually on the basis of different climatic zones duly inhabited by evolved groups of the same genera. Homo neanderthalensis, inhabited Europe and Asia from 400,000 to 28,000 years ago. There exist various anatomical and structural differences in between modern man and Neanderthal variations; along with some sort of advancement in the population of the stock of cold climate.[264] Organic evolution secured enlargement of human brain three times than compared to those of chimpanzee or gorilla.[265] Ulnar opposition, the contact between tip of thumb and the little finger, is one of the unique qualities to the genus Homo.[266] Development of spirituality, a mental aspect of life leading towards regulation of senses, refinement of spirit, intellect and reorientation of ego, is another feature which is special to humans.[267] In modern context the term is broadened to accommodate aspects of religion, culture, traditions, rituals and Yoga.[268] In some cases such development may involve beliefs in a supernatural realm beyond the scope of ordinarily sensible world.[269]

Is Divinity special to any specialised individual? Is Divinity not accessible to any of the fellow aspirants in this world?.

A strong argument is duly advanced in this regard by considering some of the great sayings as such saying confer about the universality of

---

[263] *Mellars, Paul (June 20, 2006). "Why did modern human populations disperse from Africa ca. 60,000 years ago? A new model". Proc. Natl. Acad. Sci. U.S.A. 103 (25): 9381–9386. Bibcode:2006PNAS..103.9381M. doi:10.1073/pnas.0510792103. ISSN 0027-8424. PMC 1480416. PMID 16772383.*

[264] *Finlayson C, Giles Pacheco F, Rodríguez-Vidal J, et al. (2006). "Late survival of Neanderthals at the southernmost extreme of Europe". Nature. 443 (7113): 850–853. Bibcode:2006Natur.443..850F. doi:10.1038/nature05195. hdl:10261/18685. PMID 16971951. S2CID 4411186.*

[265] *Schoenemann, P. Thomas (October 2006). "Evolution of the Size and Functional Areas of the Human Brain". Annual Review of Anthropology. 35: 379–406. doi:10.1146/annurev.anthro.35.081705.123210. ISSN 0084-6570. S2CID 7611321.*

[266] *Young, Richard W (January 2003). "Evolution of the human hand: the role of throwing and clubbing". Journal of Anatomy. 202 (1): 165–174. doi:10.1046/j.1469-7580.2003.00144.x. ISSN 0021-8782. PMC 1571064. PMID 12587931.*

[267] *Safaria, Triantoro; Bashori, Khoiruddin (2022-10-27). "Relationship between Spirituality and Emotional Maturity with Cultural Intelligence in Preventing Culture Shock". Psympathic: Jurnal Ilmiah Psikologi. 9 (1): 45–54. doi:10.15575/psy.v9i1.15628. ISSN 2502-2903. Archived from the original on 2023-01-06. Retrieved 2023-01-06.*

[268] *Gorsuch, R.L.; Miller, W.R. (1999), "Assessing spirituality", in W.R. Miller (ed.), Integrating spirituality into treatment, Washington, DC: American Psychological Association, pp. 47–64*

[269] *Schuurmans-Stekhoven, J.B. (2014). "Measuring Spirituality as Personal Belief in Supernatural Forces: Is the Character Strength Inventory-Spirituality subscale a brief, reliable and valid measure?". Implicit Religion. 17 (2): 211–222. doi:10.1558/imre.v17i2.211*

the Divine omnipresent in all kinds of worldly manifestations. We may converge our wandering attention upon four great sayings duly adopted from Upanishad.

अहं ब्रह्मास्मि - "मैं ब्रह्म हूँ" (बृहदारण्यक उपनिषद १/४/१० - यजुर्वेद)
तत्त्वमसि - "वह ब्रह्म तू है" (छान्दोग्य उपनिषद ६/८/७- सामवेद)
अयम् आत्मा ब्रह्म - "यह आत्मा ब्रह्म है" (माण्डूक्य उपनिषद १/२ - अथर्ववेद)
प्रज्ञानं ब्रह्म - "वह प्रज्ञान ही ब्रह्म है" (ऐतरेय उपनिषद १/२ - ऋग्वेद)
सर्व खल्विदं ब्रह्मम् - "सब ब्रह्म ही है" (छान्दोग्य उपनिषद ३/१४/१- सामवेद)

मनुष्य देह, इंद्रिय और मन का संघटन मात्र नहीं है, बल्कि वह सुख-दुख, जन्म-मरण से परे दिव्यस्वरूप है, आत्मस्वरूप है। आत्मभाव से मनुष्य जगत का द्रष्टा भी है और दृश्य भी।

Consciousness is the Divine (Brahman).

The self is Divine (Brahman).

The entire substratum of universal manifestation is Brahman.

Only Brahman is Truth, rest of the other manifestations are mere illusions. It also encompasses that human beings are not only the unit of bodily manifested organs and system; Soul force is the ultimate reality of such manifestation and because of such self illuminated existence human beings sees and exhibits entire creation; viewer of the all kinds of manifestation through which only Divine can be recognised at the ultimate level of reality. Only Soul force can feel the Divine omnipresence during certain instance when mind remains free from turmoils of sensory and motor functions; when the fellow aspirant gains a steadfast status of intellect and ego; when assimilative ego mounts upon the mind and intellect to make the fellow aspirant capable of exhibiting self luminous nature of the soul force.

It is obvious that all types of organisms can have such status of self luminous nature of Atma (Soul force) which also equip them in a better way to let the very self feel the Divine omnipresence. We have some higher level of thoughts and respect regarding origin and propagation of Divine knowledge embedded in Vedas: Vedas manifested from the breath of God.[270] Before accepting and popularising any spiritual principles the same must be validated on the authority of

---

[270] *Bṛhadāraṇyak Upaniṣhad (4.5.11)*

Vedas.[271]   The field of activities, as per the exhibits displayed by organisms, is composed of the five great elements: the ego, the intellect, the unmanifest primordial matter, the eleven senses (obtained from five sense organs, five action organs, and mind), and the five objects of the senses duly gathered during live activities. All such sense and action organs work under abled supervision of the mind to feel the sensible parts of surrounding; they also make themselves qualified differently to gather a potential to feel the non-sensible and non—perceivable entity of supreme master (the Divine) besides all sorts of worldly manifestations which ensures all such orientations a reality. It also confers the qualification of Atma (the Soul force) to get merged in the widest consciousness of the Divine. It is not limited to any specific organism, but availed uniformly for all organisms with identical impetus. None of the organisms can be disqualified at any instance because of any reason in exercising the process of attaining spiritual ascent for reaching the ultimate destiny for experiencing Divine omnipresence.

Scopes of our discussion remains restricted to instances of Vedic Scriptures and related literary sources alongside some of the relevant sources from Science and Technology. The scope of the Gita in our daily life is enormous for which saints often continue serving their discourses to attend all sorts of doubts of fellow aspirants having adequate faith upon the ways and means of all the teachings which brought in practice through Epics; from such Epics "The Gita" got the prominence because of the approach with which it started addressing different types doubts and worries of performers like prince Arjun; such a symbolic presence of a prince amidst a battle field duly inflicted with sorrow, agony, doubts, worries and probabilities of violent encounters from either sides.

Address to Knowledge and Wisdom

Knowledge, as the term envisages, has a direct link with mind and intellect. It is absolutely a brain function and depends to a greater extent upon the interaction of senses and memory. It has some

---

[271] *"bhūtaṁ bhavyaṁ bhaviṣhyaṁ cha sarvaṁ vedāt prasidhyati"*...... *Manu Smṛiti 12.97*

involvement of motor and sensory involvements which often people acquire through practices. Some sort of knowledge enriches an individual tradition by tradition. We cannot abruptly claim that knowledge will enrich an individual all on a sudden. It moves through a series of instructional steps and a series of practices.

The Yoga of Knowledge and Science is duly explained by the Divine Master:[272]

With complete attachment of mind in the Divine subject one can attain mastery in knowing real nature of the Divine Manifestations. Attainment of knowledge after gaining which nothing in this universe may remain unknown. Amongst thousands of persons, hardly one strives for gaining perfection; attainment of mastery or gain of superiority; and amongst those who have achieved such perfection, hardly any fellow aspirant knows the Divine in its real sense. Earth, water, fire, air, space, mind, intellect, and ego—these are eight components of material energy of the supreme master (or The Divine); a set of inferior energy upon which soul energy (ATMA) is the superior energy which comprises basis of the Divine manifestations. The Divine is the source of all sorts of manifestations and all such manifestations diffuse finally in the supreme source. There is nothing higher than such kind of supreme source and everything rests on such source; similar to beads remain restricted in a string; as similar as the restriction with which celestial bodies like stars continue emitting radiations; as similar to the restrictions with which stars ensure their membership to a galaxy; similar to taste of water; the sacred syllable OM (the Pranava); the sound of ether; similar to the ability in individuals; similar to the pure fragrance of the Earth, and the brilliance in fire, the life-force in all beings, the penance of the ascetics, the eternal seed of all beings, the intellect of the intelligent, the splendour of the glorious; similar to strength of individuals devoid of desires and passion; similar to the sexual activities not conflicting with virtue or scriptural injunctions. The three states of material existence[273] are manifested by the Divine while remaining ignorant about presence of such kind of supreme master; which often remains beyond the scope of

---

[272] *The Bhagavadgita , Chapter 7*
[273] *goodness, passion, and ignorance;*

access merely remaining dependent upon any of the sensible desires or mental passion. Remaining inflicted with three modes of illusions people remain ignorant of such kind of Divine omnipresence which is imperishable and eternal at all instances. [274] They also remain ignorant of the presence of such kind of doer of actions and consider themselves as the master of all such acts and conducts taken up individually by them or by imparting themselves in a group along with other performers of such action.

Aspirants who keep complete faith on the Divine will easily cross the entire world of illusions which often becomes a difficult task to accomplish by any of the common individuals remaining inflicted with complete faith on the supreme master. People who remain ignorant of knowledge, who lazily follow their lower nature of absolute knowledge, individuals inflicted with demonic nature and people having deluded intellect may not be able to recognise the Divine omnipresence. Four kinds of aspirants (the distressed, the seekers of knowledge, the seekers of worldly possessions, and those who are situated in knowledge) are capable of recognising the Divine and remain engaged in Divine subjects without deviating from the path of spiritual ascent; among these the fellow aspirant who worship the Divine will be considered as the highest; such individual gains the Divine love. Such kind of worshippers having devotion to the supreme master are indeed noble; their acts and conducts are noble; they are of steadfast mind; their intellect remains merged in the Divine subject; such individuals made the Divine alone as supreme accomplishable goal; they are considered as very self of the Divine master.[275]

Gainer of absolute knowledge having faith on the universality of the Divine is very rare in our surrounding; such knowledge always surrounds on the supreme master (BRAHMAN).[276]

A state of mental and intellectual dualities during which diffusion of knowledge becomes evident because of the mental engagements in worldly sensible desires is the condition during which

---

[274] *The BhagavadgitaVII. 5-13*
[275] *. (The Bhagavadgita VII.14 – 18)*
[276] *The Bhagavadgita VII. 19*

aspirants rarely recognise presence of the supreme commander (BRAHMAN) in all instances of creations. Those whose knowledge has been diffused by material desires surrender to the celestial gods. Following their own nature, they worship the devatās[277], practicing rituals or meditations meant to propitiate the specified celestial personalities. [278]

Aspirants may rely on any of the godly idol or any of the masterly guide as per sincere sanction of their mind and intellect which must not generate instances of confusion or unrest;[279] for stability of mind and intellect is extremely important to enable the fellow aspirant in gaining spiritual ascent; for such kind of spiritual ascent will ensure the spiritual refinement of mind and intellect; for refined mind and intellect gradually start recognising presence of the Divine; for recognition of the Divine omnipresence will pave a path of union (Yoga) of ATMA and PARAMATMA which is the ultimate goal of life of any aspirant.

Endowed with faith, the devotee worships a particular celestial god as per development of faith in their intellect and obtains the objects of desire accordingly. Actually, the Divine alone arranges access to all sorts of benefits. Aspirants keeping faith on celestial gods get blessings accordingly and those who worship the Divine gets renunciation bit by bit.[280]

The less intelligent think that I, the Supreme Lord Shree Krishna, was formless earlier and have now assumed this personality. They do not understand the imperishable exalted nature of my personal form. The Divine is not recognisable to everyone, although without receiving such omnipresence of the supreme master nothing can be accomplished; it is because of the persistence of the illusion (YOGAMAYA); because of the prevalence of confusion in mental state; because of the shadow of ego duly inflicted with I-ness; because of the falsehood duly mounted in

---

[277] *Hindi/ Sanskrit term which means the God, or the Divine; or any supreme guide having potential of taking role of a masterly guide.*
[278] *The Bhagavadgita VII.20*
[279] *Whatever celestial form a devotee seeks to worship with faith, the Divine confers steadiness of that faith upon the specified form. (The Bhagavadgita VII. 21)*
[280] *The fruit (or result of worships) gained by aspirants alongwith little understanding is perishable. Those who worship the celestial gods move towards the celestial abodes, while devotees of the Divine finally come to the supreme master. (The Bhagavadgita VII.23)*

mind and intellect because of the attachment to passion and desire of seeking pleasure; because of vulgar nature of the mental state; because of attachment to bodily recognisable senses of pleasure; due to lack of adequate awareness of the real nature of the soul; due to sustaining faith on the illusion which remains prevalent in the immediate surroundings. That is why, those without real knowledge about the supreme master (the DIVINE) do not know that ATMA sustains without change and remains beyond the scope of birth and death.

We must acknowledge real nature of the Divine.[281] One can have freedom from all kinds of delusion.[282] Remaining involved in noble conducts one can gain freedom from development of all sorts of illusions and start recognising the real nature of the Divine manifestations at all instances.[283] One should know the principle of Karma (nature of assigned duties and performances in nature). After recognising the Divine omnipresence, striving for liberation from sequences of old-age and death, aspirants start recognising the Brahman, the individual self (ATMA), and the entire field of karmic action (KARMA).

Those who know Me as the governing principle of the adhibhūta[284] and the adhidaiva[285], and as adhiyajña[286], such enlightened souls are in full consciousness of the Divine even at the time of the disintegration of soul from the bodily manifestations.

One cannot escape from oneself without performing duties duly assigned by the system designed for ensuring interactions at different trophic levels of the eco system. It is also true that none of the advancement and modernisation can compel us to come out of that system and behave differently to violate the basic rules of the nature. If we start claiming that tigers should not be allowed to kill deer, cats

---

[281] *The Divine (or the supreme master) knows instances of past, present, and future, and also knows all living beings along with their true nature; but no one perfectly knows presence of the Divine at all instances.*

[282] *Dualities of desire and aversion arise from illusion. All living beings in the material realm are deluded by these.*

[283] *Aspirants, whose sins have been destroyed by engaging in pious activities, become free from the illusion of dualities; they worship the Divine (or the supreme master) with utter determination*

[284] *The recognisable field of matter.*

[285] *The entire group of celestial gods, masters and the Divine guide;*

[286] *the Supreme master of all sacrificial performances or YAJNA.*

should not chase rats, snakes should not feed on frogs and owls should not puncture ripe fruits then our claims will violate the laws of nature. With certain natural instincts and for maintaining a proper balance in nature organisms ensure their definite role as per the assignments. Human beings are playing a role with some sort of exceptions. One can intend to kill deer for obtaining food; one can trap fishes, kill birds, smash snakes and chase bulls for fulfilling the need of grabbing food. With a modified vigil of registering one's presence in the cycle of energy transfer one can cultivate grains, harvest fruits and maintain mulching animals for fulfilling the requirement of food. For rest of the world the role of that human will be of a protector.

With such dual principles human beings can register the presence of oneself in between the highest and middle order of the trophic level[287]. In another aspect we people maintain our difference from others due to our ductility, capabilities to speak, performance of exhibiting our emotions and affinity of remaining linked with others. Here comes the essence of socialisation and acculturation for the same. On the basis of such involvement in the society parents cannot escape from their duties of nourishing their children, young ones cannot escape from their duties toward elders and seniors cannot escape from their affinity of helping young ones. Escapism of any type and any degree is the affinity of human beings for which the entire community may face sufferings, loss of trust and agony. Escapism of any type can also create individual differences, depending upon which human beings often start ascertaining one's role in society.

We cannot claim that all people make themselves capable enough to escape from the acts of escapism and make them more active, more responsible, perfectly awakened and properly adjusted.

Standard of Living

---

[287] This is an indicator with which position of an organism in an ecosystem and also in a food pyramid can be worked out. Trophic level of green plants, for an example, is one as they are capable of making their own food by using the energy of the sunlight. Herbivores are at level two and carnivores are at level three.

Sometimes we claim that people living in some cultured civilisation lead a higher standard of living. For all instances of life process they are more equipped and more perpetuated than compared some other people belonging to sub human standard of living. Objection regarding the Standardisation of living in terms of mechanisation of life process is not the only scale depending upon which one can classify different society and different culture. Standard is the relative term having some limitations of its own. People involved in the process of standardising a society or a person may consider some parameters on the basis of the knowledge base that the person possesses. Differences in the observation will be observed on the basis of the knowledge base of people involved in such mechanism.

Every individual in this society differ from the other at any of the points. There may remain more differences or may remain any one difference. It may be in terms of capabilities; it may be in terms of skills or may be in terms of competence. On the basis of such formats of differences none of the individuals in this world are of useless type. Everybody has a definite role to play here. We can correlate attitude of any individual with those of some olden times in terms of similarities and differences. Such comparison is of less importance because of the reality that every individual is of its own type. Then question arises, how do people encompass some similarities in attitudes and conducts with those of some characters remained prevalent in olden times? Is it true that Lord Rama can take birth again? If yes, how?

Similarities and differences that we come across are due to the system of socialisation and cultural blend that people come across during the process of acculturation. A child, for an example, rarely agrees to sit alongside other fellow students during early days of schooling. It is more prominent if we try to isolate a child from their parents. The kind of mental adjustment is developed on the basis of faith that grows inside the mind of the fellow learner. Learning of any type, at this critical juncture should not be a forced one. It should not try to suppress the individual identity by imposing any unbalanced curriculum having no adjustment with the immediate context. Epics like Ramayana, Mahabharata and holy book like Gita became evident only because of the ease that these scriptures and allied literature provided for accelerating the pace of learning. Another such famous creation that gained adequate attention of people is Ramcharitmanas written by Goswami Tulsidasa. People found their intellect more adjusted with the narratives of Goswami Tulsidasa.

When we talk about the philosophy of peace, it points out toward doctrines of certain fundamental human aspirations in which the human mind attains a constructive status. Peace never stands simply for diffusing anger, tension or any other unrest. It is not the exhibit of any termination of tension or war. It cannot be considered as a dogma opposite to violence, unrest, struggle or fighting. In its absolute sense, peace is a part of the yoga based life duly proposed by Vedic saints as a state of mind. It even ascribes the entire human effort to re-establish that state of peace in the immediate surroundings, and finally in the entire world. It can be stated that Veda describes the attainment of utter calmness and establishment of harmony in the world as an exhibit of peace. Peace is the only state of dwellings in which one can cultivate the possibilities of practicing all sorts of cooperation, brotherhood leading the entire creation finally toward harmony.

Synthesis of the spiritual convergence on the basis of the efforts made by sage Veda Vyasa is addressed perfectly by Acharya Vinoba Bhave and was perfectly reflected through his narratives as was delivered by him during imprisonment. It also indicates the way with which the saint has assimilated the teachings of the Holy Scripture through repeated studies. Points to be worked out from the teachings of the Holy Scripture will be enormous. One may become free to sort out such kinds of relevant points and may try to make their own unique combinations. It will finally open up a wider horizon of thinking and executions.

One can gain knowledge simply by following masterly instructions. Some other people can gain knowledge by indulging in the process of instructional activities. Knowledge of doing some sort of activities often enhances our skills and makes us competent in performing our specified duties in particular. Another band of knowledge makes us aware of the situation which confers our understanding of the cyclic process of creation and destruction. From certain understanding of facts and figures it is becoming evident that entire universe will be destroyed in due course of time. We cannot sit idle and wait up to the moment of destruction with an aspiration of remaining off the side of any activities in our surrounding. We must move on with a positive apprehension for performing our duties in society for which we consider ourselves quite competent. Our commitment to society and to our dearest ones resides on our effort of indulging in the process of making them happy and contented.

Wisdom is the state of mental balance at which an individual identifies wright and wrong, permissible and objectionable acts; duties to be performed and instances to be avoided. It ensures self –actualisation, ethics and benevolence.[288] It is the capacity of fore-knowledge of something, may be right or wrong, or may be with immediate implications or having implications in near future.[289] Development of wisdom is ensured through a series of masterly guidance.[290] We can also confer with our clear understanding that wisdom is a kind of expertise with which one can do things perfectly and also perform assigned duties with quite perfectness.[291]

Philosophy of Nonviolence

Ahimsa is often referred as nonviolence in English. But the term, nonviolence is not reflecting the absolute nature of the term ahimsa as the absolute form duly projected through theories of yoga in Vedic Philosophy. Special emphasis of elaborating the term ahimsa is implied in the works of Patanjali, Buddha, and Mahaveera and in a more practical way through the life of Mahatma Gandhi. Still then, we accept the term and replace ahimsa by the negative aspect of violence that often stretch out the meaning of the term nonviolence for accommodating some of the

---

[288] Staudinger, U.M.; Glück, J. (2011). "Psychological wisdom research: Commonalities and differences in a growing field". Annual Review of Psychology. 62: 215–241. doi:10.1146/annurev.psych.121208.131659. PMID 20822439.

[289] Meacham, J. A. (1990). The loss of wisdom. In R. J. Sternberg (Ed.), Wisdom: Its nature, origins, and development. Cambridge: Cambridge University Press. Pp. 181 211

[290] Karunamuni N, Weerasekera R. (2019). "Theoretical Foundations to Guide Mindfulness Meditation: A Path to Wisdom". Current Psychology. 38 (3): 627–646. doi:10.1007/s12144-017-9631-7. S2CID 149024504.

[291] "Can Humanity Learn to become Civilized? The Crisis of Science without Civilization" Nicholas Maxwell

absolute aspects of the philosophy of ahimsa. The term ahimsa took its first appearance in the Vedantic Philosophical theories and doctrines. Patanjali considered ahimsa as one of the prominent part of the eight part yoga philosophy (Astanga Yoga Darshan). Ahimsa was accommodated under the yama part of the Yoga theory. Without truth and nonviolence, one cannot make oneself fit for moving across the yoga practices duly reflected by Patanjali.

Ahimsa alone can make a situation suitable for all the organisms staying within certain confinement and facilitating in casting off all sorts of minute differences such as caste, colour, creed, customs etc. Patanjali described the philosophy of ahimsa by coining a simple theory of the concept that reflects the entire beauty of the inherent dogma. According to his theory, "Where nonviolence is established in its absolute sense, organisms living within that surrounding will cast off their individual differences and start leading a life like that of a single family." People living under such confinement of philosophical convergence even forget their all sorts of individual differences of caste, creed and colour.

Philosophy of nonviolence even secured its prominent position in Buddhism, Jainism and other schools of religion duly developed and practiced in the Indian context. Mahaveera delivered his doctrines of practicing nonviolence at its absolute level to be followed by Jain Saints. Buddha perpetuated his teachings by placing peace and nonviolence in the central position and instructed fellow followers not to move towards the impulse of violence for putting oneself and the community in trouble. Not to think about creating harm to any individual or to any system even in dream was the absolute doctrine delivered by saints like Buddha and Mahaveera. Most remarkable feature of such ahimsa is the convergence of culture, tradition and rituals towards attaining a communal harmony through sacrificing individually apprehended wants for the facilitation of community welfare. Balancing the need and want is another practical aspect of ahimsa or nonviolence that leads an individual toward attaining satisfaction.

Attainment of such satisfaction, in turn, will make the individual stable by mind, intellect, deed and creed. A follower of peace and nonviolence with such attainment of satisfaction and stability can ascend toward a state of self-regulated individual having adequate faith upon the self. Here becomes the union of both external as well as internal power of the individual.

Scholars and saints collected different flowers from the garden of Upanishad to prepare a Holy Script of instructions for a fellow warrior to diffuse his states of illusion as he was to face a large number of enemies amidst a battle field. Recognising the Divine and performing according to instructions duly issued by the supreme master to fellow aspirant is the real objective of a life form. Even after acknowledging the effort of saints and scholars to integrate all sorts of thought process and spiritual understanding which were prevalent during the Epic Age and which were springing out from the core concepts of the Spirituality, the approach of Gita cannot be accepted as a refinement of the effort of linking up all aspects of Knowledge and Wisdom to aspirations of saints and scholars. Tendency of addressing identical state of the Divine manifestation in real life from different angles also rest upon the understanding with which saints and scholars start conferring the reality related to involvement of the common source of Divine creator in all sorts of manifestations throughout the universal presence of both living and non-living forms. Here lies the involvement of a common core of spirituality which ensures the oneness of all sorts of manifestations we have in the living planet; as there exists no scope of bifurcating our conceptual approach to address diversities.

When Manifestation becomes a Reality

Upanishad rightly maintains views related to universal reality of the Divine; presence of the same at all instances of creations; one should recognise presence of such masterly guide besides all creations; by doing so one should not try to grab resources belonging to others.

Affinity to work actively for hundreds of years for betterment of society and humanity never puts the fellow aspirant in the bondage of works by any means. Individual who violates the verdict of Soul force finally move towards the world of utter darkness devoid of sources of illuminations.[292] A stationary entity which can move even faster than the mind, even non-accessible to Gods, for it remains frontwardly progressive; passes beyond the progressive aspirant whenever they move forward. Master of Life establishes waver of ether and water in that ever expanding zone of creations; that moves and even remains stationary, that is far and also besides all creations, remains both inside and outside of all the worldly manifestations. [293] All sorts of hatred and violence will be diffused if fellow aspirant start recognising presence of all manifestations in the Divine and can recognise Divine omnipresence in all kinds of manifestations. Person of such self luminous intellect, having a clear vision of recognising presence of Brahman (the Divine) in all instances of manifestations, remains free from agony, illusion, greed and sorrow. [294]

अन्धं तमः प्रविशन्ति येऽविद्यामुपासते।
ततो भूय इव ते तमो य उ विद्यायां रताः ॥

"Person inflicted with illusion comes under the confinement of darkness and individuals relying exclusively on knowledge remain trapped amidst more darkness; for only knowledge without judicious actions cannot bring knowledge in action; such bands of knowledge without effective action brings agony, develops sorrow and often puts aspirants in a state of confusion."[295]

Aspirant who recognises Truth as a combination of knowledge and illusion experiences death due to wrong deeds and also becomes famous due to assimilation of knowledge. Person exhibiting devotion to birth alone comes under the trap of utter darkness of illusion and confusion. We receive something by birth and some other thing by non-birth; such thought process is transmitted to us from nobles. After

---

[292] *Ishopanishad, Verse 2 and 3.*
[293] *Ishavasyopanishad, Verse 4-5.*
[294] *Ishavasyopanishad Verse 7*
[295] *Ishavasyopanishad, Verse 9*

recognising birth and dissolution of birth as identical process aspirants gain fame even after getting restricted due to regulations of death. [296]

Discussion implies that absolute knowledge alone cannot bring fame, truth exists in the combination of illusive knowledge and true knowledge; aspirants are exposed equally to fame and death; fame alone cannot restrict an individual to escape regulations of death and birth. It also implies accessibility of individuals to both fame and illusion and progress of the same towards attainment of Divinity while remaining under the abled guidance of any Divine master.

Aham (alternatively Ego) is the regulator of senses and actions through mind and intellect and also acts under the three scale parameters of qualities (such as SATWA or good qualities, RAJAS or ignorance and TAMAS or animism). It can be shifted from one quality scale to the other during worldly manifestations of life; it cannot be diffused completely; even it cannot be made absolutely free from any of the quality scales; we cannot limit our efforts to guide all actions and knowledge assimilation merely on the basis of any one quality parameter.

The Ego acts in accord to reality principle.[297] Besides sense of the very self it includes psychic functions such as judgment, tolerance, reality testing, control, planning, defence, synthesis of information, intellectual functioning, and memory. It can be considered as an organisation principle upon which thoughts, propositions and interpretations of the world are based.[298] The self, as considered as a driving force of development and shifting of Ego from one quality to the other, is the culmination of several archetypes.[299] The self (along with

---

[296] *Ishavasyopanishad, Verse 11-14*

[297] *Noam, Gil G; Hauser, Stuart taque chinaz #14 T.; Santostefano, Sebastiano; Garrison, William; Jacobson, Alan M.; Powers, Sally I.; Mead, Merrill (February 1984). "Ego Development and Psychopathology: A Study of Hospitalized Adolescents". Child Development. Blackwell Publishing on behalf of the Society for Research in Child Development. 55 (1): 189–194. doi:10.1111/j.1467-8624.1984.tb00283.x. PMID 6705621.*

[298] *Snowden, Ruth (2006). Teach Yourself Freud. McGraw-Hill. pp. 105–107. ISBN 978-0-07-147274-6.*

[299] *Le Grice, Keiron (2016). Archetypal Reflections Insights and ideas from Jungian Psychology. Muswell Hill Press. pp. 23–73. ISBN 978-1-908995-19-3.*

embodiment of Ego) is the autonomous centre of the psyche which also works as the principal source of dream and real life experiences; it (the Self) works as the authority figure in dreams.[300]

All the regulatory mechanism with which ego works is quite difficult to identify and categorise; we simply predict the probable reason with which ego often diverts differently to accomplish false-self organisation during various real life instances; such organisation can have poor knowledge base; some kind of ignorance related to self-advancement may play a definitive role during that moment; a kind of false- notion may be the probable reason which directs ego to accomplish false-self organisation. There are some instances of such organisation: closure to health for supporting individual to regain normal health status by the true self; doing the same to support social behaviour, manners and courtesy; protects the unactualised true self; removes true self completely during severe conditions.[301] Ego of a parent, in case of general instances of parental cares evident in higher group of animals including human beings, has its back reference through which such behaviours are transmitted from one generation to the other; a trend of gradual ascent from humanism to animism can be observed in certain cases.[302]

Wider dimensions and expanded coverage of the teachings of Gita often make people worried about what to follow and what not to follow in real life. Also in some cases it becomes difficult to think about propositions in the actual ground. Because of lack of timely relevant practical knowledge of the situation, people even keep themselves aside from following and internalising teachings of the holy book in the real life situation. Approach of such religious and cultural teaching, therefore, should have proper considerations of some practical aspects of rituals and worships.

---

[300] Thompson, E (2017). *Waking, Dreaming, Being. Self and Consciousness in Neuroscience, Meditation, and Philosophy.* Columbia University Press. ISBN 9780231538312.
[301] D. W. Winnicott, *The Maturational Processes and the Facilitating Environment* (New York 1965) p. 121
[302] "Solomon, Carol, Ph.D. "Transactional Analysis Theory: the Basics." *Transactional Analysis Journal 33.1 (2003): 15-22*" (PDF).

Some people maintain a view regarding Gita is that the entire aspects depicted in this holy book are a confusing one. Saints from olden times worked differently to show that Gita is much relevant in terms of rituals and propositions presented in it. Here also we are trying to trace out a link up in between rituals, traditions and practices that we have in nature to re-establish the age old faiths of the omnipresence of divine within us at its varying formats.

We can see things as they occupy a definite shape. We cannot see energy and power due to their in capabilities of occupying space. To feel the presence of such powers in our surrounding, we often take the support of our senses and feelings. In some cases our observations are evidence based, in some other cases it may have some imaginary propositions. Here comes the act of limitations that restrict us to feel Ultraviolet and Infrared [303] radiations which remained off the band of the visible spectrum and duly restricted our sense of vision seven visible waves of light.

There arises another question related to our effort of analyzing the relevance of the teachings of The Gita in present day situation. It was the instructions delivered by Lord Krishna to Arjun during the epic age of Vedic Civilisation. That time war had its presence in the scope of royal management. That time conflicts had a final termination to war for making efforts a result oriented. Sins and sinners had their presence in olden times and are still there with us today; format and geo-locations might vary; arms and ammunitions might differ. Even from the pages of history we can see how Prince Ashoka smashed the Kingdom of Kalinga only because that kingdom had refused to hand-over the murderer of his mother to him. Later on the war and the loss of lives of many innocent people had implied a deep impression in his mind and he had decided to refuse to take part in any other battle simply meant for territorial expansion. Teachings of The Gita have worked differently during different instances of the development of conflicts and agony.

---

[303] Both Ultraviolet and Infrared Radiations are the parts of the invisible band of spectrum incorporated in the Solar Radiation. Our visual sense organ can feel the presence of only visible spectrum comprising seven different colours.

Since conflicts and agony are beyond the scope of any historic time line, we can correlate teachings of any instances to prepare strategic actions of any other present day sectoral management plans. It has the impetus of the absolute knowledge of human actions, wishes, wills and conducts with absolute apprehension of delivering the needful.

The reason of discontentment, sorrow and agony of Arjun after entering the battle field was rejected instantly by Lord Krishna through implying a sanction of his indulgence in the war. Killing any individual or creating another one is not the role of any warrior. A warrior can deliver the duty in time with a clear impetus of making the wiser side victorious. Sinners will lose their lives because of their mis-conducts only.

It is the right place to mention about Upanishads, often referred as Vedantas, as they exhibit doctrines, rituals and worship patters prevalent in later Vedic Civilisation.[304] Those rituals and doctrines were duly incorporated in the great epics to make all sorts of teachings easy to understand. The Bhagavadgita along with majority of Upanishads and Brahmasutra are known as PRASTHANATRAYEE.[305] These three scriptures were studied extensively time to time to inculcate more relevant knowledge related to Divinity and Spirituality. Out of 108 known texts of Uapnishads only a dozen from the initial collection are considered as Primary (MUKHYA).[306] Concluding parts of Brahmans and Aranyaks are also filled with Mukhya Upanishads.[307] Authorship of all the anonymous tests duly collected from the garden of Upanishads is unknown. Group of saints might have collected and represented their lessons in the form of a collection.[308] Conversation between women like Maitreyi and Gargi are also inscribed in the holy texts of Uanishads.[309]

---

[304] Jan Gonda (1975), Vedic Literature: (Saṃhitās and Brahmanas), Otto Harrassowitz Verlag, ISBN 978-3447016032

[305] *Ranade, R. D. (1926), A constructive survey of Upanishadic philosophy, Bharatiya Vidya Bhavan*

[306] E Easwaran (2007), The Upanishads, ISBN 978-1586380212, pages 298-299

[307] Mahadevan, T. M. P (1956), Sarvepalli Radhakrishnan (ed.), History of Philosophy Eastern and Western, George Allen & Unwin Ltd

[308] *S Radhakrishnan, The Principal Upanishads George Allen & Co., 1951, pages 22, Reprinted as ISBN 978-8172231248*

[309] Ellison Findlay (1999), Women and the Arahant Issue in Early Pali Literature, Journal of Feminist Studies in Religion, Vol. 15, No. 1, pages 57-76

Root of all such creations is principally radiated out time to time in different forms and also in different sectorian units from Vedas.

Pluralism of world view was characterised by the Upanishadic age; gradually inclined more towards dualism by combining Sankhya and Yoga doctrines efficiently.[310] The Bhagavadgita moved on a step forward by incorporating Vedanta along with Upanishadic dcotrines with an aspirations of delivering a common pattern of rituals, social formats and political will to the youths of the olden times.

Maitri Upanishad aspires for attainment of reverence and completeness by human beings with the help of the knowledge of Brahmans and repeated practices of meditation on such knowledge by the self.[311]

Further study of the Bhagavadgita reveals all such studies like the gradual unfoldment of petals of a lotus. In the modern world we have various types of cultural and religious thought process possessing rituals, customs and traditions of different types, which are equally competent to enrich people in terms of knowledge, devotion, courage, will power and dedication. The way we receive each culture to enrich our multiplurality will specify our degrees and ranges of success. Our motive force will guide accordingly to explore possibilities of working out converged cultural segments from all the rituals to move up towards vibrant waves of multi plurality.

India, at this juncture of the development of multiplurality, will be a best example for all of us. Here people learned a lot to live with each other, tolerate each other and enrich each other differently.

We cannot see light. Even we cannot see the propagation of sound through the material medium. Light strikes our eye, reaches our brain and develops a sensation of vision through certain life process of vision. With some sort of illusion, or lack of true knowledge only, we often claim that we can see light. Even all the colours radiated out from the sun

---

[310] Glucklich, Ariel (2008), The Strides of Vishnu: Hindu Culture in Historical Perspective, Oxford University Press, ISBN 978-0-19-531405-2

[311] Hume, Robert Ernest (1921), The Thirteen Principal Upanishads, Oxford University Press, pp. 412–414

are not recognisable by us. If God resides inside the individual, if all mysteries related to the ascent of a person on the path of divinity, then why any devotee search it out for gaining the blessings of any Divine power located outside the physically existing body? Why such a dwindling situation any individual face during the tenure of worship?

Lord Krishna narrated essence of feeling the Divine communion with the physically existing life through witnessing cultivation of knowledge, actualisation of the presence of any supreme power in sub conscious mind and possible ways and means to follow that power. It enables an individual to come across the feeling of the advent of some completeness in the mind through knowledge transformation. Cultivation of knowledge regarding the relationship of the divine and disciple is enrouted from the age old traditions through the turmoil of the organic evolution. That evolution brought some change in the process of exhibits, but the core remained the same. It was even more perpetual and more profound regarding the ability of harnessing the relationship of matter and energy. We cannot imagine the existence of matter without the involvement of energy, and similarly energy takes a definite visible form to occupy certain space in this universe.

How do people see things and how do they correlate such unavoidable relationship of energy and matter is depend upon the level of understanding that one adheres with. A master of Physics and a master of Philosophy must have varying degree of explanations for putting forth the mystery behind the mechanism involved during inter-conversion of matter and energy. All organic combinations have certain physical and chemical sets of combinations in such a definite ways that they inculcate the abilities of interactions and abilities of giving birth to senses. Even evolution of sensory structures and related orientations became much collaborative in case of human beings. Here occurs a change which brought us near the state of explorations meant for examining the hidden mysteries behind creation and orientation of life forms in the living planet.

These days, things are known to us that earth like situation exists in the universe. Only the matter of concern is that we may not be able to reach the place even after attaining the speed as that of light in a year or two. Only we can admire the presence and orientation of such creations within our visibility. Only we can explore and examine such things with the help of optical and electronic instruments. With an understanding of such limitations human beings never arranged any voyage to explore the inner world of senses that can allow us to explore the outer orientation of time and space. Such an inner world exploration may require a little effort to culminate senses within a confinement for feeling the presence. There also resides a tremendous flux of energy accumulated within such a small space. Those mysterious combinations taking the form of life were explored differently by saints during olden times.

There developed a science of explorations of the correlations of the Creation and the Divine. Matter and energy indulged in a perfect orientation for letting senses flow through them. Arrangement and orientation of all our senses are directed outwardly. That is why we are bound to receive waves and sparks from the outside world. Our inner world remains unexplored in most of the cases. Only adherence of true knowledge and the journey of senses through inner world during meditation can pave a way out for exploring our own self. Meditation is the doorstep where orientation of senses get diverted towards the inner world and bring out mysteries associated to the fact of accommodation of the Divine power inside the living being.

Is that Divine power is restricted to the human beings only? The answer is, obviously and surely without any doubt, No. human beings has gained some sort of evolutionary supremacy in due course of time, but other beings are also of same potential and courage with a domination of animism in them. Dogs are loyal to their master, cats exhibit better vigilance power, elephants are more socialised beings having better memory power and tigers are the masters of their own territory. Taking hold upon the surrounding and defining the role according to trophic [312] level, we can easily arrange these beings and others without any difficulty.

---

[312]. A Trophic livel signifies the food habit of organisms during their representation as they exhibit in a food chain. Green Plants, for example prepares their own food with the help of sunlight and

Philosophical and Spiritual supremacy is a step forward that makes a distinction between other animals and human beings. Then also we can witness inhuman acts from human beings and humanly acts from some inhuman animals. The orientation of sense organ and correlation of senses and sensory responses with memory and intellect is the only factor regulating such varying degrees and conducts of animismic and hunmanismic behaviours.

Presence of such a Divine power within the creation is the reason behind the maintenance of an idea of serving humanity with a correlated apprehension of serving God. Only God cannot put a direct access to the feelings of the presence of such immense power within us. It is the approach with which we offer our services to living beings can develop a way out for us to feel the difference.

Once during pre-independent period in Bombay (at present Mumbai) a youth from some semi urban place approached a saint for offering himself at the service to divine. It made the saint happy. He wanted to know the exact reason behind his stand of doing so. Saint also enquired about his capabilities and considered his offering a wise one. Actually the fellow was searching jobs in the city. He was also a normal Graduate from any sub –urban area and his financial situation was also not so good. Perhaps the sacrifice might make him temporarily happy and contented, but will become a burden in due course of time. With happiness saint suggested him for searching out a suitable job and helping the parents and inmates of the family financially. Only After gaining some wealth and knowledge the person can really enjoy the glory of sacrifice. Right now the person has nothing special to sacrifice. Such sacrifice inflicted with sorrow and agony may put both the master and the disciple in trouble.

Even divine cannot allow any individual to put oneself and families in trouble and agony. It is the only state of contentment that helps a person during movement from the physical world to the spiritual world. Offerings of any kind and in any particular form will bring happiness.

---

secures the first position in a food chain and basic position in the food pyramid. Second trophic level is occupied by herbivores, followed by carnivores at the third.

Learning even continued beyond the scope of interactive curriculum transaction with aspirations of enhancing critical skills and confidence of the active members of the society. In simple words, we can say that the advanced Value system enabled people to understand and maintain their fundamental value system on the basis of the popular cultural and traditional base of olden times. For widening this type of practice with an aspiration of collective progress, people started sharing minute particulars of their feelings on any specified thing or propositions to keep the progressive trend active and to ascertain its ascending mode.

The gradual refinement in value system has come in the form of rituals and observations. In modern day context the human value system has a character of an exhibit of a convergence of differently developed value systems. The kind of convergence of both eastern and the western value system has enabled the development of Missionary Culture in the Indian context. Such missionary culture has enabled people to readjust their acts and conducts on the basis of some masterly instructions that they duly received through scheduled discourses of their masterly guide. None of such value system is entirely aligned towards the west and not even towards the Vedic culture. Combination and recombination of value system always reflect some sort of Yoga Philosophy with an affinity towards naming it differently for making oneself satisfied. Lord Buddha, for a simple example, has cultivated eight fold simple path of worship having a proposition identical to that of the Yoga Philosophy and acts and conducts duly proposed by Saint Patanjali. The path proposed by Lord Buddha became popular in some of the society due to advent of easiness in the worship.

The missionary culture in Bengal duly introduced by Shri Ramakrishna has the identical affinity of bringing the Yoga based acts and conducts to people with easiness. It has also designed a service oriented mechanism of worship based on the principle of "Serving Man, Serving the Divine." It has also gained success and brought its prominence through cultivating ideals of Saint Patanjali. Ramakrishna wanted people to keep faith on the presence of the Divine. As we cannot feel the presence of all kinds of waves of energy because of our limitations of senses, similarly we cannot feel the omnipresence of the supreme power within us because of our in-capabilities of imbibing the waves of the supreme power. Only because of this reason we cannot deny the presence of such divine power within ourselves and within the others.

We can see things as they occupy a definite shape. We cannot see energy and power due to their in capabilities of occupying space. To feel the presence of such powers in our surrounding, we often take the support of our senses and feelings. In some cases our observations are evidence based, in some other cases it may have some imaginary propositions. Here comes the act of limitations that restrict us to feel Ultraviolet and Infrared radiations which remained off the band of the visible spectrum and duly restricted our sense of vision seven visible waves of light.

Once several scholars and aspirants of Kolkata wanted to judge the knowledge base of Saint Ramakrishna. A group of learned persons and veterans from the city visited the temple where Ramakrishna used to deliver his services by preying goddess Kali in his own language and also by claiming incidents of his conversation with Goddess Kali. The matter became very critical when Raasmani, the main patron of Ramakrishna, came to know about this incident. Inmates of the temple and the royal family wanted to work out any alternatives, but firmness of Ramakrishna made them more confident about the knowledge enrichment that the saint had.

People came in and took their respective seats within the small residential block of the fellow saint. His happiness and contentment exhibited his firmness and fearlessness. People prepared to throw questions towards him. With a gentle smile Ramakrishna described a narration in short, "Once an idol made of salt moved on to measure the depth and expansion of ocean. We all can easily imagine what happened to that idol. Returning back from his status became impossible. I have nothing more to say, now it's your turn. Ask me."

The kind of voice and firmness to face all sorts of questions made people worries about their own limit of knowledge. Ramakrishna had narrated an incident which was from Vedantic teachings. It made people confirmed about the knowledge enrichment of the saintly person having a common look with some uncommon adherence to the immediate divine. The judgement went on differently and some among them had accepted Ramakrishna as their true guide in their respective path of spiritual ascent.

Spirituality, in its true sense, should not put any individual off the track of society and culture. It should cultivate the essence of true knowledge for the purpose of the collective enrichment of the referred commune through making their overall spiritual ascent towards integral progress more and more confluous. Instead of having all such knowledge of Veda, Epics and other spiritual worshipping mechanism, Ramakrishna preferred offering food to Goddess Kali in the way people offer to any other living beings. The kind of contentment itself exhibited his effort of linking people of some common living to their holy mother and immediate divine.

Most critical aspect that Saint Ramakrishna had to handle appeared in front of him in the form of Narendranath Dutta, later on popularly received the name Swami Vivekananda. Naren wanted to judge the actual claim of Ramakrishna regarding his conversation with the divine power. Repeatedly he started approaching his master and repeatedly started blaming him for his claim of enjoying divine communion as a false one. Ultimately the day came when the young Naren had something to beg during his divine communion. It was arranged by his master to nullify the doubts and confusion which was hampering the intellect of the young student of Philosophy. The conflict in the mind of Narendranath was going on due to his contradictory knowledge of Western and Eastern Philosophical ideas, due to his affinity of examining divine power with an intention of jotting down scientific evidences, due to his lack of true knowledge regarding non-avoidable coupling of matter and energy and due to his lack of faith in exploring the divine omnipresence in some incidents of immediate surroundings.

Depth and expansion of the knowledge is so enormous that we can simply feel it and try to acquire it by part on the basis of our capabilities, willingness and interests. Once people of Kolkata wanted to judge the knowledge base of Saint Ramakrishna. A group of learned persons and veterans from the city visited the temple where Ramakrishna used to deliver his services by preying goddess Kali in his own language and also by claiming incidents of his conversation with Goddess Kali. The matter became very critical when Rani Raasmani, the main patron of Ramakrishna, came to know about this incident. Inmates of the temple and the royal family wanted to work out any alternatives, but firmness of Ramakrishna made them more confident about the knowledge enrichment that the saint had.

People came in and took their respective seats within the small residential block of the fellow saint. His happiness and contentment exhibited his firmness and fearlessness. People prepared to throw questions towards him. With a gentle smile Ramakrishna described a narration in short, "Once an idol made of salt moved on to measure the depth and expansion of ocean. We all can easily imagine what happened to that idol! Returning back to his original status became impossible. I have nothing more to say, now it's your turn. Ask me whatever you want to ask."

The kind of voice and firmness to face all sorts of questions made people worries about their own limit of knowledge. Ramakrishna had narrated an incident which was from Vedantic teachings. It made people confirmed about the knowledge enrichment of the saintly person having a common look with some uncommon adherence to the immediate divine. The judgement went on differently and some among them had accepted Ramakrishna as their true guide in their respective path of spiritual ascent.

Spirituality, in its true sense, should not put any individual off the track of society and culture. It should cultivate the essence of true knowledge for the purpose of the collective enrichment of the referred commune through making their overall spiritual ascent towards integral progress more and more confluous. Instead of having all such knowledge of Veda, Epics and other spiritual worshipping mechanism, Ramakrishna preferred offering food to Goddess Kali in the way people offer to any other living beings. The kind of contentment itself exhibited his effort of linking people of some common living to their holy mother and immediate divine.

Most critical aspect that Saint Ramakrishna had to handle appeared in front of him in the form of Narendranath Dutta, later on popularly received the name Swami Vivekananda. Naren wanted to judge the actual claim of Ramakrishna regarding his conversation with the divine power. Repeatedly he started approaching his master and repeatedly started blaming him for his claim of enjoying divine communion as a false one. Ultimately the day came when the young Naren had something to beg during his divine communion. It was arranged by his master to nullify the doubts and confusion which was hampering the intellect of the young student of Philosophy. The conflict in the mind of Narendranath was going on due to his contradictory knowledge of Western and Eastern Philosophical ideas, due to his affinity of examining divine power with an intention of jotting down scientific evidences, due to his lack of true knowledge regarding non-avoidable coupling of matter and energy and due to his lack of faith in exploring the divine omnipresence in some incidents of immediate surroundings.

Is it difficult for any ordinary person to have an experience of witnessing the holy touch of the divine master? Is divinity something special which can open up horizon for its follower after ascertaining the balanced state and enrichment of mind and intellect?

There is no such correlation between literal enrichment of mind and experiencing process of divinity. Divinity is the state of mind where people start recognising one's role in the society and all other acts and conducts of that individual are duly accorded. It cannot ascribe any state of attainment of such perfection without adhering oneself entirely in the path of worship. Divinity cannot even make a person off the track of society and cannot allow oneself to be entangled amidst any rituals and conducts. King Gopal Singh of Malla Dynasty once refused to fight against the Maratha invaders. The reason was that there was a ceremonial worship of Madan Mohan in the state capital. All the citizen of that state were also observing the week for worshipping their lord. Bhasker Pandit, the headman of the Maratha oppressors moved in easily and reached up to the state capital with an easy confluence. There occurred the miracle, which has created some argument. Bhasker Pandit and his men were smashed badly by two strange and unidentified warriors. Their bravery were the exemplar ones. Some of the fellow inmates of the state capital identified one of the warriors as none other than the Madan Mohan, the divine power of the kingdom, himself. Some other fellow thinkers lost their faith on any chance of occurrence of such a miracle.

Keeping faith is, therefore, with its genuine format, an individual apprehension that guides the person considerably in maintaining or rejecting any ideas and propositions. Ascent of the individual on the path of divinity is also ascertained by the state of mind on the ground of any intention of accepting or rejecting any ideas. We have two different segments in our brain meant specifically for memorising things and analysing things. Both the format of brain functions are compared and maintained perfectly with an involvement of one intermediary sensory power. Perfectly balanced mind maintains adequate balance in between memory and intellect. It is also regulated considerably by our wish factor. What we wish that we often do perfectly. Gita , on the one side, intends to bring forward those essential propositions people should make oneself acquainted with. It also aspires for integrating all principles of Yoga in a true gatherable format for making the soul enlightened. Such an enlightened spirit is the doorstep where the individual identifies the hidden mystery related to the inwardly embedded divine power. After such identification one can reallocate spheres of rights and duties for ensuring the assent of the individual on the path of spirituality.

Exhibits of a proper coordination of rights and duties in our surrounding can be explained differently by pointing out different incidents from our surrounding. Once there was a saintly person from Bengal. He was in a wandering state and was moving from place to place to ascertain the real reason of problems and agony that the motherland was moving through during that time. During one of such turn of his visit, he was in a remote village of Gujarat. There the saintly person delivered lectures. People even approached him for discussion some common personal problems. Gradually all the fellows left the place where the arrangement of night halt for the saint was duly made by villagers. Amidst the dim light of the earthen candle saint recognised that one person was still waiting there in the room. Perhaps the person might be in trouble! May be, due to some critical problem, he wants to discuss with the master alone! Whatever be the case, saintly person approached the fellow villager, "It's too late my dear brother! You are waiting here for anything?"

With jointed hands and respectful eyes, the fellow farmer came little bit closure to the saint and said, "All people went away. You had lots of interaction with many people. Now, what about your dinner, my master?"

Situation was entirely different. The farmer was not worried because of his any individual level or family level problems. It was his worry about the hospitality of the saint. He was much worried about wellbeing of the saint. The duty delivered by him during that time has melted the ego of the saint for his state of a claim regarding his much religious, much spiritual and much awakened status. The kind of quality exhibited by the farmer in practical way was a lesson for the saint. It was a lesson for him in a way of enabling him to consider every soul in this universe a potent divine nucleus. A powerful mind filled with knowledge can ascribe the exhibit of such noble conducts.

Actually the farmer was from an untouchable community and was feared of being trapped by villagers while offering food to a saintly person. But, the saint wanted him to feel the joy of offering cooked food to a saint; a state of pure and selfless sacrifice. It was a kind of lesson for the saint to have an opportunity of witnessing the manifestation of divine conduct in an ordinary farmer. He had exhibited his spiritual supremacy over the saint by fulfilling his timely need.

Once upon a time all inmates of an Ashram instructed a youth to accept his master without indulging in any argument. But the youth was not ready to go on such a way. He had a clear apprehension of examining the excellence of his master regarding spiritual enrichment, then only the fellow can be accepted as a true master. He went on examining his master repeatedly for diffusing all his doubts before accepting the saint as his master. Such kind of approach exhibits a devotion with clear understanding of one's role in society.

Repeated examination of the fellow master incarnated him towards attainment of perfectness in worshipping the Divine. There he came to know about the language with which one can talk to the Divine Almighty. It is actually the state of mind from which any disciple can correlate a conversation with the supreme power and a perpetuated guide. That was the state where the dialect of the masterly mind was relying on to the acquired ones. In that sense the act of the fellow disciple to come out of the state of confusion through examining the masterly mind was also a justified one. There was no trace of any absurdity.

***

The Circle of Birth and Death

Cessation of functioning of the whole brain and associated sensory branches, including the brain stem and other related tracks of sensory structure, is often termed as death (a legal term "brain death"[313] is often used to signify it differently); an inevitable process during which disintegration of bodily parts become a reality; a mechanism followed by cessation of breathing and heart-beat (clinical death).[314] Any clinical anomaly, just like cardiovascular disease affecting the heart, may cause death.[315] It is the junction which ensures finishing line of living forms followed by disintegration of physically recognisable living body and functioning of senses; only one thing, often titles as energy (nuclear energy at the atomic level) is the ultimate manifestation, retains its existence and continuation within the scope of the universal existence; a

---

[313] *Parent, Brendan; Turi, Angela (1 December 2020). "Death's Troubled Relationship With the Law". AMA Journal of Ethics. 22 (12): 1055–1061. doi:10.1001/amajethics.2020.1055. ISSN 2376-6980. PMID 33419507. S2CID 231300316. Archived from the original on 23 July 2022. Retrieved 23 July 2022.*
[314] *United States. President's Commission for the Study of Ethical Problems in Medicine and Biomedical and Behavioral Research (1981). Defining Death: A Report on the Medical, Legal and Ethical Issues in the Determination of Death · Part 34. The Commission. p. 63. Archived from the original on 17 August 2023. Retrieved 19 March 2023.*
[315] *Richtie, Hannah; Spooner, Fiona; Roser, Max (February 2018). "Causes of death". Our World in Data. Archived from the original on 20 May 2018. Retrieved 14 February 2023.*

uniform distribution of elements and compounds in our surrounding from which a life got its obligatory physical support; a systematic withdrawal of senses, memory and intellect from the physically recognisable body; a regulation induced by nature to ensure cyclic shift of elements from one form too the other. Affinity of defining "death" is still a matter of debate; approaches differ if we consider the same doctrine from view point of different faculties, such as science, spirituality, philosophy, yoga and psychology.[316] Different schools of spirituality and psychology specify death differently on the basis of their approaches of considering manifestation of living forms.

At certain instances there exists a minute distinction in between living forms and non-living forms; any intermediate form, like viruses, rarely lose their living- non-living status in terms of their chemical combinations; for they attain non-living status after becoming detached from a site of infection and again gains living status whenever brought to any other sites of infection.[317] A permanent cessation of blood circulation and pulmonary[318] breathing can be considered as a circulatory definition of death; [319] often considered as the instance during which electrical activity of sense organs and central regulator of senses is lost due to cessation of consciousness;[320] signifies permanent suspension of the consciousness;[321]

Most significant observations which made scholars reconsider instances of death related to partial anatomical and physiological activities supported by some of the automatized sensory responses duly recorded in some of the cases of brain death; as such patients maintained

---

[316] Antony, Micheal V. (2001). "Is 'consciousness' ambiguous?". Journal of Consciousness Studies. 8 (2): 19–44. Archived from the original on 6 March 2023. Retrieved 14 February 2023 – via PhilPapers.

[317] Metcalf, Peter; Huntington, Richard (1991). Celebrations of Death: The Anthropology of Mortuary Ritual. New York: Cambridge Press.

[318] "Pulmonary"is the term which clinically signifies events related to lungs and exchange of gases performed by an organism with the help of lings.

[319] Bernat, James L. (2018). "Conceptual Issues in DCDD Donor Death Determination". Hastings Center Report. 48 (S4): S26–S28. doi:10.1002/hast.948. ISSN 1552-146X. PMID 30584853.

[320] National Health Service of the UK (8 September 2022). "Overview: Brain death". National Health Service. Archived from the original on 12 November 2008. Retrieved 15 February 2023.

[321] National Health Service of the UK (8 September 2022). "Overview: Brain death". National Health Service. Archived from the original on 12 November 2008. Retrieved 15 February 2023.

the ability to sustain circulation and respiration, regulate temperature, excrete wastes, heal wounds, fight infections and, most dramatically, to gestate fetuses (in the case of pregnant "brain-dead" women); as such kind of neural collapse was not signifying complete withdrawal of senses and consciousness from all the levels of bodily organisations; as such kind of sensory pause was not the final destiny of the living form; as such a silence cannot be defined as a silence and decay of all the individual living cells which were taking part actively to manifest living forms during instances of activities; as such kind of sensory failure may too signify immediate withdrawal of the organism from different organs and systems; as the situation can be considered as a transition from life and death; as a transition is paved for the organism to ensure gradual shift from physical existence and disintegration of all kinds of bodily organisations; as such a collapse cannot signify the immediate collapse of participant molecules and atoms from the living form to ensure material identity of the living body; [322] as brain function can be stopped temporarily due to hypoglycaemia, hypothermia, hypoxia or by applying certain drugs.[323] All kinds of efforts of reviving neural, psychological, mental and intellectual distinction of organism will be lost permanently if cerebral cortex of human brain collapses during dormancy or non-functioning of the nervous system.[324] Coma with clear etiology, cessation of breathing, and lack of brainstem reflexes are some of the diagnostic parameters depending upon which permanent brain death can be confirmed.[325]

Biological ageing, a reason other than any kinds of accident or clinical anomalies, is a natural and obligatory fate of living forms duly

---

[322] Magnus, David C.; Wilfond, Benjamin S.; Caplan, Arthur L. (6 March 2014). "Accepting Brain Death". New England Journal of Medicine. 370 (10): 891–894. doi:10.1056/NEJMp1400930. ISSN 0028-4793. PMID 24499177.

[323] Nicol, A. U.; Morton, A. J. (11 June 2020). "Characteristic patterns of EEG oscillations in sheep (Ovis aries) induced by ketamine may explain the psychotropic effects seen in humans". Scientific Reports. 10 (1): 9440. Bibcode:2020NatSR..10.9440N. doi:10.1038/s41598-020-66023-8. PMC 7289807. PMID 32528071.

[324] Zaner, Richard M. (2011). Death: Beyond Whole-Brain Criteria (1st ed.). Springer. pp. 77, 125. ISBN 978-9401077200.

[325] Bernat, James L. (March 2013). "Controversies in defining and determining death in critical care". Nature Reviews Neurology. 9 (3): 164–173. doi:10.1038/nrneurol.2013.12. ISSN 1759-4766. PMID 23419370. S2CID 12296259.

regulated by time.[326] About two third individuals of all the cases as recorded across globe die due to age. Several factors are reported in modern science which often causes death of foetus before birth.[327] Death before old age (senescence) is another instance during which a living form ensures withdrawal of the life from the bodily recognisable living form.[328] Better diet, planned physical activities, following good habits, calorie restrictions, yoga and meditation are some of the practices which may enhance the living form and endure ageing.

Attainment of maximum lifespan may become an accomplishable reality if tissue level damages can be replaced by rejuvenation of such levels of organisation periodically.[329] Most of the cases of modern death (nearly 20 to 25% of all such records by the start of 21st Century) in modern time died outside clinics and hospitals.[330] Anxiety and fear while remembering the situation related to death can be avoided by enhancing self—esteem and cultural enrichment.[331] In reality a person dies without experiencing it and without getting aftermath of fear. Epics and Scriptures of Indian origin (Vedic Schools of Spirituality) interpret the situation differently by address the fact while rejecting regulations of life and death upon the non-perishable entity (like Atman, Brahman or Soul).

[326] Aubrey D.N.J, de Grey (2007). "Life Span Extension Research and Public Debate: Societal Considerations" (PDF). Studies in Ethics, Law, and Technology. 1 (1, Article 5). CiteSeerX 10.1.1.395.745. doi:10.2202/1941-6008.1011. S2CID 201101995. Archived from the original (PDF) on 13 October 2016. Retrieved 20 March 2009. roughly 150,000 deaths that occur each day across the globe
[327] Goldenberg, Rl; Kirby, R; Culhane, Jf (1 August 2004). "Stillbirth: a review". The Journal of Maternal-Fetal & Neonatal Medicine. 16 (2): 79–94. doi:10.1080/jmf.16.2.79.94. ISSN 1476-7058. S2CID 218875617.
[328] "The top five causes of premature death". familyserviceshub.havering.gov.uk. Archived from the original on 21 September 2021. Retrieved 15 August 2023.
[329] Blagosklonny, Mikhail V. (1 December 2021). "No limit to maximal lifespan in humans: how to beat a 122-year-old record". Oncoscience. 2021 (8): 110–119. doi:10.18632/oncoscience.547. PMC 8636159. PMID 34869788.
[330] Ahmad, S.; O'Mahony, M.S. (December 2005). "Where older people die: a retrospective population-based study". QJM. 98 (12): 865–870. doi:10.1093/qjmed/hci138. PMID 16299059.
[331] Harmon-Jones, Eddie; Simon, Linda; Greenburg, Jeff; Pyszczynski, Tom; Solomon, Sheldon; McGregor, Holly (1997). "Terror management theory and self-esteem: Evidence that increased self-esteem reduced mortality salience effects". Journal of Personality and Social Psychology. 72 (1): 24–36. doi:10.1037/0022-3514.72.1.24. PMID 9008372. S2CID 32261410. Archived from the original on 17 February 2023. Retrieved 17 February 2023 – via APA PsycNet.

Death is not the ultimate experience of all kinds of living organisms; as organisms like Hydra and Jelly Fish often experience death less manifestation of their living forms in our surrounding.[332] It is also not an obligatory regulator in case of some of the perennial plants. Organisms having a limit of life –span are mostly from the advanced forms in terms of their evolutionary trend. Such organisms experience a pre-determined span of ageing as per the regulations specified by their levels of organisations; highest of which is possessed by organisms belonging to primates and human beings. Power of repairing organ system and worn out tissues also became feeble in hominids; as any deeper wounds developed in organisms belonging to this group may cause death; as repairing of worn out tissues may not confer rejuvenation of organ system in these animals; as development and maturation of organ system becomes irreversible and non-rearable after certain age (onset of adulthood); as such maturation leads to loss of the divisibility power of cells of neural origin; as maturations conger specialisation of entire system in terms of functional identity.[333] Lower organism like volvox[334], because of diversification of specialisation of bodily functional cells, gained regulations of life and death of somatic line of manifestation as a regular, genetically regulated part of its life.[335]

It is becoming clear from the discussion that worldly manifestations cannot be generalised within the restricted cycle of life and death; as such death cannot specify spiritual withdrawal of the individual from the immediate surrounding; as such regulations cannot wipe out emotional, intellectual and spiritual withdrawal of the fellow aspirant from the context; spiritual and intellectual horizon related to individual can be restricted up to a limit in the context but it cannot be brought to a halt immediately after physical disintegration of the physical body. There

---

[332] *National Institute on Aging (2020). "The National Institute on Aging: Strategic Directions for Research, 2020–2025". National Institute on Aging. Archived from the original on 4 June 2020. Retrieved 16 February 2023.*

[333] *Gilbert, S.F. (2003). Developmental biology (7th ed.). Sunderland, Mass: Sinauer Associates. pp. 34–35. ISBN 978-0878932580.*

[334] *Volvox is a polyphyletic genus of chlorophyte green algae in the family Volvocaceae. Volvox species form spherical colonies of up to 50,000 cells*

[335] *Hallmann, A. (June 2011). "Evolution of reproductive development in the volvocine algae". Sexual Plant Reproduction. 24 (2): 97–112. doi:10.1007/s00497-010-0158-4. PMC 3098969. PMID 21174128.*

exists more enriched explanation of the situation which confers freedom of jeevatma (the soul force) from the bodily restrictions of life and culmination of the same in the collectively broader manifestation of the supreme power (Paramatma)[336]; as such kind of liberation ensured convergence of both the manifestations the death cannot be confirmed within the limit of such manifestations in reality; as such a kind of sensory withdrawal of fellow individual cannot confer complete removal of ideals and contributions duly made by the living form during instances of manifestations; as all sorts of worldly manifestations may experience creation and destruction as per the sanction of all the dimensions duly provided to the same by supreme master; as all sorts of worldly manifestations are not sensible to any of the specific organism; as worldly regulations are availed to all the particles within the scope of a specific realm of creation; as, in a broader way to specify, there exists several other instances of cyclic process of creations and destructions; as adaptation, mutation and evolution are the steps followed by organisms within the realm of worldly manifestations of living forms; as highest order of manifestations ignited spiritually to converge progressive focus towards following exploration of "(Satya) Truthfulness"[337].

Instructions in The Bhagavadgita also maintains the fact that we cannot kill the Soul force by any means, only disintegration of bodily organ systems and material combinations can be accomplished; one should not go on claiming that any individual is killed by any means; as we cannot kill the waves of spiritual ascent of any aspirant.

जातस्य हि ध्रुवो मृत्युर्ध्रुवं जन्म मृतस्य च |
तस्मादपरिहार्येऽर्थे न त्वं शोचितुमर्हसि || ॥. 27||

jātasya hi dhruvo mrityur dhruvaṁ janma mritasya cha
tasmād aparihārye 'rthe na tvaṁ śhochitum arhasi

---

[336] *The Hindu Kama Shastra Society (1925). The Kama Sutra of Vatsyayana. University of Toronto Archives. pp. 8–11, 172.*
[337] *Truthfulness (Satya) is second of the Yamas in Patanjali Yoga Sutras : "Satya pratiṣṭhāyāṁ kriyā phalā 'śrayatvaṁ" – As truthfulness (satya becomes established in the context) is achieved, the fruits of actions naturally result on the basis of wills of the fellow aspirant.*

It is also confirmed while relying by Prince Yudhishthir to Yaksha (the lord of death) regarding identification of most strange thing in the world. Prince said: People see other dying, they also know the ultimate fate of all the living forms, and then also they consider themselves beyond the regulations of death.[338] All manifested created beings remain unmanifest before birth, gradually manifest while remaining alive and again unmanifest while bodily disintegration is ensured on death.[339] Gross body (five gross elements of nature—earth, water, fire, air, and space.), Subtle body (eighteen elements—five life-airs, five working senses, five knowledge senses, mind, intellect, and ego) and Casual body (the account of karmas from endless past lives, including the sanskārs (tendencies) carried forward from previous lives) ensures complete manifestation of an individual in the immediate context. There exist several other instructions of similar types to facilitate fellow individuals not to lament on death of any living form, as such kind of mere physical regulation of creation and destruction never kills the non-perishable soul force (ATMA).[340] Some can describe, some can see and some can describe the soul as amazing; as the soul force remain beyond the scope of quality distinctions; as there is no physical identity of the soul force in the exhibits of living forms; as one cannot meditate quite easily on the manifestation of soul force through reflections of mind and intellect.[341] Teacher having experience of self-realization is rare; obtaining masterly instructions from such a teacher by any aspirant is also very rare; after getting such a rare opportunity attainment of self-realization by fellow aspirant is also rarest.[342] Fellow warrior of a country fights enemy violently to protect people of that country and also to maintain territorial law and order while fighting the brute.[343] Human birth is a rare opportunity granted by the Divine to an individual; one should utilise it

---

[338] *ahany ahani bhūtāni gachchhantīha yamālayam*
sheshāḥ sthiratvam ichchhanti kimāśhcharyamataḥ param (Mahabharat) [v30]
[339] *The Bhagavadgita II.28*
[340] *lamentation is only attachment that arises out of illusion... Shrimadbhagavatam 1.13.44 [V31]*
[341] *The Bhagavadgita II.29*
[342] *Kathopanishad 1.2.7 [V 32]*
[343] *Parāśhar Smṛiti 1.61 [context The Bhagavadgita II.33]*

with utmost care otherwise the life will put the aspirant at sufferings of great ruin.[344]

Aspirants, who practice the ostentatious rituals duly prescribed in the Vedas merely for enjoying the celestial pleasures of the higher abodes, are like the blind leading another blind;[345] as they rarely move on for experiencing the real nature of the soul force. The masterly guide instructs fellow aspirants to move on further through the path of spiritual ascent after rejecting fluctuations on mind and senses. The ultimate goal of all the Vedic mantras, the ritualistic activities, spiritual practices, sacrifices, assimilation of knowledge, and conducts of duties, is to help the soul force of fellow aspirants to feel the Divine omnipresence.[346] The Vedas prescribe varieties of social and ritualistic duties for individuals. But those who grasp their underlying motive while escaping intermediate instructions, fulfill their duty toward the Divine with utter devotion will be considered as wisest of all. [347]

A clear distinction between doing duties and claim of result for the same is made in The Bhagavadgita.

कर्मण्येवाधिकारस्ते मा फलेषु कदाचन।
मा कर्मफलहेतुर्भूर्मा ते सङ्गोऽस्त्वकर्मणि ॥ II. 47 ॥

karmaṇy-evādhikāras te mā phaleṣhu kadāchana
mā karma-phala-hetur bhūr mā te saṅgo 'stvakarmaṇi

"One should deliver duty, but must not concern oneself with the results………"

It also encompasses the real status of the living form which moves beyond the regulations of life and death; as all events are happening on the basis of nature's regulation; as all accomplishments are obligatory for individuals having affinity towards performing specified duties in society; as individuals rarely confine oneself within the physical regulations of life and death; as only death cannot restrict spiritual

---

[344] *Kenopanishad 2.5 [The Bhagavadgita II.35]*
[345] *Mundakopanishad 1.2.8 [Context The Bhagavadgita II.37]*
[346] *The Bhagavatam 1.2.28—29 [context The Bhagavadgita II. 38]*
[347] *The Bhagavatam 11.11.32*

manifestation of any of the fellow aspirants. One should remain steadfast while delivering duties by abandoning attachment to success and failure (a state of equanimity which is often called Yoga).[348] Aspirants having adequate enlightenment (as per the acquisition of knowledge) because of soul force (ATMA) remain devoid of affinity towards results of any actions duly performed.[349]

The supreme indestructible and inducer element of the creator power is called Brahman (the Divine or the Purush Element). The supreme Divine power becomes helpful when one assimilates its reflection on the intellect with its proper exhibits and its role in the creation and destruction. We can correlate the ways of functioning of the Divine by observing any luminous object like that of the sun. Some of the hidden mysteries responsible for the luminous nature of the sun have become known to us, and there exists several mysteries still unexplored because of our limitations in terms of senses and intellect. Mystery behind the inter-conversion of matter and energy is the main process responsible for liberating such a tremendous amount of radiation in the form of electromagnetic waves that radiating out from the celestial bodies like that of the Sun. Before such radiation the energy remained trapped inside the atomic nuclei were in the form of Nuclear Energy. We also came to know about presence of such king of tremendous amount of energy within all types of atoms of different elements. This phenomenon indicates the presence of creation elements and destruction elements inside the atomic nuclei. It is also confirmed that such nuclei remain inactive during all kinds of chemical reactions. Such a tremendous concentration of creation element ensures its presence during the process of creation but remains off the system of bindings. It registers its presence in the form of powerful particles.

All the above phenomena indicate the way supreme power becomes functional whenever time comes. The Divine energy ensures its presence in all sorts of creation. Even stars were created in olden times under the influence of such Divine power. It can be ascribed as the supreme power with which balance of matter and energy is ensures. It is

---

[348] *The Bhagavadgita II.48*
[349] *The Bhagavadgita II.49*

also true that matter alone or energy alone cannot make the creation possible. Both of these supreme creation elements interact in a coordinated fashion to make creations possible. We rarely recognize the presence of energy element in the creation because of their non-sensible characters. We can feel the presence of such electromagnetic waves through the activities of reflections accomplished by other earthly visible elements or through any other celestial elements. The sun itself registers in the universe as a successful combination of matter and energy through which the presence of matter is guarded by the intense power of outwardly directed radiations. This discussion encompasses the scientific basis of the Vedic, Sankhya and Yoga Philosophy. Living things always rest on Divine in same way the blowing wind rests in the atmosphere.[350] Only ignorant ones behave differently by violating prescribed rules of the nature and intend knowingly or unknowingly to put oneself in trouble. People can worship that Divine differently through varying degree and nature of contributions. Aham (or the ego centre) is everything perceivable in the surrounding in varying forms of relatives, friends, parents, masters and other living forms. Supreme goal for all the life form is, therefore, to have an exploration of working out the instances during which one start recognizing the Divine omnipresence.

Worshippers of other forms or god or other forms of power or faiths worship the supreme Divine because of the universal existence of such power at various instances in our surrounding. Similarities of the characters of the Nature elements itself indicate the presence of a uniform supreme inducer of creation element at all instances in the form of the Divine.[351] People should offer all acts and conducts with absolute sincerity to the Divine for enriching one's knowledge base. Worship described in Bhagvadgita is for all irrespective of their individual differences. By doing so it has registered the fact regarding the universality of the worship methods and the processes of spiritual ascent duly narrated at different portions of the holy book Gita. It is, therefore, exclusively not meant for any specific group of worshippers.[352]

---

[350] *Bhagvadgita, Chapter 9, Verse 6-12.*
[351] *Bhagvadgita, Chapter 9, Verse 23,24.*
[352] *Bhagvadgita, Chapter 9, Verse 29,30-32.*

The Divine knowledge passes on from one generation to the other through the process of orientation and extensive training. During such training a devotee generally maintains the stability of mind, body and intellect for ensuring proper and timely maintained confluence of knowledge from the master to the follower. The degree of involvement of master and followers in the synthesis of knowledge will ensure the degree and instances of success. Divine knowledge also enables an individual to redefine the role duly prescribed for him or her in the society. It also ensures the onset of a repeated refinement process which aims ultimately towards the instance during which renunciation of the soul is duly accomplished.

Different functional exhibits of knowledge duly enlisted by saints are as follows : a state of humbleness; freedom from hypocrisy; non-violence; forgiveness; simplicity; service offered to the master; maintaining cleanliness of body, mind and intellect; steadfastness; self-control; dispassion toward the objects of the senses; establishing a hold and control on egoism; recognising the evils of birth, disease, old age, and death; non-attachment to sensible objects; absence of clinging to relatives, children, home, and other worldly objects; even-mindedness amidst desirable and undesirable events in life; spontaneous and exclusive devotion towards the Divine; inclination of mind towards a state of calmness and stability through ensuring detachments from socially inclined gatherings of subjects other than the scope of study and experimentations; strong adherence towards the Divine, related subjects and spiritual knowledge; a long lasting aspiration of the thought processes related to the truth.[353] Contrasting bases of above mentioned knowledge will be considered as acts of an ignorant mind and intellect. At the final stage of our understanding regarding the alignment three different horizons through which the Divine ensure manifestation will be discussed in particulars.

Three different portions of the Divine consciousness that remained active in the Natural world have the following orientations:

---

[353] *Source: Bhagvadgita, Chapter 13, Virses 8 to 12*

1. **Adhyatm** or the Divine of an individual (the inner world consciousness of an individual) : it registers its omnipresence beside the Nature elements and gets reflected during certain instances through intellect.
2. **Jeevatm** or the Divine getting manifested through rest of the other individuals including plants and animals.
3. **Paramatm** or existence of the Divine beyond the scope of all the living forms and duly ensures the wider dimensions of creations and destructions at the levels of the celestial supremacy like Universe, Galaxy, Nebula etc.

Modern science has created an instance due to which we can easily go through evidences related to the vast expansion of the Universe. We can even claim that we all were earlier not aware of the presence of such a vast expansion over the ether which appears blue during day time and dark during night. Both the contrasting colours are not the actual character of the limitless sky. We also confirm that the presence of all the celestial bodies can be recognized even during day time with the help of specially enabled devices. Such kind of limitless expansion of the Universe and information related to the varying nature and orientations of all such bodies were depicted during olden times by Vedic saints. They have also pointed out about our limitations with which we may not be capable enough in ensuring our access to all those knowledge.

We can correlate the Vishwaroopa (or the vision of the Universal expansion of creations) through explanations registered in the chapter 11 of Bhagvadgita. Names of different characters were pointed out symbolically to narrate the true nature of the Knowledge confluence from one generation to the other. Saints always played a vital role in preserving, cultivating and transferring the holy knowledge from generation to generations. Lord Krishna recognized himself as Kapil amongst all sages. This recognition has confirmed the alignment of the Philosophical alignment of Gita towards Sankhya Philosophy. Other schools of thought process will register their presence in the light of Sankhya narratives. The converging nature of the synthesis of Divine Knowledge is also confirmed by different instances of discussions depicted in Bhagvadgita. From all the above discussions it is becoming absolutely clear that a Soul (atma) cannot take the role of a killer and even cannot be killed by any other Soul (atma) at any instance of the worldly manifestations. After knowing this fact one should consider reward-seeking actions inferior to works performed with the intellect established in divine knowledge.[354] Instruction is also advanced by the Divine master that one should "strive for Yoga, which is the art of working skilfully." [355] The Bhagavatam states that individuals engage in fruitive works to get happiness never attains satisfaction; these activities only aggravate the misery. [356]

Waves of Impulse

Being an advanced living entity, human body is perfectly equipped with different organ systems specialised for conducting various specialised functions; nervous system is one of such unit responsible for generation, conduction and regulation of electrical impulse; a system which imposes direct or indirect regulations upon rest of the other organ or system; a mechanism which never rests on any other system other than supply of nutrients to alter impulse transmission.

While addressing real nature of the Soul force of an individual it would be better if we prefer moving through instances of brain function. Human brain is the zone where intellect, memory, emotions, ego and rest of the other centrally regulated processing of senses (such as vision, hearing, smelling, taste and feelings) are perfectly accommodated.[357] Presence of functional overlappings in between different lobes of the central unit of this organ is also acknowledged by scholars.[358] Functional areas of this organ (popularly known as Brodmann's area) differ considerably when seen under microscope.[359] Cortex portion is

---

[354] *The Bhagavadgita II.49*
[355] *"buddhi-yukto jahātīha ubhe sukrita-dushkrite*
tasmād yogāya yujyasva yogaḥ karmasu kauśhalam" ... The Bhagavadgita II.50
[356] *sukhāya karmāṇi karoti loko na taiḥ sukham vānyad-upāramam vā*
vindeta bhūyas tata eva duḥkham yad atra yuktam bhagavān vaden naḥ (The Bhagavatam 3.5.2)
[357] *Standring, Susan, ed. (2008). Gray's Anatomy: The Anatomical Basis of Clinical Practice (40th ed.). London: Churchill Livingstone. ISBN 978-0-8089-2371-8.*
[358] *Ackerman, S. (1992). Discovering the brain. Washington, D.C.: National Academy Press. pp. 22–25. ISBN 978-0-309-04529-2.*
[359] *Hall, John (2011). Guyton and Hall Textbook of Medical Physiology (12th ed.). Philadelphia, PA: Saunders/Elsevier. ISBN 978-1-4160-4574-8.*

distinguishable functionally as sensory cortex and motor cortex.[360] Primary sensory areas collect senses from different sense organs and process the same for enabling central unit to recognise all such signals. Attention, abstract thinking, problem solving and behaviour are principally regulated by the frontal lobe.[361] There exists several minute regulators deeply embedded in the brain and make the functions little bit complex. It also confers the accommodation of wishes and wills amidst rest of the other neural responses of specific types. Movement regulation and behaviour design is the subject of basal ganglia.[362] We may not go deep into the structural details of this organ system. Our focal attention is to analyse some sort of functional complexities with which human brain accommodates mind, intellect and ego and also restricts the fellow individual from recognising involvement of soul force in making the entire structure functionally active. Some of the obligatory and acquired reflexes are regulated locally by spinal branches while bypassing central regulation of the brain. Some of the functions, such as breathing and heart beat, are regulated by automatized system embedded in the nervous system (parts of Hypothalamus and Pons). Chemical control of different glands and organ systems is also a subject of the master gland (Pituitary) which remains under the regulation of nerve-regulators duly provided by active part of Hypothalamus. Sleep, also considered as the inactive phase of human brain, is also considered very important as it ensures removal of toxins from functional sites which often develops due to prolonged functioning of the nervous system; it also ensures restoration of energy giving molecules at functional sites of the brain.[363] Lateralisation of function (because of which right part of brain controls function of left half of body and left half regulates the right portion) is the speciality of

---

[360] *Hall, John (2011). Guyton and Hall Textbook of Medical Physiology (12th ed.). Philadelphia, PA: Saunders/Elsevier. ISBN 978-1-4160-4574-8.*
[361] *Kolb, B.; Whishaw, I. (2009). Fundamentals of Human Neuropsychology. Macmillan. pp. 73–75. ISBN 978-0-7167-9586-5.*
[362] *Purves, Dale (2012). Neuroscience (5th ed.). Sunderland, MA: Sinauer associates. ISBN 978-0-87893-695-3.*
[363] *"Brain Basics: Understanding Sleep | National Institute of Neurological Disorders and Stroke". www.ninds.nih.gov. Archived from the original on December 22, 2017.*

this organ system.[364] Regulation of emotion is a multi component processes involving elicitation, followed by feelings, appraisal, expression, autonomic response and tendencies of performing actions.[365] Involvement of basal ganglia in regulating happiness is duly acknowledged by scholars.[366] There exists several other evidences to ascertain the real nature of localised functions of various parts of brain.

Regulation of cognition is also a brain function; as it works to filter information and removes irrelevant ones; as it holds ability of processing information and holding the same in functional part of memory; as it ensures ability to think upon multiple subjects simultaneously and with attention from one subject to the other; as it ensures ability to inhibit impulses and to ascertain importance of certain sets of information.[367] Higher order of executive and exploratory function of human brain requires networked use of multiple basic executive functions, such as planning, prospection and fluid intelligence (a combination of reasoning and problem solving abilities).[368] Prefrontal cortex of brain plays an important role in this regard.[369]

Entire brain function is made possible because of the network of interconnected neurons; and their ability to recognise process and transmit electrical signals.[370] Almost one fourth of the energy giving

---

[364] de Lussanet, M.H.E.; Osse, J.W.M. (2012). "An ancestral axial twist explains the contralateral forebain and the optic chiasm in vertebrates". Animal Biology. 62 (2): 193–216. arXiv:1003.1872. doi:10.1163/157075611X617102. S2CID 7399128.

[365] Sander, David (2013). Armony, J.; Vuilleumier, Patrik (eds.). The Cambridge handbook of human affective neuroscience. Cambridge: Cambridge Univ. Press. p. 16. ISBN 978-0-521-17155-7.

[366] Phan, KL; Wager, Tor; Taylor, SF.; Liberzon, I (June 1, 2002). "Functional Neuroanatomy of Emotion: A Meta-Analysis of Emotion Activation Studies in PET and fMRI". NeuroImage. 16 (2): 331–348. doi:10.1006/nimg.2002.1087. PMID 12030820. S2CID 7150871.

[367] Malenka, RC; Nestler, EJ; Hyman, SE (2009). "Preface". In Sydor, A; Brown, RY (eds.). Molecular Neuropharmacology: A Foundation for Clinical Neuroscience (2nd ed.). New York: McGraw-Hill Medical. p. xiii. ISBN 978-0-07-148127-4.

[368] Diamond, A (2013). "Executive functions". Annual Review of Psychology. 64: 135–168. doi:10.1146/annurev-psych-113011-143750. PMC 4084861. PMID 23020641.
Figure 4: Executive functions and related terms Archived May 9, 2018, at the Wayback Machine

[369] Hyun, J.C.; Weyandt, L.L.; Swentosky, A. (2014). "Chapter 2: The Physiology of Executive Functioning". In Goldstein, S.; Naglieri, J. (eds.). Handbook of Executive Functioning. New York: Springer. pp. 13–23. ISBN 978-1-4614-8106-5.

[370] Pocock, G.; Richards, C. (2006). Human Physiology: The Basis of Medicine (3rd ed.). Oxford: Oxford University Press. ISBN 978-0-19-856878-0.

nutrient is utilised by the brain which represents only 2% of the body weight.[371]

Electrophysiology, a branch of science and technology, is developed to record different types of brain functions and response of sense organs to stimuli; it is also used in cortical stimulation mapping; used to predict interactions of cortical area and systemic functions; often used at certain instances to specify exact reason of neural malfunctions; used frequently to specify zonations of brain functions.[372]

Only 400 out of 20,000 different genes are identified specific to signify structure and function of the central nervous system;[373] such specialities can be altered due to long term use of alcohols by the individual; as such kinds of use may alter the systematised gene expression and may induce cellular architecture involved in regulating brain functions.[374] Alteration and decline of synaptic functions in ageing brain is also confirmed by scholars; as changes in gene functions alter the levels of proteins involved in different pathways of neural functions; as such kind of alterations leads to loss or decline of neural functions; as such kind of sensory malfunction leads to synaptic contact dysfunction or loss of senses.[375]

It is also confirmed from studies that multiple head injury may lead to long lasting chronic traumatic encephalopathy (a neurodegenerative disease leading to repeated trauma to the head).[376] It can affect different

---

[371] *Clark, D.D.; Sokoloff. L. (1999). Siegel, G.J.; Agranoff, B.W.; Albers, R.W.; Fisher, S.K.; Uhler, M.D. (eds.). Basic Neurochemistry: Molecular, Cellular and Medical Aspects. Philadelphia: Lippincott. pp. 637–670. ISBN 978-0-397-51820-3.*

[372] *Towle, V.L.; et al. (January 1993). "The spatial location of EEG electrodes: locating the best-fitting sphere relative to cortical anatomy". Electroencephalography and Clinical Neurophysiology. 86 (1): 1–6. doi:10.1016/0013-4694(93)90061-y. PMID 7678386.*

[373] *"The human proteome in brain – The Human Protein Atlas". www.proteinatlas.org. Archived from the original on September 29, 2017. Retrieved September 29, 2017.*

[374] *Warden, A (2017). "Gene expression profiling in the human alcoholic brain". Neuropharmacology. 122: 161–174. doi:10.1016/j.neuropharm.2017.02.017. PMC 5479716. PMID 28254370.*

[375] *Flores, CE; Méndez, P (2014). "Shaping inhibition: activity dependent structural plasticity of GABAergic synapses". Frontiers in Cellular Neuroscience. 8: 327. doi:10.3389/fncel.2014.00327. PMC 4209871. PMID 25386117.*

[376] *Dawodu, S.T. (March 9, 2017). "Traumatic Brain Injury (TBI) – Definition and Pathophysiology: Overview, Epidemiology, Primary Injury". Medscape. Archived from the original on April 9, 2017.*

parts of brain and can affect movement, memory and cognition.[377] Mental disorders (such as depression, schizophrenia, bipolar disorder, posttraumatic stress disorder, attention deficit hyperactivity disorder, obsessive-compulsive disorder, Tourette syndrome, and addiction) are known to relate to the functional anomalies of the brain.[378] Such anomalies can be addressed effectively by using psychotherapy, psychiatry or social interventions; as such anomalies are often caused by different types of complicated social, economic, spiritual or cognitive issues; as such anomalies rarely become recognisable by any physical or physiological means; as such anomalies can be addressed by adopting multiple approaches of therapy.[379] Our scientific temperament and clinical research approaches of various types indicates that brain development is also regulated considerably during pregnancy by nutritional disorders, use of recreational drugs and by infectious diseases.[380]

There is no common concern related to instances of brain death and diagnosis of the same which can be recommended for wider practices. Concerns related to such kind of neural collapse are prepared locally at different places and is in practice with slight variations.[381] Poor communication with family members and associates of patient makes the diagnosis of brain death quite complicated.[382] Absence of breathing and

---

[377] Colledge, Nicki R.; Walker, Brian R.; Ralston, Stuart H.; Ralston, eds. (2010). Davidson's Principles and Practice of Medicine (21st ed.). Edinburgh: Churchill Livingstone/Elsevier. ISBN 978-0-7020-3085-7.

[378] Volkow, N.D.; Koob, G.F.; McLellan, A.T. (January 2016). "Neurobiologic advances from the brain disease model of addiction". The New England Journal of Medicine. 374 (4): 363–371. doi:10.1056/NEJMra1511480. PMC 6135257. PMID 26816013.

[379] Simpson, J.M.; Moriarty, G.L. (2013). Multimodal Treatment of Acute Psychiatric Illness: A Guide for Hospital Diversion. Columbia University Press. pp. 22–24. ISBN 978-0-231-53609-7.

[380] Perese, E.F. (2012). Psychiatric Advanced Practice Nursing: A Biopsychsocial Foundation for Practice. F.A. Davis. pp. 82–88. ISBN 978-0-8036-2999-8.

[381] Wijdicks, EFM (January 8, 2002). "Brain death worldwide: accepted fact but no global consensus in diagnostic criteria". Neurology. 58 (1): 20–25. doi:10.1212/wnl.58.1.20. PMID 11781400. S2CID 219203458.

[382] Urden, L.D.; Stacy, K.M.; Lough, M.E. (2013). Priorities in Critical Care Nursing – E-Book. Elsevier Health Sciences. pp. 112–113. ISBN 978-0-323-29414-0.

response to stimuli often signify the onset of "brain death" but the entire thing is still under the consideration of research scholars.[383]

If we start considering entire thing from spiritual angle then all sorts of propositions and functional linkages of human brain to sensory and motor responses become manageable at all instances; as all such anomalies related to function of senses, mind, intellect and ego becomes adjustable and self-regulating for having access to timely as well as masterly guide to the fellow aspirant. It is the critical juncture where we are allowed to shift from evidence based medication to need based guidance which may ensure spiritual ascent of the individual; such guidance will qualify the fellow aspirant for gaining such ascent.

Impulse transmission and its central regulation makes the idea confirmed that cortical regulation of senses is the main functional superiority with which human brain works. Question arises about the masterly regulation of mind, intellect and ego for materialising all sorts of sensory and motor regulations duly exhibited by the living entity. Science rarely permits us to move beyond the scope of recognisable evidences to configure the real zonation of mind, intellect and ego; as only frontal cannot encompass loss or gain of memory; as memory formation is accomplished layer by layer; as intellect is the regulation housed within any part embedded in the cortex but cannot be confirmed by providing evidences; as ego is mounted on all sorts of sensory and motor functions just like superimposition of a blanket upon any object without encompassing any specialised neural zonations; as ego confers the recognisable quality parameters (three qualities duly explained in Vedas, Upanishads and Epics as satwa, Rajas and Tama); as ego experiences a shift from one quality to the other. There are instances like good qualities, moderate ignorance and animism which develop, transform and perish time to time. Masterly guide always works to develop and enhance good qualities in an individual; such guidance also works to remove affinities of animism from ego; refinement of such type is the desirable progress which spiritual master wants to accomplish.

---

[383] *Colledge, Nicki R.; Walker, Brian R.; Ralston, Stuart H.; Ralston, eds. (2010). Davidson's Principles and Practice of Medicine (21st ed.). Edinburgh: Churchill Livingstone/Elsevier. ISBN 978-0-7020-3085-7.*

Spirituality, is therefore, the only way out for enhancing creative brain function for ensuring development and manifestation of good qualities, friendly nature in aspirants; for such kinds of progress will ensure human to human bond in society; for such kind of acculturation will minimise instances of sensory and motor difficulties in individuals; for such kinds of approaches work considerably as confidence building measures; for enhancement of aspirants of this type will work as a hidden current of river aiming ultimately to ascertain spiritual and intellectual progress of the individual.

Here develops the situation when relevance of the Bhagavadgita in our daily life is brightly established by nullifying almost all sorts of our doubts and worries. We cannot simply dispose the Holy Script for immediate consideration by fellow aspirants without making them fit for analysing the situation; even without letting them recognise the difficulties they are facing in the context; also we do it after making them concerned of the type of ego, intellect and mind with which they are remaining active in the context; also by making them aware of the real linkages which exist in between knowledge, works and devotion.

The work, titled The Bhagavadgita as taken out from Bhishma Parva of the Mahabharata is dated to the second half of first Millenium BCE.[384] Situation of war developed during the Epic age when Kuru princes refused to deliver rights to Pandavas; which led to exhibit fellow prince Arjun to declare war against Kuru Princes; after getting assembled at the battle filed the fellow prince Arjun started thinking about ultimate fate of the war; as such war would bring calamities in the form of death and loss of properties; as such war was going to claim lives of relatives, masters and Kuru Princes; as such war was developing by rejecting doctrines of peace, nonviolence and brotherhood. Considering all these results in advance Arjun, the fellow warrior from Pandava's side, became emotionally preoccupied with dilemma.[385] Masterly instruction duly

---

[384] "Bhagavadgita | Definition, Contents, & Significance | Britannica". www.britannica.com. Archived from the original on 21 August 2018. Retrieved 27 December 2022.
[385] The Song Celestial, Or, Bhagavad-gîtâ (from the Mahâbhârata) Being a Discourse Between Arjuna, Prince of India, and the Supreme Being Under the Form of Krishna. Roberts Bros. 1885. pp. Book one the first, page 19.

issued to him suggested to deliver duty of a warrior amidst the battle field for ensuring victory of wise people by destroying the brute.[386]

It was the timely instruction issued to the fellow warrior which made them contented and aware of the real fate of life after death; for such instructions equipped the fellow prince in identifying duty of a person in society; for such instructions enabled the fellow aspirant to recognise real nature of the self (Aham) alongside omnipresence of the Divine (Paramatma); for such instructions enabled the fellow Yogi to recognise the nature of Soul force which remains free from three dimensions of quality parameters; for timely instructions delivered by the fellow master was fruitful in removing dilemma and diffusing illusions; for all kinds of instructions aimed finally towards "Knowing Thyself"[387]. Wide range of instructions accommodated in the Gita covers a broad range of spiritual topics, touching upon moral and ethical dilemmas, and philosophical issues that go far beyond the war of Epic Age.[388] It can be considered as an allegory for the struggles of human life; as human beings also face different kinds of problems at work places and even in the family; as human beings often get confused of what to do and what not to do; as individuals remain ignorant of delivering duties duly issued by society; as individuals seek timely guidance before moving on towards delivering duties, claiming rights or for facing enemies; as the individual delivers duties in accord to the Divine sanctions and seeks utter culmination of the individual self (Atman) to that of the supreme self (Paramatma). Entire creation can be considered as embodiment of the supreme Divine from which a tiny part in the form of individual is duly manifested; after understanding this reality fellow individuals start recognising the Divine omnipresence.

---

[386] Easwaran, Eknath (2007), The Bhagavad Gita, Nilgiri Press, ISBN 978-1-58638-019-9

[387] "I am Brahman." ... as the concept developed on the basis of instructions of Vedas, Upanishads, Epics and Puranas delivered to Aspirants.

[388] Sargeant, Winthrop (2009), Christopher Key Chapple (ed.), The Bhagavad Gītā: Twenty-fifth Anniversary Edition, State University of New York Press, ISBN 978-1-4384-2841-3

Treasure of Perfect Synthesis of Spirituality

The Bhagavadgita presents a perfect synthesis of the Yoga, Sankhya and Vedanta philosophy; as this Holy Scripture provides a perfect analysis of absolute Spirituality which can be considered as a doctrine free from the realm of different schools of religion.[389] It also encompasses a perfect combination of Jnana (the path of knowledge), karma (the path of actions), Bhakti (the path of devotion) and Raja Yogas.[390]

One can acquire knowledge by listening to master, following masterly instructions and through experiences. It implies an everlasting impression on the mind of the fellow worshipper and remains with the individual even up to the last pulse of life. People having no faith in masterly instructions may fail to gain the true knowledge and may remain at the state of confusion. Only true follower of masterly instructions can have an easy access to the true knowledge. Only true knowledge can unfold the real reason lying behind the creation of billions of life forms of varying types and their interactions with other natural objects. Trend of such evolutionary transformation of life forms of varying types are also regulated by the organic interactions of elements and compounds. The part of supreme energy can be traced out in the individual life forms but such an individual life form cannot accommodate the entire cluster of celestial lump of energy. Such a lump of energy may give birth to a new galaxy or it may withdraw itself from any previously existing galaxy. Organism may restrict oneself up to the planetary realm of interactions. One cannot even dare to cross the celestial boundary of the star system from which it has originated. Subject of manifestation itself is regulated up to the realm of luminous intensity. Beyond such intensity we have no chance to prosper.

It is also true that the divine power has made the creation possible by influencing the nature elements to manifest and interact accordingly for ensuring the onset of a conscious spark of life. All

---

[389] *Raju, P.T. (1992), The Philosophical Traditions of India, Delhi: Motilal Banarsidass Publishers Private Limited*

[390] *Eliot Deutsch; Rohit Dalvi (2004), The Essential Vedānta: A New Source Book of Advaita Vedānta, World Wisdom, Inc, ISBN 978-0-941532-52-5*

material elements are thus influenced and guided by the divine power to pass on through the cyclic process of creation and destruction. Although divine power plays a vital role in creating an organism the power of such type is not restricted only up to the organismic sensitivity , it has a limitless expansion and remains without being influenced by the fellow organism or organismic conducts[391]. The mighty wind blowing everywhere rests always in sky. In the same way all the organisms rest always in the divine lord and get manifested accordingly when time permits. At the end of one creation cycle all the organisms duly created will be merged into the realm of materials and energy and the entire collection of such kind of lump will be directed towards any of the black hole towards which the centrally located star system will feel the power of attraction. The situation of such a dramatic withdrawal of the diversity of creation may be initiated at any moment. None of the creations and destructions of any types are ever capable of binding the divine power in them. This creator power (the PURUSH element in accord to Sankhya Philosophy) remains independent of the realm of creation and destruction. It ensures the process without being involved actively in the entire process of manifestation.

Divine power of such a doer type may often remain non-recognisable because of the non-association of such power in the process of creation. We often recognize the intellect and soul holding such intellect as the creator element. The soul and intellect can have a reflection of the creator superconscious doer element but it cannot be ascribed directly as a doer. We also recognize the soul of an individual as a non-destroyable entity as that of the divine power. It is similar to that of a stream of water joins the other and a beam of light joins the other. All such sources lose their individual identity before joining. Similar the thing is true regarding diffusion of soul in the surrounding when any individual dies. Band of energy get absorbed in the celestial collection and may be utilized at some other instances randomly during some other phases of creations.

---

[391] *Bhagvadgita, Ix. 5:*

न च मत्स्थानि भूतानि पश्य मे योगमैश्वरम्।
भूतभृन्न च भूतस्थो ममात्मा भूतभावनः ॥9.5॥

Everything being created does not rest in me. Although my role as a maintainer and creator of this entire cosmic manifestation is confirmed then also I am not residing in any of such creations.

Because of this reason material world moves through series of changes and one change is followed by series of other changes of varying degree and intensity. The person having true knowledge of the cycle of creation and destruction keep faith on the divine power and start exploring the existence of such power within the self. Two types of individuals see such a divine power in two different ways: one can recognize it as an inseparable part of the self and other can recognize it as a separate entity having no linkage to the self. Vedic rituals, medicinal herbs, worships of all types and cultivation of knowledge are nothing but different aspects of realising the omni-presence of divine power.[392]   One can recognize the role of the divine power in different realms of creation and destruction.

Person having noble conducts in society remain there in the memory of individuals for a considerable time and may secure a prominent position in the history of development. Such an individual even secure a prominent position amongst nobles because of noble deeds. They even imply a notable influence upon the social conducts. Their contribution in terms of knowledge enrichment may even become the part of the treasure of Vedas. The only lord worshipped by people is the divine power or the creation element (Purush). Common individuals do not know that they worship the supreme creation elements in varying forms. All actions, conducts, rituals and worships should be aimed ultimately towards worshiping the supreme creation element (Purush). We can even maintain our utter faith on the role of such a creation element in making the process of all the creations true.

Even sinners come out of the clutches of sin after knowing the ultimate fate of such sins and start residing in the process recognizing the

---

[392] *Bhagvadgita IX – 15-18:*

ज्ञानयज्ञेन चाप्यन्ये यजन्तो मामुपासते ।   एकत्वेन पृथक्त्वेन बहुधा विश्वतोमुखम् ॥१५॥

अहं क्रतुरहं यज्ञः स्वधाहमहमौषधम् ।मन्त्रोऽहमहमेवाज्यमहमग्निरहं हुतम् ॥१६॥

पिताहमस्य जगतो माता धाता पितामहः । वेद्यं पवित्रमोंकार ऋक्साम यजुरेव च ॥१७॥

गतिर्भर्ता प्रभुः साक्षी निवासः शरणं सुहृत् । प्रभवः प्रलयः स्थानं निधानं बीजमव्ययम् ॥१८॥

Cultivators of knowledge worship sureme lord as an entity. They recognize the diversified forms of such divine power at different instances. Divine power are the worship, vedic chantings, the fire , the butter and the rituals. Divine is the object of knowledge, the creator element and the Pranava (Om). It is the basis of everything that we see. It has its presence as a creator as well as destroyer element in the universe.

presence of creator element (Purush) by the side of the holy creations. They even start recognizing the wider form of the divine manifestation and start delivering their duty in the society with an altered conducts. They quickly get the shelter of the divine and start defining their role in society.

Life is restricted to the cycle of birth, development and death. The span between birth and death may be a prolonged one or may be followed by an immediate succession. Some fellow worshippers of knowledge understand this trend easily and consider the divine power as an immortal entity. Some other individuals remain in the clutch of confusion for a long time and fail to recognize the divine as any separate entity. Varieties of qualities in humans; such as intellect, knowledge, clarity of thought, forgiveness, truthfulness, control over the senses and mind, joy and sorrow, birth and death, fear and courage, non-violence, equanimity, contentment, austerity, charity, fame, and infamy; all develop from the supreme sense which implies a command upon memory, intellect and ego.[393] Combination of all such qualities may vary considerably. Combination of such qualities finalise the nature of an individual. Some of the combination may be wiser and some other combination may be demonic.

The yoga of devotion makes the individual linked to the divine power and with such inclination a devotee gains the sense of divine omnipresence quite easily. Such individual considers the diversity of all the living forms as a form radiated out from the divine. All such forms even remain restricted to the divine and get merged to the source after completion of life. It is similar to the act of the formation of clouds at the ocean bed and development of streams due to down pour from the clouds. All these acts jointly ensure the cyclic movement of water from ocean to mountains and again from mountains to oceans through streams. Intermediate results may be of many types and many forms, but the real identity of water droplet remains unchanged.

Whatever we acquire in the form of knowledge will enrich the society in different ways and even it will enrich our efforts of feeling the

---

omnipresence of the divine power. Lord describes himself as an inseparable entity of different forms and capacities which remain prevalent in the surrounding. Lord Shiva, for an example, among Rudras is divine. Every individual in this universe are capable of feeling the oneness with the divine, but they may not be capable of accommodating the source as we may not be able to accommodate the sun in our immediate surroundings. We can feel the warmth and illumination of the sun from a safest distance. Before reaching the ground such radiation is even filtered by the realm of atmosphere. We are absolutely incapable of assimilating the ultraviolet radiations at even a fraction of a percent. Such radiations are competent enough in killing any life forms. On the other hand we cannot think about birth and manifestation of any life form without the sun.

Scholars and saints collected different flowers from the garden of Upanishad to prepare a Holy Script of instructions for a fellow warrior to diffuse his states of illusion as he was to face a large number of enemies amidst a battle field. Recognising the Divine and performing according to instructions duly issued by the supreme master to fellow aspirant is the real objective of a life form. Upanishad rightly maintains views related to universal reality of the Divine; presence of the same at all instances of creations; one should recognise presence of such masterly guide besides all creations; by doing so one should not try to grab resources belonging to others.

Affinity to work actively for hundreds of years for betterment of society and humanity never puts the fellow aspirant in the bondage of works by any means. Individual who violates the verdict of Soul force finally move towards the world of utter darkness devoid of sources of illuminations.[394] A stationary entity which can move even faster than the mind, even non-accessible to Gods, for it remains frontwardly progressive; passes beyond the progressive aspirant whenever they move forward. Master of Life establishes waver of ether and water in that ever

---

[394] *Ishopanishad, Verse 2 and 3.*

expanding zone of creations; that moves and even remains stationary, that is far and also besides all creations, remains both inside and outside of all the worldly manifestations. [395] All sorts of hatred and violence will be diffused if fellow aspirant start recognising presence of all manifestations in the Divine and can recognise Divine omnipresence in all kinds of manifestations. Person of such self luminous intellect, having a clear vision of recognising presence of Brahman (the Divine) in all instances of manifestations, remains free from agony, illusion, greed and sorrow. [396]

अन्धं तमः प्रविशन्ति येऽविद्यामुपासते।
ततो भूय इव ते तमो य उ विद्यायां रताः ॥

"Person inflicted with illusion comes under the confinement of darkness and individuals relying exclusively on knowledge remain trapped amidst more darkness; for only knowledge without judicious actions cannot bring knowledge in action; such bands of knowledge without effective action brings agony, develops sorrow and often puts aspirants in a state of confusion."[397]

Recognition of Truth as the Divine

Aspirant who recognises Truth as a combination of knowledge and illusion experiences death due to wrong deeds and also becomes famous due to assimilation of knowledge. Person exhibiting devotion to birth alone comes under the trap of utter darkness of illusion and confusion. We receive something by birth and some other thing by non-birth; such thought process is transmitted to us from nobles. After recognising birth and dissolution of birth as identical process aspirants gain fame even after getting restricted due to regulations of death. [398]

We never claim our absolute isolation from the immediate surrounding because of the intimate relationship we regularly exercise on a daily basis for claiming basic facilities needed for

---

[395] *Ishavasyopanishad, Verse 4-5.*
[396] *Ishavasyopanishad Verse 7*
[397] *Ishavasyopanishad, Verse 9*
[398] *Ishavasyopanishad, Verse 11-14*

living. Entire population of human beings living in cities and villages are directly or indirectly rely upon the natural resources (Prakriti in terms of The Gita).

True beliefs and true statements correspond to the actual state of affairs or doctrines can be considered as Truth.[399] Being a traditional model duly popularized by great thinkers and philosophers this model correlates thoughts and things in a better way. A judgement can be considered as "True" if it correlates the external reality and facts.[400] Truth is also considered as an objective reality which is often ascribed through thoughts, words and other means.[401] Obstacle due to variations of language and dialect is considered as a limiting factor due to which any universal definition of the doctrines related to "Truth (SATYA in Sanskrit) cannot be generalised. If we put concepts into practice then the result or outcome of such practice will confirm the nature of Truth (a Pragmatic Approach)[402]. Concordance of abstract statements with the ideal limit towards which hundreds of investigations can be advanced to bring out essential ingredients of Truth is considered as a basis through which one can assess Truth.[403] True is the expedient in our way of thinking and Right is the expedient in our way of behaving.[404] Truth is a quality the value of which is confirmed by the effectiveness when applying concepts into practice.

From another angle it is confirmed that what works may or may not be considered as Truth, but what fails cannot be considered as a representation of Truth. It can be advanced only because Truth never

---

[399] *Encyclopedia of Philosophy, Vol.2, "Correspondence Theory of Truth", auth.: Arthur N. Prior, p. 223 (Macmillan, 1969).*

[400] *"Correspondence Theory of Truth", in Stanford Encyclopedia of Philosophy (citing De Veritate Q.1, A.1–3 and Summa Theologiae, I. Q.16).*

[401] *See, e.g., Bradley, F.H., "On Truth and Copying", in Blackburn, et al. (eds., 1999),Truth, 31–45.*

[402] *Encyclopedia of Philosophy, Vol. 5, "Pragmatic Theory of Truth", 427 (Macmillan, 1969).*

[403] *Peirce, C.S. (1901), "Truth and Falsity and Error" (in part), pp. 716–20 in James Mark Baldwin, ed., Dictionary of Philosophy and Psychology, v. 2. Peirce's section is entitled "Logical", beginning on p. 718, column 1, and ending on p. 720 with the initials "(C.S.P.)"*

[404] *James, William, The Meaning of Truth, A Sequel to 'Pragmatism', (1909).*

fails.[405] We cannot confer with facts and figures that we are right during all instances, but we can easily identify instances when we are wrong.[406] Nothing considered absolutely true as some other angles of observation may specify a fact true after altering the collections of facts and figures. This is a kind of superficial examination with which nature of Truth is defined. It has limitations of approach which remained restricted to the materialistic view of facts, figures, propositions and concepts. Deflationary theory maintains a clear view that "Truth" is an expressive predicate requiring no additional explanation.[407]

Regarding Nonviolence we must maintain our mind-set in such a way that it should not be judged from the angle of violence. From the view point of the regulation of senses Nonviolence (AHIMSA) is a state of mind which ensures the realm of our relations which distinguishes other human beings as relatives, strangers, friend, enemy or any other entity. Nonviolence will finalise the demarcation line within which our relatives gain some special treatment. Such kind of sense charged with the ritual of Nonviolence can consider a number of individuals as family members. With highest degree of such ritual filled with Nonviolence the individual start considering animals with care and respect. Animals are well treated in the family having higher state of Nonviolence as a ritual. In that context, with clear identification of the age old ritual, we can say that Nonviolence is the highest pursuit of socialisation and acculturation in a community. We cannot, even at any instance we should not, restrict the doctrine of Nonviolence to a limited quarter of any religious or social teachings. We should make it widely acceptable ritual irrespective of any social, cultural, physical or any geographical boundary. Restricting beauty of this ritual due to any reason is also a sin. There are instances during which we gain several common resources from the nature. We are also getting equally exposed to global problems like pollution, depletion of ozone layers, war, cross border terrorism and many other problems.

---

[405] *Sahakian, W.S. & Sahakian, M.L., Ideas of the Great Philosophers, New York: Barnes & Noble, 1966, LCCN 66--23155*
[406] *Feynman, The Character of Physical Law, New York: Random House, 1994, ISBN 0-679-60127-9.*
[407] *Encyclopedia of Philosophy, Supp., "Truth", auth: Michael Williams, pp. 572–73 (Macmillan, 1996)*

We are also getting exposed to the globally developed economic crisis due to various reasons. World Economic Forum formulated a list of most pressing points to be considered jointly to address majority of global problems (better we say it as issue).[408] These were: Food security, Inclusive growth, Future of work/unemployment, Climate change, financial crisis of 2007–2008, Future of the internet/Fourth Industrial Revolution, Gender equality, Global trade and investment and regulatory frameworks Long-term investment/Investment strategy and Future healthcare. It is also suggested that no single issue can be isolated or analysed individually at any instance. All the issues as incorporated in the list are directly or indirectly influenced by states of Peace and Nonviolence. The reason is very simple: Peace and Nonviolence signify the spiritual, mental and emotional set up of an individual. We all are, in that context, in the state of such situation where our alignment towards Truth and Nonviolence will be quantified. Truth is absolute and is beyond any doubts. Truth also resides in our knowledge base with which we start examining facts and figures.

Truth is considered as the second obligatory doctrine of first order of life process with which an individual prepares oneself efficiently which is required for attainment of an advancement of the path of gaining Spiritual Contentment.

Truth and Nonviolence are two wheels upon which the chariot of personality moves towards attainment of completeness in live. More perfectly to say truth is god and nonviolence is the way of living with which we can experience the presence of truth in our life.

Mahatma considered truth as God. His doctrines of truth and nonviolence remain relevant even today. In accord to the format of truth and nonviolence the service life of an individual gains advancement and perfectness in gradual succession. I am considering my life as "a pilgrimage to Truth".

---

[408] *Hutt, Rosamond (21 January 2016). "What are the 10 biggest global challenges?". World Economic Forum. Retrieved 18 January 2018.*

Surrender without knowing the exact fate of such pursuit in our daily life may not bring any fruitful result. What nature expects from us should be made clear before moving for implementing any process of renunciation. Wisdom and knowledge culminates in a definite fashion for ensuring the soft process of renunciation. Theoretical model of wisdom should be tested empirically for ensuring the existence of a broad link in between reasoning and well-being.[409]

During the condition of ill-defined life situation wisdom intends to move through unbiased judgement;[410] such as recognition of the limits of one's knowledge, appreciation of perspectives as broader than the prevalent issues, sensitivity to the probable changes in social relations and integration of different perspectives in particular. Contextual factors, such as training, educational practices and repeated practice of the masterly instructions, collectively play a vital role in the development of wisdom in an individual.[411] Evidence based methods are duly advanced for making the instructions more easy for the fellow scholars. Because of that reason only saints started linking up masterly instructions with stories and real life facts for making the fellow disciple properly actualised and wiser. Such a kind of wisdom inflicted with true knowledge is an expected outcome of the study of The Bhagavadgita. It is a source of knowledge and wisdom, but not the ultimate one. It has its linkages from wider streams of Vedic instructions, Yoga Philosophy and the philosophy of Sankhya. There rarely exists any profound relationship between age and exhibits of wisdom in any individual.[412] Knowledge enrichment aiming ultimately towards development of wisdom may be initiated at any time and may even start reflecting at the tender age, as the situation developed in the life of Shankaracharya. It may even bring completeness to a holy life even at the tender age. In

---

[409] Grossmann, I.; Gerlach, T.M.; Denissen, J.J. (2016). "Wise reasoning in the face of everyday life challenges". Social Psychological and Personality Science. 7

[410] Grossmann, Igor (20 July 2017). "Wisdom and how to cultivate it: Review of emerging evidence for a constructivist model of wise thinking".

[411] *Grossmann, Igor (20 July 2017). "Wisdom and how to cultivate it: Review of emerging evidence for a constructivist model of wise thinking".*

[412] Orwoll, L.; Perlmutter, M. (1990). R. J. Sternberg (ed.). Wisdom: Its nature, origins, and development. New York: Cambridge University Press. pp. 160–177. ISBN 978-0-521-36718-9.

some other cases it may not bring any chance of culmination of the soul and the divine. Attachment to the worldly belongings is considered as a major obstacle in attaining the awareness of the divine omnipresence.

Universe as a Divine Truth

The collection of time and space along with rest of the other constituents can be considered as the Universe.[413] Earlier cosmological model of the Universe during early stages of research and innovation were geocentric, keeping earth in the middle.[414] Modern studies suggested that the Universe is expanding periodically since beginning.[415] Contents of inter-galactic space are there in the Universe.[416] Elementary particles, like protons and neutrons, took part to form atomic nuclei of various types giving the universe a versatile status.[417] Gradual expansion of the Universe results in gradual decline of energy of each of the photons, as it is cosmologically re-shifted.[418]

From the status of the features and extensions of the Universe we came to know about the probabilities of the limitations of the radio signals as it may not reach the terminal portion of the Galaxy as it expands rapidly compared to the speed of light.[419] It is also estimated that distance between Earth and the observable universe is 46 billion light years.[420] It is also not a permanent structure as the entire collection

---

[413] Zeilik, Michael; Gregory, Stephen A. (1998). *Introductory Astronomy & Astrophysics* (4th ed.). Saunders College Publishing. ISBN 978-0-03-006228-5. *The totality of all space and time; all that is, has been, and will be.*

[414] Glick, Thomas F.; Livesey, Steven; Wallis, Faith (2005). *Medieval Science Technology and Medicine: An Encyclopedia.* Routledge. ISBN 978-0-415-96930-7. OCLC 61228669.

[415] Hawking, Stephen (1988). *A Brief History of Time.* Bantam Books. p. 43. ISBN 9780553053401.

[416] *"Universe". Dictionary.com.* Archived from the original on October 23, 2012. Retrieved September 21, 2012.

[417] Johnson, Jennifer A. (February 2019). *"Populating the periodic table: Nucleosynthesis of the elements". Science.* 363 (6426): 474–478. Bibcode:2019Sci...363..474J. doi:10.1126/science.aau9540. ISSN 0036-8075. PMID 30705182. S2CID 59565697.

[418] Steane, Andrew M. (2021). *Relativity Made Relatively Easy, Volume 2: General Relativity and Cosmology.* Oxford University Press. ISBN 978-0-192-89564-6.

[419] Kaku, Michio (2008). *Physics of the Impossible: A Scientific Exploration into the World of Phasers, Force Fields, Teleportation, and Time Travel.* Knopf Doubleday Publishing Group. pp. 202–. ISBN 978-0-385-52544-2.

[420] Bars, Itzhak; Terning, John (2018). *Extra Dimensions in Space and Time.* Springer. pp. 27–. ISBN 978-0-387-77637-8. Retrieved October 19, 2018.

moves gradually towards some unidentifiable space and may lose its identity afterwards.

Analysis of Type la Supernova indicates that expansion of the Universe is accelerating[421] It is also ascertained that whatever sensible particles we have in our surrounding are not created permanent; they are going to disintegrate in due course of time and can have some other dimensions after moving off the realm of black hole; the stipulated vigil with which entire creation has to tolerate the instances of creation and destruction. The cyclic process of creation and destruction is not restricted exclusively to living creatures only; it has a wider applicability to rest of the other sensible objects. If all such creations are not permanent then we should not have any passion of retaining the will of gaining a hold upon all sorts of manifestations. Truth is the basis with which we come across the structural and functional regulations of worldly objects. Expansion of creation also ensures our limitation of exploring the entire creation within the limited span of our life; as such kind of life impulse may not permit us to reach up to the farthest point of the universe; as such limitations never confer our momentum of such mark which ensures speed of our explorators having speed greater than the speed of light.

Integration of Schools of Yoga

As evident from the Gita, warrior Arjun lost his balance of mind after seeing his master, his elders and other relatives standing on the opponent's side. He refused to kill his masters and relatives simply for gaining a state. He even expressed his desire to cast off all his wishes to stop such a mass killing.

Such a state of confusion comes during a loss of proper coordination between the mind and intellect. One may lose any challenge

---

[421] *Perlmutter, S.; Aldering; Goldhaber; Knop; Nugent; Castro; Deustua; Fabbro; Goobar; Groom; Hook; Kim; Kim; Lee; Nunes; Pain; Pennypacker; Quimby; Lidman; Ellis; Irwin; McMahon; Ruiz-Lapuente; Walton; Schaefer; Boyle; Filippenko; Matheson; Fruchter; et al. (1999). "Measurements of Omega and Lambda from 42 high redshift supernovae". Astrophysical Journal. 517 (2): 565–586. arXiv:astro-ph/9812133. Bibcode:1999ApJ...517..565P. doi:10.1086/307221. S2CID 118910636.*

immediately if they impart themselves in any action by keeping such a state of confusion in mind. The stand of Arjuna amidst the battle field was vividly explained by lord Krishna. There developed the conversation of Krishna with Arjuna to enlighten the role of Pandavas in the battle. As parent, grand parents, friends and masters joining the opponent sides had not delivered their duties properly they all lost their special status and became a culprit responsible for the development of tension and conflicts, which ultimately led two different segments of the same family to declare war against each other.

Such a state of confusion developed in the mind of Arjun because of his state of attachment with fellow relatives, masters, friends, brothers and sisters who were joining the opponent side and were planning to hold and use weapons against Pandavas, the five brothers including Arjun.

At this critical juncture lord Krishna explained the essence of maintaining balance of mind by bringing out oneself from the state of confusion through gaining true knowledge. There exists a clear distinction between the soul of the individual and the respective physical body. Physical body may perish, elements present in bodily organs may disintegrate, physically the body may die, but waves and propositions of the soul will remain active in this world for centuries. In forthcoming days people may remember them through their acts, attitudes and conducts.

After knowing such differences and knowing about the importance of perfectly planned actions in life Arjun gradually prepared himself for the war. Entire Gita is the exhibit of the journey of Arjun from the state of confusion, sorrow and agony to the state of self-confidence, self-esteem and enlightenment. At his ultimate state of awareness he felt the presence of the Divine beside himself; it was also there within himself. His failure in feeling such omnipresence was due to lack of true knowledge only. It was also due to his unwanted attachment to the physical world and worldly things.

Yoga is the state of communion of the divine master and the studious disciple meant for feeling the state of communion through acts and conducts. Yoga might make the communion of the individual with Knowledge (Jnan Yoga), with actions (Karma Yoga) or with sacrifices (Sanyasa Yoga). Such communion of various types may not invade the individual senses differently. Their senses and conducts work on the individual jointly. These different realms of acts and conducts internally make any one of them with a bit prominence upon the others. We can understand this phenomenon with an incident from the Ramayana, where Lord Rama wanted his brother Laxmana to behave like a true learner having enough affinity to gain knowledge, even from any sworn enemy. After the completion of the battle of Sri Lanka, when both the fellow brother came to know about the state of the final breathes of demon King Ravana, Lord Rama instructed his fellow brother to move closure to Ravana with an aspiration of learning something from the demon King.

Laxmana moved on to obey the instructions of his brother only. There was no true affinity towards the divine knowledge developed in him. Then also he was considering the demon King as his sworn enemy. Such a state of discontentment forced him to take the position beside the head side part of the demon King, the place where one can rarely glance with a bit comfort. They remained silent for a long time. During another move with such approach of learning something pure from the demon King, Lord Rama positioned himself in such a way that the fellow King can see him with an ease. It made the King convinced perpetually and compelled him to deliver a timely relevant lessons infiltrated with his life time experience. It was the learning for a politically motivated individual. Lord Rama wanted his brother to listen the teaching of Ravana with proper attention and respect. His stand and approach was to make his fellow brother a learned one. Here the mechanism of integral Yoga worked perfectly for making them aware of the state of mind duly required for any individual for gaining aspirations and timely relevant instructions from a sworn enemy.

Ravana pointed out the difference between both the fellow brothers regarding their abilities of utilising senses, memory and intellects for materialising their political and social will. Wish factors arranged properly with an intention of materialising the common good made Lord Rama special amongst the group of warriors. It has also made him perpetually contented because of the proper culmination of Yoga based acts and conducts.

Integration of senses with a clear understanding of the timely relevant acts and conducts is also a subject of the culmination of different Yoga. It is the seat of philosophy, meant for individual and a collective ascent, where the referred individual can actualise oneself through a clear correlation with the centrally active Divine. Integral Yoga can even make the individual perpetually clear regarding the role in further manifestation of the self-actualised power of mind and intellect. Saints worked tirelessly to converge these philosophical ideals through representative conversation of the Divine and individual duly displayed in the Gita. Integration of individual with Yoga is the core of the principle materialised in Gita with an aspiration of enabling a doer of actions in attainment of completeness by all means. The presentation of such conversation has also exhibited the existence of such Yoga philosophy from olden times in the universe. It has evolved differently in due course of time and also narrated differently by saints time to time. Gita was, obviously without any doubt, a successful effort amongst all of them. Gita comprehends the teachings incorporated in Upanishads and Uanishads comprehend teachings prescribed in Holy Scriptures like Vedas. It also links up the thought process of Vedantic, Yoga and Sankhya Philosophy of Indian origin. All these schools of thought process instruct an individual to lead a life on the basis of a divine goal of feeling the presence of supreme power by the side of immediate creations. All forms in this universe are nothing but the manifestation of the Divine. It is the only truth that can link up all the human beings throughout the world and can materialise the dream of a peaceful world order.

Credit goes to saint Patanjali for the development of a most scientifically actualised Yoga conduct meant for the advancement of individual followed by a collateral advancement of the society and of the commune. His proposal is even perpetually designed for accommodating different aspects of a noble life process duly meant for experiencing feelings of collective ascent through the paths of spirituality.

The journey begins with a proposition of following rules of Yama (a set of acts meant for individual purity). It proposes that a person having aspiration of moving through the Octagonal path of Yoga should be nonviolent, truthful, altruistic, self-contented and worshipper of knowledge. While explaining the core philosophy of Nonviolence, the saint proposed the state of mind that considers all the other beings as a family member can claim that the individual is experiencing a true state of nonviolent life.

The second fold in this life comes in the form of some rituals for gaining purity and perfectness of organs and senses. There lies the importance of cleanliness, contentment, self-study, sacrifices and worships of the divine. It will simultaneously purify both the mind and body for making the individual and the referred community fit for the ascent up to the third state of this Yoga conduct.

Third stage is meant primarily for balancing the body, mind and intellect through positioning oneself in some proposed postures, termed popularly in Indian Philosophy as Asana, and regularising the same through day to day routine works. While describing such positioning, the saint says that the kind of position which offers a stability of mind, body and intellect is the Asana in its true sense. Whatever may be the posture and whatever may be the name for such posture, true Asana can only bring desired stability of mind and body.

Fourth stage of the Ascent is vital one because of its involvement in diverting senses towards the inner conscious mind through regulation of the breathing and confluence of senses through specified neural transmission. The core philosophy ascribes the establishment of a hold on the breathing and bringing it down at least below 15 per minute. It is also designed for channelizing the breathing through different nerve channels for infusing senses in the deep conscious mind for making it awakened and contented. This process is most vital one because of its importance in making the individual capable of diverting senses towards the inner world for roaming around the acquired knowledge and rearranging such acquisitions by repeatedly meditating on them. It can be also described as a process of self-actualisation and self-contentment. Such contentment only can enable a person to move through the inner world of senses and knowledge. It can be more confluent because of its mild infiltration through all the senses. It can make a person see what the mind wants to see, it can listen in accord to the inner sense, and even taste, smell and touch things accordingly. Development of positive waves in mind because of the prolonged meditation, the individual makes oneself fit for experiencing the practice of withdrawal from the external world for enabling oneself perpetually confined upon the attained knowledge and quantify oneself for further attainment of true knowledge. Such a withdrawal (PRATYAHARA) makes the person competent for making oneself refined and more perpetual for the ascent of the soul a step ahead for the attainment of a feeling related to the presence of the divine in the life process. It can even imply a guiding force for the individual duly required for rearranging the absolute knowledge for the purpose of making it more vibrant, more confluent and more actualised.

All the five stage practice brings a state of enlightenment for the individual and make the person fit for feeling the true meaning of life, real goal of life and all sorts of lively involvements in the community and lately , in a broader sense, in the universe. Such an actualisation (DHARANA) makes the person fir for meditating upon the stand point repeatedly with an aspiration of bringing refinement. Movement and journey of any person through this stage depends entirely upon the degree and expansion of the knowledge duly acquired by the person in life. It can ascertain the attainment of such a state of mind at the stage where senses, memory and intellect culminate perpetually with an apprehension of spiritual ascent.

Sensual, intellectual, spiritual and social convergence mounted voluntarily in an individual brings a state where the conscious mind intends to meditate repeatedly. This state of Concentration (DHYANA) enables a person to feel the presence of such a divine power in so many different states of individual and different life forms of all types moving around in nature. Their purpose of survival, their inter dependence and other hidden mysteries start becoming clear during concentrating upon the related process and propositions. A warrior, for example, can concentrate properly at the specified target. Such a perpetual concentration can bring further refinement in senses, memory and intellect with an objective of making them more actualised, more contented and more balanced.

Fixing mind, intellect and senses upon the true attainable goal in life is the final stage (SMADHI) where the person can feel the presence of Divine in the centrally actualised Memory, intellect and senses. It will become a guiding force for the individual and make the person competent for gaining spiritual advancement in life. It will even make the life a meaningful and perpetually contented. It is the desired stage of life where person aspires to ascend through practices, acts and conducts. At all instances it is not necessary that all people should move through all the eight folds of Yoga. The state of mental and spiritual contentment or a state of saturation aspiring for mental stability will exhibit the advent of Samadhi.

We cannot claim that individuals imparting oneself in society for delivering services or for playing some other definite role are perfect by all means. They work ceaselessly in due course of time for attaining perfectness in a gradual succession. Some people may consider an individual as perfect as compared to some other. One player may be considered a best one in his or her team. In gradual succession best ones will be identified through tournaments and some other best ones may be compared globally to select the globally best one. But, what about that skilful player who had decided not to take part in any tournament? The kind of art exhibits the limitation of the evaluation process as a whole.

The comparative process of examining and assessing perfectness parameter is standing on the basis of certain directives usually made by a group of people. Because of that reason any perfectness parameter cannot claim that individuals moving through the screening of the perfectness examinations are absolutely perfect. We can work put billions of questions from any specific field of study. Moving through such a massive task might make the life of any aspirant a hell. The type of testing in the form of written interaction is usually made limited by incorporating a set of planned interactions and content areas with a pre – planned format of study.

Karma Yoga is often defined by thinkers and philosophers as "Yoga of Actions and Performance.[422]" "Selfless actions perfumed by any individual for the benefit of others", on the other hand, as per narratives and postulated described in the Bhagavadgita, is considered as Karma Yoga.[423] Duties performed without maintaining aspiration of implying any claim on the result of fruit of action being performed leads an individual, with utmost contentment, to spiritual liberation.[424] Any work can be done with the spirit of a Karma Yogi as Karma Yoga.[425] Actions inflicted with, or more prominently to say in the context of the Bhagavadgita, driven by "equanimity, balance", with "dispassion, disinterest", avoiding "one sidedness, fear, craving, favouring self or one group or clan, self-pity, self-aggrandizement or any form of extreme reactiveness are the actions performed by a Karma yogi. Karma Yogi performs all the actions as the duty duly assigned by the nature to an individual and cannot maintain any claim on the results whatever comes out of the actions duly performed.[426] Selfless services performed with right feelings and positive attitude to serve the community, and ultimately to the nature, to which the indaba belongs, are considered as Karma Yoga.[427] The action, which are categorised as Karma Yoga in the Holy Scripture the Gita, can be motivated by body or manipulated by external influences.[428] Even, with certain alteration, it can be motivated by one's inner reflection and true self (soul, Atman, Brahman).[429]

A person engaged in delivering services to others and performing duties duly assigned by the nature efficiently and properly

---

[422] P. T. Raju (1954), The Concept of the Spiritual in Indian Thought, Philosophy East and West, Vol. 4, No. 3 (Oct., 1954), pp. 210.

[423] James G. Lochtefeld (2002). The Illustrated Encyclopedia of Hinduism: A-M. The Rosen Publishing Group. p. 352. ISBN 978-0-8239-3179-8.

[424] Mulla, Zubin R.; Krishnan, Venkat R. (2013). "Karma-Yoga: The Indian Model of Moral Development". Journal of Business Ethics. Springer Nature. 123 (2): 342–345, context: 339–351. doi:10.1007/s10551-013-1842-8. S2CID 29065490.

[425] William L. Blizek (2009). The Continuum Companion to Religion and Film. Bloomsbury Academic. pp. 161–162. ISBN 978-0-8264-9991-2.

[426] Harold G. Coward (2012). Perfectibility of Human Nature in Eastern and Western Thought, The. State University of New York Press. pp. 132–133. ISBN 978-0-7914-7885-1.

[427] Stephen Phillips (2009). Yoga, Karma, and Rebirth: A Brief History and Philosophy. Columbia University Press. pp. 99–100. ISBN 978-0-231-14485-8.

[428] The Bhagavadgita III.6 and III.8;

[429] Eliot Deutsch; Rohit Dalvi (2004). The Essential Vedanta: A New Source Book of Advaita Vedanta. World Wisdom. pp. 64–68. ISBN 978-0-941532-52-5.

moves towards an inward journey, in the other word spiritual enrichment (withdraw of senses from desires and compulsions and aspiring for spiritual contentment), which is inherently fulfilling and satisfying.[430] Seeker of rewarded for the duties performed may get inflicted with some sort of disappointment, frustrations or self-destructive apprehensions after completion of the work or in the middle.[431] Working without maintaining attachment to the actions, or without adhering to the fruit of actions one can easily move towards the supreme master and can feel the Divine omnipresence.[432]

Out of three means of liberation, Karma Yoga, as described in Sri Bhagavad Purana, is an easy way out. It can be followed by individuals while remaining at services and performing duties.[433] The first six chapters of the Bhagavadgita describe the essence of Karma Yoga in our daily life.[434]

Is there any liberty from Karma (performing duties or offering services to the nature or community) to a person who is aspiring to move towards complete renunciation? Absolutely, and speaking frankly without maintaining any alignment, No. one cannot escape different biological activities for remaining alive; the person is offering services to the nature, may be knowingly or unknowingly, while performing breathing, taking food and maintaining belongings. Karma Yoga is the part of life and can be judged as an inseparable part of life of all standards and all levels. Offering services to other and also services to oneself is a part of daily activity which, at any cost and at any instance, cannot be avoided.

---

430 Dharm Bhawuk (2011). Spirituality and Indian Psychology: Lessons from the Bhagavad-Gita. Springer Science. pp. 147–148 with footnotes. ISBN 978-1-4419-8110-3.
431 Jonardon Ganeri (2007). The Concealed Art of the Soul: Theories of Self and Practices of Truth in Indian Ethics and Epistemology. Oxford University Press. pp. 67–69. ISBN 978-0-19-920241-6.
432 "Bhagavad Gita 3.19". vedabase.io. Retrieved 3 November 2020.
433 T.R. Sharma (2013). Karel Werner (ed.). Love Divine: Studies in 'Bhakti and Devotional Mysticism. Taylor & Francis. p. 85. ISBN 978-1-136-77468-3.
434 Brian Hodgkinson (2006). The Essence of Vedanta. London: Arcturus. pp. 91–93. ISBN 978-1-84858-409-9.

Bhakti Yoga is a spiritual path, more prominently to say, a way of life with focussed on loving devotion towards any personal deity.[435] It has ancient Upanishadic root, and also is considered as one of the three paths leading a person towards attainment of liberation from the cycle of birth and death.[436] The personal God varies with devotee considerably.[437] It is devotee loves devotion to the personal God with an aspiration of growth in terms of spirituality.[438]

There are four types of devotees who practice Bhakti Yoga[439].

1. Devotees who are pressed or stressed by anxiety or their daily life circumstances.

2. Devotee often aspires to learn about god out of curiosity and intellectual intrigue.

3. Some devotee seeks reward in this Yoga or in afterlife.

4. Some devotees continue expressing devotion to the master simply for devotion and for nothing else.

The traditional doctrines, as often termed as Shaivism in Indian tradition, teaches ethical living, service to the community and through one's work, loving worship, yoga practice and discipline, continuous learning and self-knowledge as means for liberating the individual soul from bondage.[440] This tradition also focussed considerably on abstract ideas of spirituality.[441]

---

[435] Cutler, Norman (1987). Songs of Experience. Indiana University Press. pp. 1–2. ISBN 978-0-253-35334-4.

[436] Max Muller, Shvetashvatara Upanishad, The Upanishads, Part II, Oxford University Press, page 267

[437] Karen Pechelis (2011), Bhakti Traditions, in The Continuum Companion to Hindu Studies (Editors: Jessica Frazier, Gavin Flood), Bloomsbury, ISBN 978-0826499660, pages 107-121

[438] Gordon S. Wakefield (1983). The Westminster Dictionary of Christian Spirituality. WJK Press. pp. 46–47. ISBN 978-0-664-22170-6.

[439] Gordon S. Wakefield (1983). The Westminster Dictionary of Christian Spirituality. WJK Press. pp. 46–47. ISBN 978-0-664-22170-6.

[440] S Parmeshwaranand (2004). Encyclopaedia of the Śhaivism. Sarup & Sons. pp. 210–217. ISBN 978-81-7625-427-4.

[441] Sanderson, Alexis (1988). "Saivism and the Tantric Traditions". In S Sutherland; et al. (eds.). The World's Religions. Routledge.

Instructions on nine different types of devotion[442], as described in Bhagavad Purana and Ramayan, displays the way a devotee can practice Bhakti Yoga: (1) śravana ("listening" to the scriptural stories of Divine powers and their companions), (2) kīrtana ("praising"; generally and broadly refers to ecstatic group singing), (3) smarana ("remembering" or fixing the mind on the Divine master; such master will from the collection of characters upon which the devotee is maintaining absolute faith), (4) pāda-sevana (rendering service to the lord or the creations made by the lord), (5) arcana (worshiping an idol, image or any other symbol which can represent the divine power in terms of physical status), (6) vandana (paying homage to the master), (7) dāsya (servitude without expecting anything in return), (8) sākhya (friendship with the divine master), and (9) ātma-nivedana (complete surrender of the self with an aspiration of seeking liberation from the world).

The perfect explanation of characters of a true devotee is properly presented in the context where Sage Veda Vyasa pointed out such features in chapter 12 of the Bhagavadgita. It was delivered by the divine master in the form of a synthesis of all the nine types of devotions as pointed out earlier in old scriptures. Bhagavadgita (XII – 2 to 20)[443]

Quality of a devotee as preferred by the Divine master is described in this section.

1. Those who fix their minds on master and always engage in such state of devotion with steadfast faith will be considered as one of the best worshipper.

2. Those who worship the formless aspect of the Absolute Truth (the imperishable ones, the indefinable source, the all-pervading form, the unthinkable one, the unchanging type of the source of inspiration, the eternal, and the immoveable one) by restraining their senses, holding commands upon all the senses and by remaining even-minded everywhere, such progressive and

---

[442] Hagerman, David L. (2001). Acting as a Way of Salvation. Motilal Banarsidass. pp. 133–134. ISBN 978-81-208-1794-4.
[443] Shri Madbhagvadgita Chater 12.

balanced persons, while remaining engaged in the welfare of all beings, also without any doubt attain the Divine omnipresence.

3. Worship of the divine master will become easy for individuals having absolute focus on the goal of life.

4. Person worshipping the master without exacting anything in return will pass through a state of liberation during which the divine master will deliver that devotee from the ocean of birth and death, for their consciousness is united with and is gradually becoming non-separable by any means.

5. Person gains the omnipresence of the divine master instantly if that devotee prepares to keep faith on the master alone and surrender the very intellect to master. By doing so, devotee start always living in the beloved master.

6. Person having difficulties in remembering the divine master can have an alternative of fixing the mind steadily on master or alternatively on any other subject related to the divine master. Such devotee can practice remembering the fellow master with devotion while constantly restraining the mind from worldly affairs and also from other attachments.

7. Devotees having difficulties in remembering the divine master with devotion can simply try to work for the fellow master with utmost sincerity. Thus performing devotional service to the master or to the subjects related to the master with continuation and prolonged regularity shall achieve the stage of perfection without any failure.

8. Another type of devotee can try to renounce the fruits of actions or duties duly performed in society and can attain utter contentment by focusing on the waves of the inner self.

9. A devotee knows well about the states of renunciation which is the best alternative of devotion. Knowledge is better than mechanical practice; better than knowledge is meditation. Better than meditation is renunciation of the fruits of actions or results of duties delivered in society or to nature, for peace immediately follows attainment of such renunciation without any failure?

10. Those devotees are very dear to master who are free from malice toward all living beings, which are friendly in nature, and are also compassionate. They are free from attachment to

possessions and egotism, equipoised in happiness and distress, and ever-forgiving one. They are ever-contented, steadily aligned to the side of the divine master and remain in absolute state of devotion; remain self-controlled, of firm resolve, and dedicated to the master in terms of mind, spirit and intellect.

11. The person capable enough in maintaining the sensible balance of body, mind and intellect with an aspiration of retaining the balanced state even during adversities; and who are equal in pleasure and pain, free from fear and anxiety; such devotees are the preferred one by the master.
12. Person keeping balance of mind and action during profit or loss, happiness or sorrow, good or evil deeds; and even retain balance of the mind during adversities are the real devotees.

Devotion impregnated with knowledge is considered as a best way out which leads an individual towards renunciation. Even absolute devotion without much knowledge can bring the same result of renunciation. Remaining loyal to the fellow master and considering all the instructions delivered by the master as final is the ultimate expectation that the Divine expects from an individual. This doctrine was explained in detail time to time in scriptures and epics through different events. Event related to mother SABARI, as was narrated by Sage Valmiki in RAMAYANA, is one of such example. True devotion never puts any argument and even never intends to indulge in any kind of dispute. It always rests upon the verdict of the Divine master and prepares to offer services to the nature at the will of the Divine. Such kind of living and dwelling brings absolute happiness for the devotee and inspires others for doing the same. There is a kind of absolute surrender with which a true devotee prepares oneself to reach the fellow master with an instantaneous pace. It also harnesses oneness of devotee and the Divine. Such a state is, and finally will be, the final destiny of an individual.

Jnana Yoga emphasizes "the path of yoga meant primarily for assimilation and becoming enriched with knowledge."[444] This yoga primarily addresses the questions of an individual to actualise oneself in the realm of creations. Questions like: "Who am I", "What am I", and "What is the goal of my life", etc. are some of such questions with which a person advances in this path.[445] The purpose of true knowledge is to attain liberation for the person aspiring for it.[446] The entire mechanism related to this path of yoga context is better understood, along with some sort of examples and needful narratives, as "realization or gnosis", referring to a "path of study meant primarily for the attainment of liberation" wherein one knows the unity between self and ultimate reality called Brahman.[447] This path of knowledge is preferred by those who aspires for attaining some sort of advancement while delivering mental and spiritual services to the nature and also, with some broader apprehension, to the community.[448]

Enrichment of an individual in terms of attainment and utilisation of knowledge is an ever continuing act. It will continue throughout the life of an individual. One can even assimilate knowledge with a normal day to day confluence by seeing the services and qualities of other natural objects. Entire nature, more perfectly to say in a broader sense, is filled with knowledge. One may attain such kinds of true knowledge without putting much effort. Realisation of oneness of an individual (ATMAN) with the Divine master (BRAHMAN) is the ultimate goal of JNANA YOGA.[449] The Bhagavadgita efficiently

---

[444] Flood, Gavin (1996), An Introduction to Hinduism, Cambridge: Cambridge University Press, ISBN 0-521-43878-0

[445] [a] Ravi Dykema---- (2011). Yoga for Fitness and Wellness. Cengage. pp. 10–11. ISBN 978-0-8400-4811-0.;
[b] Orlando O. Espín; James B. Nickoloff (2007). An Introductory Dictionary of Theology and Religious Studies. Liturgical Press. p. 676. ISBN 978-0-8146-5856-7.;
[c] John M. Rector (2014). The Objectification Spectrum. Oxford University Press. pp. 198–201. ISBN 978-0-19-935542-6.

[446] Matilal, Bimal Krishna (2005), "Jnana", in Jones, Lindsay (ed.), MacMillan Encyclopedia of Religions, MacMillan

[447] Jones, Constance; Ryan, James D., eds. (2006), Encyclopedia of Hinduism, Infobase Publishing

[448] M. V. Nadkarni (2016). The Bhagavad-Gita for the Modern Reader: History, interpretations and philosophy. Taylor & Francis. pp. 45–46. ISBN 978-1-315-43898-6.

[449] J.J. Chambliss (2013). Philosophy of Education: An Encyclopedia. Routledge. p. 271. ISBN 978-1-136-51168-4.

integrates the thought process of Sankhya, Vedanta and Yoga to explain the real goal of Jnana Yoga in the life of an individual. After knowing about the science of such integration of individual and the Divine master one can feel the omnipresence of that supreme power. That supreme power is considered as a whole and the individual being aspires for gaining that totality and reverence through the path of Jnana Yoga.

Levels of emphasis may differ, but a worshipper of knowledge can have, and in actual sense must have, the combination of Karma Yoga and Devotion, to encompass the path leading towards liberation. One cannot claim at any instance that the person is exclusively or solely relying on Yoga of Knowledge (JNANA YOGA). It is even absurd to think and absolutely difficult to implement as the law of creation and biological processes cannot allow us to continue in the realm of creation without delivering some of the obligations. The related doctrine of Yoga of Knowledge is properly systematised earlier than Karma Yoga and Bhakti Yoga.[450] This yoga also offers an enlightenment to the soul with which the person start recognising the very self as an inseparable part of the nature, and finally as an inseparable part of the entire realm of the universal creation. The same individual is also a subject of the ever going cycle of the creation and destruction, which will at any circumstances remain unavoidable.

The Bhagavadgita also emphasises that Divine master is the jīva Shakti (the soul energy), which comprises the embodied souls of an individual and, with proper incorporation of sensible sparks of the energy, which forms the basis of life in this world.[451]

Divine master is the source of creation and ultimately all the creations diffuse in the supreme source. In that sense we can say that the

---

[450] Robert W. Roeser (2005), An introduction to Hindu Indiaís contemplative psychological perspectives on motivation, self, and development, in M.L. Maehr & S. Karabenick (Eds.), Advances in Motivation and Achievement, Volume 14: Religion and Motivation, Amsterdam: Elsevier, ISBN 978-07623-12-597, pp 305-308

[451] The Bhagavadgita (VII -5)

Divine master is the source of the entire creation, and it diffuses once again at the ultimate moment to the source from which it diverged out[452].

Persons who cannot advance, or may experience some sort of obstacle in the path of knowledge, are pointed out in the Holy Scripture: those ignorant of true knowledge, those who lazily follow their animal or demonic nature though capable of knowing the Divine, those inflected primarily with deluded intellect, and those with a demon like attitude and apprehensions.[453] Chapter 7 of the Bhagavadgita entirely narrates the true quality of a person who aspires for gaining knowledge for establishing oneself in the path of Jnana Yoga with proper affinity towards feeling the omnipresence of the Divine master, that person may then worship any of the idol or any of the cosmic form to feel the presence of such Divine spark within the self. That state of knowledge is the ultimate destiny towards which all the individuals are actually progressively and continuously advancing. Some of them are relying primarily on knowledge, some others take the support of knowledge for performing with enhanced efficiency and some other, along with a bit deviation, refers surrendering oneself at the feet of the Divine master.

Advancement of all of such kinds are finally free to locate themselves in the broader realm of creations along with the waves of further manifestation of their individual soul some sort of higher purposes of life. Life of such kind impregnated primarily with divinity is the ultimate goal of life.

The Purushottam Yoga, as vividly narrated by Saga Vyasa in Chapter 15 of the Bhagavadgita, signifies the quality and aspirations depending upon which an individual can feel the ascent of the soul towards harnessing the desired omnipresence of the Divine. It also enshrines the quality with which such person can move on through the path of spirituality for feeling oneself being enlightened.

A true worshipper of knowledge having devotion to the Divine master can move successfully without much obstacle towards the

---

[452] The Bhagavadgita (VII – 6)
[453] The Bhagavadgita (VII – 15)

supreme lord and it leads the individual ultimately to renunciation. That Divine world, having enough potential of offering liberation to a soul, is not illuminated or exhibited by solar, lunar or any other illuminations of any luminous or non-luminous objects of any form.[454]

Integration of almost all schools of Yoga, as represented in various sections of the Holy Scripture, is becoming evident at various instances; as a renunciation without performing scheduled performances and assigned duties is considered an aspect of falsehood; as different practices, such as cultivation of knowledge, maintaining devotion to the supreme master and becoming responsible while delivering duties are considered as interlinked aspects of life; for which aspirants could make oneself considerably competent.

Sensitivity of Aspirants

Teachings of Veda and Epics are from age old traditions. After the Epic Age we have passed on a span of thousands of years. Are such age old teachings becoming irrelevant day by day? Is the discussion on such teachings becoming useless in present day context?

If we start searching proper answer to these questions then we have to rely on the fact of the exact relationship with which the time and philosophy move on.

Actually Philosophy and Religion never take the support of the confluence of time. Time can even repeat itself through predetermined actions. Philosophy never intends to influence the normal cycle of the confluence of time. Therefore, both of these aspects of our daily life are independent of each other and reflect themselves independently.

What happened in Epic Age and the way Lord Rama handled the situation during that time had a deeper impact in the society during that time. It has exhibited the value system with which a State and a family can define their role in society. Those values are still relevant. Advent of any change in the material world has no power of influencing the fundamental value system with which a community leader should work.

---

[454] Bhagavadgita (XV – 6)

There are millions of books and narratives with some noble initiative available for explaining and elaborating the propositions of teachings of Gita. Gita is relevant for both learners and teachers. It has something to say even to a layman having less knowledge about the mysteries hidden amidst the conversations displayed in the holy book of Gita.

The term Gita directly links our thinking with the conversation that took place in between Arjuna, a Warrior from the side of Pandavas, and his friendly guide Krishna. It was going on amidst a critical situation in which Arjuna lost his power of finalising something justifiable to have a sanction of war and killings. Involvement in a series of killing of such a type in which his beloved ones were standing at a threshold of death made the warrior discontented. Krishna took the role of his charioteer to normalise the situation and to let Arjuna understand his own status in a better way. The agitation, as described in the holy book of Mahabharata, was against the stand of his own family members having intention of grabbing all the resources by taking advantage of some conspired game-fares. The game-fare of such type with in infliction of opportunistic ideals was moved on differently and both the segments of a single family took a stand against each other.

Lord Krishna defined his stand by putting himself in the side of Pandavas with a sheer commitment of not to use his weapon at any instances. It was his stand that made him free from direct indulgence of the warfare and made it possible to guard Pandavas through delivering timely relevant instruction. In this way he has secured his position similar to that of the brain in our body. Conversation of Krishna and Arjuna amidst the battle field was also an act of holy instructions duly issued for Arjuna to signify his timely need. It had linked senses with duties, established correlation between rights and duties, issued bands of things to be done and things not to be done, entangled a spirit with its higher source, conferred the juxtaposition of creation and the creator and finally re-established need of knowing the self.

Madbhagvad-Gita, as the complete term coined for the holy book, had also defined the role of divine power in infusing values within the intellect and senses of a fellow devotee. It has also established a perfect correlation between knowledge and devotion. None of the paired combination alone can succeed in bringing fame. Through all the eighteen chapters of the holy book, Godly propositions were incorporated by saints and philosophers who have created it for commons. It has a perpetual compilation of various combinations of practical aspects of Yoga and Meditation. It has also narrated the true nature of Knowledge that often receive a confluence more confluous than that of a stream. Attainment of such knowledge is a subject of individual apprehension and resides solely on the purity of mind. Our discussion up to this point has made a point clear about the nature and proposition of knowledge confluence remaining evident amongst us since centuries with a clear impetus of facilitating its follower for gaining an ascent through divinity and perfectness. There exist narratives in different forms and in different languages meant primarily to make people aware of the eternal philosophical aspects related to teachings of Gita.

Another effort of making Gita simple, easy to understand, more confluous to attend aspirations of people, more perpetuated to incorporate aspirations of millions and more conferred to actualise role of senses. Efforts may be of varying kinds to satisfy aspirations of people in different ways out. It may have some more relevant narratives that can efficiently link up the need of fundamental values reflected by Gita at different instances. Effort is also made to curtail unwanted explanations for maintaining the flow of the vibration of thought process intact. Discussion on any philosophical aspects should not go in a hurry and also it should not be too slow. It should have adequate stress of combined segments of knowledge and information to keep things enlightened and actualised.

It will be even more perfectly balanced to contingent human efforts of ascent towards the state of the unification of conscious mind with that of masterly guide. Effort is also made to encompass the segregation of individual differences from the common philosophical knowledge to make it more people friendly and more relevant, as well as time tested one.

Gita, in its actual sense, stands for some sort of compilation that people can sing. It can be discussed with some beautiful rhythmic tunes. Collective recitation of Gita brings out a collective wave in the form of auditory vibrations for the purpose of cleansing the immediate surroundings. It also conferred essence of collective and community level worship for making the entire effort possible and for keeping the converged senses of cooperation and brotherhood alive.

To a compilation of prayers and songs meant for the supreme lord the World Poet coined a term "Gitanjali" for it. To link up the practical aspects of life and mission of an individual with the specified spiritual destiny, Saint Vinoba coined the term "Katha Gita (Gita through a series of stories)" and incorporated all the teachings and narratives of Gita in absolutely friendly way. Examples are in plenty. It had not diffused the glory of the original compilation of Gita, also had not conferred replacing the original poetic compilation with millions of narratives. Waves of vibrations that the chanting of Gita creates is based on the assimilation of collective vibrations of saintly senses that makes a way out through the surrounding of the place of worship and gives birth to an essence of keeping the collective vibrations of cooperation, brotherhood, divine omnipresence and interlinkages of senses alive.

We, in the same manner, can successfully create hundreds and thousands of such narratives duly inflicted with fundamental human values to make the spark of Gita a confluous one, a vibrant one and a strategic one. It has enormous power of accommodations for incorporating all sorts of socially and culturally relevant directives within the scope of its teaching related to individual refinement impregnated with spiritual ascent. It also makes the relationship of creator and the creation a vibrant one. We can specify any of the particular effort as an initiative inflicted with divine power meant for accomplishing certain works. All such Gita, duly compiled by saintly people, are not with us. In due course of time we have lost many of such beautiful, relevant and time tested compilations due to various reasons. Our mind kept on imbibing presence of such powers tradition by tradition through many of our rituals. Those graceful efforts played a significant role in keeping waves of community worship alive. Gita was interpreted differently by different saints since olden times. Still we have a lot to explore from it in the true sense. The teachings and discourses duly incorporated by Saint Veda Vyasa reflect the teachings of Upanishads put together. Saint

Vyasa wanted to incorporate all the fundamental value system and yoga based life in a compact compilation to provide people an ease of access to the divine knowledge.

If we correlate different scriptures and Epics side by side then the value system duly reflected through all the propositions of saints will reflect each other's presence in common. We can better understand this aspect by taking an example of idol making. We use clay for shaping it differently to reflect our imagination and art, similarly the case is there with Philosophy of Yoga. We can correlate Yoga with all aspects of our life. In that sense we can even say that, "All Life is Yoga."

This extended philosophy and belief cannot cripple our mind and intellect. We can even, for an example, consider the life of a beggar as a manifestation on the basis of Yoga. The beggar prepares the mind for begging something from any individual. In failing to get anything the fellow beggar prefers to move on further to gain a living. Ultimately the fellow beggar surrenders himself/herself at the disposal of the almighty. Time cannot permit us to move as per our own wishes and willingness, but philosophy can do so. We can even adhere to certain principles and propositions to express our wishes and willingness to move through such doctrines.

People maintain faith on certain principles and rituals in which they feel themselves properly secured. Such security feelings will give birth to a communion having identical wishes and willingness. They even come across certain rituals to accomplish the jointly with an affinity of exhibiting a community feelings.

There exist thousands of nobles in a society. One cannot claim that all such individuals are absolutely perfect and wise by all means. Some of the notable limitations of all the individuals can be ascertained with varying evidences which may remain prevalent during their activities in a society.

Eight different components of the material element of the Nature are as follows:[455]

1. **The Earth** or worldly material things of various types.
2. **Water**: it is the greatest percentage of the physical body and also works as a basis of all kinds of biochemical reactions.
3. **Fire**: A kind of thermodynamic regulation which transforms the inter-conversion of energy and also the shift of energy from one trophic level to the other.
4. **Air:** IT ensures a basis of gaseous exchange during different metabolic activities. It also ensures it presence within the material basis of the life forms.
5. **Space**: It is the basis with which an individual registers its place in the habitat. It even quantifies the horizon of activity within the scope of a habitat.
6. **Mind:** A seat of the horizon of consciousness and confluence of impulses with the help of five different sense organs.
7. **Ego:** A state of the mental consciousness with which an individual registers its presence in the surrounding. It also makes the manifestation other components of mind and body manifested.
8. **Intellect:** A higher state of higher form of analytical brain power with which an individual implies adequate balance in between mind and body and ensures desirable presence in the surrounding. It also acts as a guiding force with which the fellow individual remains functional.

Interior energy also registers its presence in the states of creation and ensures proper coordination between different material elements. Embodiment of soul in the coordinated material elements is ensured by another element which remains off the interactive Nature elements and ensures the creations through implying adequate inductions. Such a supreme inductor of creation is nothing but the Divine (Purush) Element.

---

[455] *This classification of the materials has another back reference from the Sankhya Philosophy proposed by Sage Kapil.*
   ■ *Sankhya Karika and Sankhya Tatwa Mimansa (Resolution of Nature Elements).*

This element is beyond the scope of the exhibits of three different qualities. The Divine creates and also dissolution of Nature elements become recognizable in through the induction of that Divine only. During such disintegration all the nature elements are shifted again to their respective positions from where they had registered their participation during creation. That Divine is also different sensible sparks such as sight, taste, smell, touch and sound. It is also the intellect of an intelligent individual. We may become confused to see the presence of some qualities of the Divine in the intellect element. It should be considered as the reflection of the supreme creator and often become recognizable because of the omnipresence of intellect near the Divine.

All the Elements of Nature manifest differently on the basis of their three different qualities (Guna – Traya), such as Truth or goodness (Satwa), Rajas (the quality of activity, chaos, impulsivity and passion) and Tamas (the quality of darkness, illness, dullness etc.).[456] Character of an individual is determined on the basis of interplay of all these three qualities.[457] But the Purush Element (the Divine Power) remains off the quality parameters and people having some sort of illusion (Maya) start comparing similarities between Intellect and the Divine. The Divine manifest through Nature elements but remain off the cycle of creation and destruction because of its inductive approaches.

There exists a person who may not be capable of recognizing the real character and role of the Divine. These four different types of people are:

1. People who are ignorant of knowledge.
2. Even after knowing the real role of the divine, people who lazily follow their lower nature, mind and senses.
3. People with deluded intellect.
4. People having a nature and conducts like that of a demon.

---

[456] Refer Samkhya Karika by Ishwarkrishna.
[457] James G. Lochtefeld, Guna, in The Illustrated Encyclopedia of Hinduism: A-M, Vol. 1, Rosen Publishing, ISBN 9780823931798, page 265
T Bernard (1999), Hindu Philosophy, Motilal Banarsidass, ISBN 978-81-208-1373-1, pages 74–76

There also exist different types of people having adequate affinity towards the Divine. People having affinity towards knowledge, adequately devoted to their respective masters, distressed ones and seekers of worldly possessions can have adequate affinity towards gaining consciousness for feeling the omnipresence of the Divine. A worshipper with adequate knowledge will be the individual having highest pursuit with affinity towards gaining the Divine enlightenment. Intellect of such person remains embedded in the Divine and with such graceful pursuits the individual starts reflecting the Divine. Worshipper having material desires remains engaged in the acts of material gains and start moving through the path of Divine enlightenment by performing sacrifices and practices of Meditation.

A devotee remains engaged in the prolonged state of worship by keeping faith on any celestial god. Such individual also attains success through a fruitful arrangements made by the Divine only. Devotees reach ultimately to the Divine and other worshippers gain the desirables through the Divine arrangements only. Such Divine power knows the all creations, but none of the creators with limited knowledge rarely become capable of recognizing the true state and functioning of that Divine in the process of Creation and Destructions.

The supreme indestructible and inducer element of the creator power is called Brahman (the Divine or the Purush Element). The supreme Divine power becomes helpful when one assimilates its reflection on the intellect with its proper exhibits and its role in the creation and destruction. We can correlate the ways of functioning of the Divine by observing any luminous object like that of the sun. Some of the hidden mysteries responsible for the luminous nature of the sun have become known to us, and there exists several mysteries still unexplored because of our limitations in terms of senses and intellect. Mystery behind the inter-conversion of matter and energy is the main process responsible for liberating such a tremendous amount of radiation in the form of electromagnetic waves that radiating out from the celestial bodies like that of the Sun. Before such radiation the energy remained trapped inside the atomic nuclei were in the form of Nuclear Energy. We also came to know about presence of such king of tremendous amount of energy within all types of atoms of different elements. This phenomenon indicates the presence of creation elements and destruction elements inside the atomic nuclei. It is also confirmed that such nuclei remain inactive during all kinds of chemical reactions. Such a tremendous concentration of creation element ensures its presence during the process of creation but remains off the system of bindings. It registers its presence in the form of powerful particles.

All the above phenomena indicate the way supreme power becomes functional whenever time comes. The Divine energy ensures its presence in all sorts of creation. Even stars were created in olden times under the influence of such Divine power. It can be ascribed as the supreme power with which balance of matter and energy is ensures. It is also true that matter alone or energy alone cannot make the creation possible. Both of these supreme creation elements interact in a coordinated fashion to make creations possible. We rarely recognize the presence of energy element in the creation because of their non-sensible characters. We can feel the presence of such electromagnetic waves through the activities of reflections accomplished by other earthly visible elements or through any other celestial elements. The sun itself registers in the universe as a successful combination of matter and energy through which the presence of matter is guarded by the intense power of outwardly directed radiations.

This discussion encompasses the scientific basis of the Vedic, Sankhya and Yoga Philosophy. Living things always rest on Divine in same way the blowing wind rests in the atmosphere.[458] Only ignorant ones behave differently by violating prescribed rules of the nature and intend knowingly or unknowingly to put oneself in trouble. People can worship that Divine differently through varying degree and nature of contributions. Aham (or the ego centre) is everything perceivable in the surrounding in varying forms of relatives, friends, parents, masters and other living forms. Supreme goal for all the life form is, therefore, to have an exploration of working out the instances during which one start recognizing the Divine omnipresence.

---

[458] *Bhagvadgita, Chapter 9, Verse 6-12.*

Worshippers of other forms or god or other forms of power or faiths worship the supreme Divine because of the universal existence of such power at various instances in our surrounding. Similarities of the characters of the Nature elements itself indicate the presence of a uniform supreme inducer of creation element at all instances in the form of the Divine. [459]

People should offer all acts and conducts with absolute sincerity to the Divine for enriching one's knowledge base. Worship described in Bhagvadgita is for all irrespective of their individual differences. By doing so it has registered the fact regarding the universality of the worship methods and the processes of spiritual ascent duly narrated at different portions of the holy book Gita. It is, therefore, exclusively not meant for any specific group of worshippers. [460]

The Divine knowledge passes on from one generation to the other through the process of orientation and extensive training. During such training a devotee generally maintains the stability of mind, body and intellect for ensuring proper and timely maintained confluence of knowledge from the master to the follower. The degree of involvement of master and followers in the synthesis of knowledge will ensure the degree and instances of success. Divine knowledge also enables an individual to redefine the role duly prescribed for him or her in the society. It also ensures the onset of a repeated refinement process which aims ultimately towards the instance during which renunciation of the soul is duly accomplished.

Different functional exhibits of knowledge duly enlisted by saints are as follows : a state of humbleness; freedom from hypocrisy; non-violence; forgiveness; simplicity; service offered to the master; maintaining cleanliness of body, mind and intellect; steadfastness; self-control; dispassion toward the objects of the senses; establishing a hold and control on egoism; recognising the evils of birth, disease, old age, and death; non-attachment to sensible objects; absence of clinging to relatives, children, home, and other worldly objects; even-mindedness

---

[459] *Bhagvadgita, Chapter 9, Verse 23,24.*
[460] *Bhagvadgita, Chapter 9, Verse 29,30-32.*

amidst desirable and undesirable events in life; spontaneous and exclusive devotion towards the Divine; inclination of mind towards a state of calmness and stability through ensuring detachments from socially inclined gatherings of subjects other than the scope of study and experimentations; strong adherence towards the Divine, related subjects and spiritual knowledge; a long lasting aspiration of the thought processes related to the truth.[461]

Contrasting bases of above mentioned knowledge will be considered as acts of an ignorant mind and intellect. At the final stage of our understanding regarding the alignment three different horizons through which the Divine ensure manifestation will be discussed in particulars.

Three different portions of the Divine consciousness that remained active in the Natural world have the following orientations:

4. **Adhyatm** or the Divine of an individual (the inner world consciousness of an individual): it registers its omnipresence beside the Nature elements and gets reflected during certain instances through intellect.
5. **Jeevatm** or the Divine getting manifested through rest of the other individuals including plants and animals.
6. **Paramatm** or existence of the Divine beyond the scope of all the living forms and duly ensures the wider dimensions of creations and destructions at the levels of the celestial supremacy like Universe, Galaxy, Nebula etc.

Modern science has created an instance due to which we can easily go through evidences related to the vast expansion of the Universe. We can even claim that we all were earlier not aware of the presence of such a vast expansion over the ether which appears blue during day time and dark during night. Both the contrasting colours are not the actual character of the limitless sky. We also confirm that the presence of all the celestial bodies can be recognized even during day time with the help of specially enabled devices.

---

[461] *Source: Bhagvadgita, Chapter 13, Virses 8 to 12*

Such kind of limitless expansion of the Universe and information related to the varying nature and orientations of all such bodies were depicted during olden times by Vedic saints. They have also pointed out about our limitations with which we may not be capable enough in ensuring our access to all those knowledge.

We can correlate the Vishwaroopa (or the vision of the Universal expansion of creations) through explanations registered in the chapter 11 of Bhagvadgita. Names of different characters were pointed out symbolically to narrate the true nature of the Knowledge confluence from one generation to the other. Saints always played a vital role in preserving, cultivating and transferring the holy knowledge from generation to generations. Lord Krishna recognized himself as Kapil amongst all sages. This recognition has confirmed the alignment of the Philosophical alignment of Gita towards Sankhya Philosophy. Other schools of thought process will register their presence in the light of Sankhya narratives. The converging nature of the synthesis of Divine Knowledge is also confirmed by different instances of discussions depicted in Bhagvadgita.

. One can gain knowledge easily by observing the fellow teacher who has already experienced the Truth. The boat of the Divine knowledge can accommodate any individual irrespective of any physical or social differences.

Renunciation: When the journey begins!

There is nothing pure than compared to the purity of the Divine. With such an understanding we often move through the attainment of such purity of mind and intellect. With the aspiration of the attainment of such Divine knowledge one can attain the state of the everlasting peace of mind. Person who has already sacrificed all the actions will readily attain the peaceful state of mind and become happy by tracing out the exact nature of the Divine as an element of the supreme creator.

On the basis of different features of Karma Sanyasa and Karma Yoga duly described by Lord Krishna in Chapter 5 we can point out some aspects related to Yoga of Actions and Yoga of Inactions.

Remaining off the actions and remaining deeply involved in different actions lead ultimately towards the state of renunciation as a final fate of both the types of worships. By moving through any one of the paths we can achieve the same result. Accomplishment through both the path signifies some common aspects in both the types of worships. Person having involvement in actions can identify presence of the Divine in all creations due to accommodation of true knowledge in the intellect. Individual having steadiness in works never considers himself or herself as a doer of any action. Yogi often performs action with their mind, body and soul only for attaining personal advancement. Whatever actions we have visible in Nature are because of the involvement of three qualities of the Nature element. Nothing in special is created by the God and no external forces are responsible for such creations. Sinful or virtuous deed of anyone is not attended by the Divine. Ignorance covers up the eternal knowledge and compels an individual to lose its adherence to the fact of recognizing the role of the supreme master in the steps as well as propositions related to creation.

True knowledge also ensures the vision of an individual with which one start identifying the presence of the Divine in different creatures. With such understanding one start offering services to all the creatures. It also balances the mind and keeps the mind stable during any kind of loss or gain in terms of materials of different types or wealth in the form of money. Pleasure has a beginning and an end, due to this reason wise do not delight in them. The person with disciplined mind can work out strategies of imparting oneself in the process of development.

Shutting out all external forces, by equalizing all the incoming and outgoing breathes, by fixing mind and intellect on the Divine, an individual can feel the omnipresence of a supreme power through a sequential instances. Disciplined mind even remain involved in the welfare of millions through ensuring their participation in the duties duly assigned by the Nature and by the Divine. Balance of both the supreme creator ensures timely functioning of the intellect. That intellect starts reflecting the true nature of the Divine and, by doing so; make the individual aware of its presence by the side of the creation. Such a sage, who lives in the world remaining free from desire and fear, become eligible for the attainment of freedom from earthly attachments. Such a kind of freedom from physical bondage will ensure the timely liberation of the soul which started reflecting the true nature of the Divine (or the supreme Creator in the form of Purush)[462] . Real saints always perform duties without expecting anything in return. The path of renunciation is not different than the path of Yoga. One cannot even claim oneself as a Yogi without moving through renunciation of the worldly pleasures and comforts. A sage moves further through practices of meditation. The mind of an individual can help a lot by implying adequate sanction from the inner consent for accepting different propositions of Yoga and Meditation. A victorious upon mind can have liberation from the feelings of all sorts of dualities like happiness and sorrow, honour and dishonour. Such individual gains a state of real happiness of mind and stability for the intellect. Conqueror of all the senses and follower of the propositions of Yoga and Meditation always remain in the state of a balanced intellect. Meditation helps an individual to divert senses and impulses inwardly to ensure the instances with which the Yogi start exploring oneself through reflections of the Divine, which has registered its impression upon the intellect. With such a state of sensible ascent such individual start recognizing things with their real nature. They even start correlating similarities between iron, copper, gold and other earthly existing alloys. Such intellect attains an impartial stand and start treating friends and enemies with an equal grace.[463]

It is also made clear by the supreme Master that practice of some perfect posture (Asana) can give an individual adequate stability of body and mind. It will also nullify the chances of development of any bodily anomalies during the period of worship. Every activity in our daily life should have a kind of adequate balance. One should not go on sleeping for a long time and even should not go on working without taking a rest in the middle. Taking too much food and remaining in a fast for a longer time cannot make any individual competent in the path of Yoga. It should have adequate balance by all means. Individual with such a state of balanced mind start meditating upon the Divine. Such individual also

---

[462] *Sage KApil, Sahkhya Philosophy ; Purush (or the supreme Creator element) can be considered as the Divine power having a definitive role in making the creation possible.*
[463] *Bhagvadgita, Chapter 6 , Verse 1 to 12,*

start unfolding different mysterious layers of knowledge for understanding the new appearance of the supreme creator. It is the act similar to that of the blossoming of a flower. Such kind of awakened individual can feel a development in their mind and intellect which remove them considerably off the state of selfish acts and conducts. One cannot forcefully move any individual up to that state of mental stability as we cannot force the unfoldment of petals of a flower. These developments are automatically accomplishable alongside the practices of Yoga and Meditation. The state of inner joy develops after recognising the true reflection of the Divine on the horizon of the intellect. Such state of joy and happiness may remain permanently embedded in the mind and intellect and imply a kind of influence upon both senses and action organs. That joyous state of a being is considered as the state of Samadhi[464] or a state of the stability of mind and intellect on the subjects of the Divine.[465]

Chances of success increases considerably when one repeatedly brings the wandering mind back to the subjects of the Divine and aspire for remaining fixed to that subject. With such a state of enlightenment that individual start recognizing the presence of the Divine in all the creations. Such individual can fix up mind and intellect in Divine even remaining active at varying instances.

Renunciation and the state at which such renunciation makes the individual free from the cycle of life and birth is described perpetually by the saint through the verses of supreme creator at different instances in the holy book Gita. At the final state all individuals are driven close towards the Devine, even against their eternal will, and renunciation, in particular, is ensured. Evil forces, at certain instances, rarely become capable of bringing themselves off the cycle of life and death. It also entangles the individual in the cyclic process of birth and death.

---

[464] *The term Samdhi was originally used by Saint Patanjali in his creation titled Yoga Philosophy. The state of Samadhi comes after moving through the practices of Meditation. It can be ascribed as a state of renunciation and also a state of higher level of knowledge with which the fellow individual starts recognizing the omnipresence of the Divine through the reflections perceivable on the horizon of intellect.*
---Patanjal Yoga Pradeep, Saint Patanjali.

[465] *Bhagvadgita, Chapter 6, Verse 19 to 21.*

One more question arises in our mind regarding purity of soul. Is there any instance when a soul attains impurity? The question is obviously, no. quality parameter is restricted only up to the ego and mental status of an individual. The creator element and the intellect remain off the parameters of quality. Being a segment of energy, a soul always remains untouched by the quality parameters. A soft dissociation of the body and soul is initiated during death of an individual.

All the Nature elements having their presence in the process of creation have three different quality parameters, such as Satwa (Purity, truth, harmony, goodness and wiser state), Rajas (State of activity, passion) and Tamas (a state of darkness, destruction and choosiness). None of the elements other than the Purush (or the supreme creator power) are devoid of these three qualities. One quality may go down by percentage in certain elements and may go up by percentage by keeping simultaneous decline in the percentage of other qualities of the same element in the same state of creation. All the three quality parameters always add up to a complete whole for the specific creation element belonging to the Nature. The quality of purity, truth and goodness binds the soul by creating a sense of happiness and knowledge. Second type of quality, such as Passion, arises from the worldly desires. It also conditions a soul towards actions. It arises from worldly desires and affections. Being a causative agent of acts like negligence, laziness and sleep, the third quality (a state of ignorance, darkness and destruction) causes development of illusion for the embodied soul. Actions done in the mode of passion results in pain, while those performed in the mode of ignorance results in darkness. Result of the truth and purity results in the illumination of the soul. Mode of goodness results in the development of knowledge. We can easy recognize interactive aspects of all these three qualities in the states of manifestation of Nature elements. Wise persons having a feeling and understanding of the Divine omnipresence can recognize all the three quality parameters of the Nature elements. Such person maintains the neutral state of the intellect with a clear stand during interchange of quality triplet at all instances. Combination of three qualities along with their varying ratio implies adequate influence upon the character of the individual. Domination of first quality signifies the character of a wise person.

Self Enlightenment

Yoga of Knowledge and Yoga of Works are explained separately in Gita. Person having adherence towards work can move through Yoga of action and individual having adherence towards cultivation of knowledge can move through Yoga of Knowledge. It is also true that only Work and only Knowledge cannot lead an individual towards the state of complete renunciation. Without doing certain works one cannot move through the path of Knowledge. An individual, for an instance, cannot survive without food. Such kind of basic necessity is fulfilled through coordinated works of a group of organ system. Similar is the case related to breathing, walking, talking and other different activities. So renunciation without performing any work is technically not possible. Aspirations of doing works without taking adequate support of Knowledge cannot be ascertained in actual. Therefore we cannot justify the existence of two different Yoga processes in real life situation with their distinct identity in particular. Work must be done with an aspiration of sacrifice and it should be done without ascribing any kinds of expectations in return. Creation of human beings is objectivated towards attainment of all the accomplishable tasks with a pure aspiration of sacrifice to the Nature God. [466]

All the desired necessities of life are duly granted to the individual by the Divine Almighty. Sinners can enjoy all such gifts of nature without offering it to the Divine Almighty as like those made by wise persons. Every individual in Nature register themselves as a part of the expanded realm of Food Web. One cannot keep aside from such kind of inter-related energy cycle. Even one cannot violate the rules of Nature by implying heavy demand for energy on such kinds of energy cycles. We should practice all kinds of activities related production and harvesting only after understanding the real facts related to works and their inherent causes. Such duties of human beings in Nature are properly

---

[466] *Use of the term God is made admissible by the propositions of Saint Patanjali. On the other hand Sankhya Philosophy cannot admit the role of any external creator like God in the process of the Manifestation of the entire creation. It is the Divine (Purush) element which registers its presence and ensures the process of creation possible.*
   a. Sankhya Sutra by Sage Kapil ,
   b. Patanjal Yoga Pradeep by Sage Patanjali.

described in Vedas. That is why one should align one's life process on the basis of Vedic instructions. Only sinners can violate instructions of Veda and put oneself, and ultimately the entire community, in trouble. Person having knowledge of self –actualisation has nothing to lose or nothing special to gain. [467] One should remain engaged in prescribed duties without adhering oneself towards any affinity of losing or gaining something in particular. Real happiness resides in making the performance wilfully without compulsion or prejudices. If any individual fails to perform its duty which is duly assigned by the Divine and if the Divine also fails to perform the role during creation, then we cannot expect sustainability of any kind of stability in the surrounding. A wise person act without remaining attached to the fruit of action and the crippled minded fellow, on the other hand, will act with adherence to implying a hold upon fruit of the results. Wise person can inspire others for indulging in works as per the scope duly assigned by the Divine.

Activities duly performed by any individual are accomplished on the basis of three different qualities of the elements of the Nature. These three different qualities are the sole moderator of actions. Without knowing the exact fact, one starts thinking it as a role played by the doer individual. Here develops a state of illusion due to which a person start considering oneself as a doer. Only awakened person can identify the Divine (PURUSH) as an entity of creator element remaining off the quality triplet parameters. The worker who makes oneself free from evil forces and agony will become aligned properly towards refusing in the standpoint of the Divine. From this point onwards the prosperity of such individual on the path of spiritual ascent is properly ensured. All living beings including human beings remain active in the surrounding on the basis of their exact nature duly ascribed by the creator supreme power. It is therefore expected that all such individuals remain active in the surrounding as per their specific nature for ensuring the stability of the cycle of energy confluence in the respective blocks of the cyclic systems.

Here lies the coordination of science and spirituality with which the Sankhya Philosophy has already pointed out about the involvement of mature element and the Divine in making the manifestation of Nature

---

[467] *Bhagvadgita, Chapter 3, Verse 15,16 ,17-19.*

element possible through activation of Supreme element namely Mahat Element or Intellect. Our discussion regarding Sankhya Philosophy will be advanced separately by incorporating a special chapter alongside the main discussions.

One should establish adequate control upon all the senses for ensuring success of the intellect during execution of the specific assignments of duties. One may remain indulge in the duty duly assigned even with adherence of limited skills and should not indulge in duties of others even with any aspirations of doing that with adequate perfectness. The lust along with passion gives birth to anger and gradually make the intellect a birth place of different sinful acts and conducts. It is also true that our knowledge remain surrounded by desires like the covering of womb upon an embryo. Such kind of desire burns like a fire and is responsible for all sorts of discontentment and agony. After knowing such a role of senses in development of desires, one should imply adequate hold upon senses since the beginning.

It is already known to us that all the senses are controlled by the mind and mind in turn is controlled by intellect. Intellect is the reflection of the soul, which is nothing but the first element of the creation. Gita highlighted the role of the Divine in the process of creation at different instances and also pointed out the exact feature of the creator element. Even the Sun follows such principle and start radiating the band of energy without expecting anything in return. Such radiation plays a vital role in making creation of life in the Earth possible. While doing so, it remained off the process of creation. It had made all other elements united with an objective of establishing a coordinated function in between different elements of the creation.   Lord Krishna also highlighted the science of birth and rebirth with a graceful involvement of the Divine creator. The Divine manifests through any individual whenever need arises. Similarly the birth of Lord Krishna is made for ensuring the victory of wise over the brute for the sake of protecting religion. It is also ensured through timely involvement of the Divine in the process of creation for ensuring such definite tasks. The Divine reciprocate with individuals the way they surrender to their master. The Divine is also identifiable as a non-doer of any actions. The reason is that

Divine never comes in any direct contact with any of the Nature element during creation. It registers its presence simply by coming close to different materials with an aspiration of switching on the process of manifestation.

There are different instances through which one can successfully perform duties in society:

1. By following any sage or saints from olden times.
2. Remaining active in society after knowing the nature of the Divine.

The spark of knowledge alone cannot ensure progress on the path of spiritual ascent. It is possible through participation of the individual in definite duties naturally assigned to the individual by the Nature. While redefining one's role in the immediate surrounding one should know about three different aspects of actions, such as recommended action, wrong action and inaction. The individual remaining completely aligned in the Divine are Brahman, their acts, conducts, efforts and propositions all remain recognizable as Brahman. The sacrifice made to fire is also considered as Brahman.

Different types of offerings at different instances by different persons are also evident in society[468] :

1. Some offer food to the Divine Almighty with honesty and sincerity.
2. Some other persons offer money, wealth, land and other assets.
3. Life energy is also offered during many instances in the fire of the controlled mind.
4. Severe austerities are also offered to the supreme master by many.
5. Some of the followers and workers practice eight fold path of the Yoga as duly coined by the sage Patanjali.
6. People also offer functions of all the senses.
7. Some wise performers curtail their food and offer the same to other living beings. Such kind of fast will make the individual

---

[468] The Bhagvadgita Chapter 4, Verse 25 to 34.

more inclined towards the holy path of the attainment of renunciation.

8. Somebody offer sensible presence in the form of establishing regulations on the breathings. (Pranayaam)

9. Sacrifice performed in the form of knowledge by a master is more result oriented because of its ability of making an individual competent in terms of the character building measures.

Of all types of sacrifices, the sacrifice of knowledge is considered as superior one than compared to sacrifice in the form of any material. For nullifying the state of confusion and agony of the warrior the supreme power in the form of Lord Krishna started narrating the exact nature of an individual in accord to the context of the Sankhya Philosophy. Krishna says that any performance made by a conscious individual will bring success at all instances, in some cases it may be delayed one. Acts of Kuru Prince and all his brothers and associates are impregnated with a predetermined objective of gaining the state ownership at the cost of deprivation of their cousins. On the other hand involvement of nobles in this battle is ensured in terms of different noble thoughts for safeguarding nobles and for ensuring justice to oppressed ones.[469] People with incomplete understanding of the relationship of Nature element and divine, puts the individual in a state of illusion. Such person even comes in the influence of some beautiful Vedic words without considering the exact meaning of such words and propositions.[470] One should move out of duality and make oneself free from all the three materialistic qualities for aligning oneself to the state of truth. It can even make the individual off the attractions of the material world. One who realizes the truth and fulfils the purposes of all the Vedas. By doing so, the referred fellow can fulfill the social obligations in particular. It is similar like similarities in the role of a pond and a lake in terms of their act of providing water to remove thirst of an individual.[471]

---

[469] *Shri Madbhagvadgita, Ch ,2 Verse 40,41*
[470] *Shri Madbhagvadgita, Ch ,2 Verse 41 to 43.*
[471] *Shri Madbhagvadgita, Ch ,2 Verse 44,45,46.*

People must perform duties without expecting any fruitful result from the same. In other words one cannot wait for the desired results to come. The sun never waits for the fate of any result of its acts of illuminating objects. It repeatedly illuminates things whatever made exposed to it. By doing so, the Sun never admits its doer-ship in any of the acts of illumination. Illuminating things is the naturally assigned duty meant for the luminous objects like that of the Sun. that is why the Sun is doing nothing, nut performing its natural duty. Abandonment of attachment or expectation of success and failure will equanimity in the states of success or failure. This balanced state of mind and intellect is the highest pursuit of Yoga. [472] Works done with an expectation of reward or praise is obviously an inferior one than the works performed with adequate understanding and intellect and also is performed for the sake of the Divine. With such understanding of the balance of mind and intellect at all instances, skill of performing one's role is Yoga. Real happiness is attained when one successfully castes off all the desires of success and failure of works. It will also diffuse all states of confusion regarding exact role of an individual in performing duties in society. [473]

Qualities of an Enlightened Person[474]

With a clear understanding of the Divine omnipresence, the enlightened person will remain adequately satisfied in the realization of the self. It can also be ascribed as a state of self-contentment. Kathopanishad moves one step forward by admitting that after understanding the self-one can easily feel the Divine omnipresence and attain Divinity.[475] A sage of steady wisdom should have a mind without agony, fear, anger or attachment and even does not crave for pleasure. Such mind also remains undisturbed amidst success and failure. A sage with perfect knowledge, rarely become happy for success and sad for the

---

[472] *Shri Madbhagvadgita, Ch ,2 Verse 47. 48,49.*
[473] *Shri Madbhagvadgita, Ch ,2 Verse 50, 53.*

[474] *Shri Madbhagvadgita, Chapter 2, Verses 50 to 65. ; this section properly describes the quality of an individual having enlightenment and feelings of the Divine Omnipresence.*
[475] *yadā sarve pramuchyante kāmā ye 'sya hṛidi śhritaḥ*
atha martyo 'mṛito bhavatyatra brahma samaśhnute (2.3.14)[v48] -- Kathopanishad

failure. His happiness and sadness is diffused during both the instances because of the stability of the mind impregnated with enrichment of true knowledge. A person duly established in divine wisdom can withdraw all senses from sensible things efficiently. Taste of the sensible objects ceases considerably during the state of mind which realises the omnipresence of the Divine. Senses are so turbulent and strong that it can even trap a person having some sort of advanced knowledge alongside self -control. Their senses are established in true knowledge which empowers them perfectly to feel the omnipresence of the supreme creator in the form of the Divine (Purush).

The state of agony and misery develops in a gradual succession of the involvement of any individual who contemplates on any sensible object. Such contemplation develops attachment to them; with the state of attachment one can feel the development of desire. Such desire, if not fulfilled timely, will turn into anger. Anger destabilizes the mental stability and hypnotises the mind to certain extent and makes it illusive. With such illusions that individual lose the enrichment of memory. Memory submerged in such state of mental illusion will spoil the intellect and may lead that individual to commit a sin.

When Lord Krishna approached Duryodhan with a peace proposal before the onset of the war and said him that Pandavas may remain satisfied even by receiving only five villages. The reply of Duryodhan was absolutely unexpected, "I cannot give even a small piece of land without battle."

Lord Krishna said, "Is it Justice? Can you explain it as a religious act?"

"Obviously not, Krishna. It is not Justice. I cannot even claim that my stand is religious."

"Then why are you doing that?"

"It is only due to my strong adherence towards the acts which I am doing. May be such acts are not admissible in the context of justice and religion, but some irresistible force residing in me forces me in doing so. I always find myself trapped in that irresistible force."

Such admission of Duryodhan describes the state of mind which forces and individual with some sort to knowledge for committing a sin due to the status of an elusive mind. Person having adequate self-control and self-esteem can feel sensible objects even without becoming trapped amidst the state illusion due to presence of proper understanding of the presence of the Divine. Happiness of the intellect impregnated with true knowledge feels the presence of Divine and remains firmly established in the same. Peace and contentment is not established at the situation when individual remains off the feeling of any omnipresence of the Divine. Even focus of mind on a single sensible object can distract the stability of mind. The person who has successfully restrained oneself from all types of sensible objects can have a state of mental contentment duly impregnated with true knowledge. Relative things such as days and nights, right and wrong, success and failure are well explained with their absolute state of relativity by a self-contented individual. Such individual can even explore some aspects of darkness amidst lightness and states of sorrow amidst happiness. The kind of feeling and related reasoning grows on the basis of the relationship of works and its reasons.

Person who strives to satisfy desires cannot attain true knowledge. The person, who remains undisturbed amidst all sorts of knowledge confluence from all sides and remain admissible at all instances like that of ocean, gains a state of mind of a wise person. Perfect peace of mind is attainable only during the situation when individual castes off all the desires and successfully regulate all sorts of senses.

Here lies the similarity where sage Patanjali described his Yoga Philosophy by proposing the regulation of senses as the first step to be followed by an individual before entering the path of Yoga. Self-regulatory practice, according to Sage Patanjali, is designed perfectly for ensuring stepwise attainment of completeness alongside enrichment of the mind and intellect. One can go on ensuring one's adherence towards the states of Truth, Non-Violence, Altruism, cultivation of knowledge and self-contentment. When the state of mind regarding all the five states is confirmed alongside the adherence of true knowledge , then such individual is fit for moving up to the second stage of Yoga.[476] It is the state of individual which confers the eligibility of the self for moving towards practices of certain rules as follows:

1. Cleansing of the body and mind.
2. Making oneself satisfied at the state duly availed by the Nature and not to move towards attainment of something by violating rules ascribed by the Nature.
3. Worshipping the Divine through cultivation of true knowledge with an aspiration of understanding different elements duly imparted in different processes of creations and manifestations.
4. Study of the self with an objective of actualizing the self.
5. Contemplating mind and intellect upon the presence of a Divine power and recognizing its role in every aspect of creations.

After moving across all such rules a worshipper can successfully make oneself capable of re-aligning all such regulations of senses and intellects through repeated practices of bodily postures (ASANAS)[477]

Up to this point the Yoga is meant for regulating and aligning externally projected senses and organ systems. From here onwards the Yoga will ensure the internal state of the fellow worshipper. The shift of the individual from the external state of regulations towards the internal state of regulation is made possible by practices of the regulation of breathing and vibrant confluence of sensory impulses.

Teaching of The Gita or Lessons from The Gita?

What we think in mind that we aspire to see and experience in reality. We even plan accordingly to make things happen. If we aspire for attaining success in life and duly put our plan and efforts accordingly

---

[476] *Sage Patahjali , The Patanjal Yoga Pradeep.*
[477] ASANA refers to a bodily posture and exercises which ensures the state of mind alongside a state of happiness. It also ensures proper functioning of different organ system.

then the desired success must come in reality.

Emperor Ashoka, one of the powerful emperors from Maurya Dynasty during later Vedic Civilisation, invaded Kalinga for punishing the culprit who was also the murderer of his mother. Kalinga was maintaining a voluminous army; even they had a democratic status. With only selected army Ashoka was more organised, confident and contented regarding attainment of success. Success was supplemented with proper planning and absolute positive attitude. That was the real mystery lying behind attainment of success by emperor Ashoka.

Yoga speaks more about the strategy of actions that the actions or perfections. How to do any work is more important than the work itself. One can keep on drawing water from the well by using ropes and bucket, or it can be obtained by fitting a water lifting pump at the base of a pipe.

What to do, how to do and when to do are some of the pre-requisites of developing a strategy for designing a strategy. For throwing out Nanda Dynasty [478] and for replacing the same by a wise king, Vishnu Gupta, popularly known as Chanakya[479] or Koutilya in History, took the support of Greeks deputed there in Indian continent by Alexander. It was the strategy of developing friendship with the enemy's enemy. Such mechanism worked perfectly and he attained success by putting his efforts in bringing change in the Indian context. The result was a long lasting success which came in the form of good government.

Although Chanakya was the most powerful person and most respected master mind of his time, then also he preferred not to put himself on the throne. He preferred maintaining his status of a king maker.

---

[478] *Dhana Nanda was the last Emperor of Nanda dynasty. Chanakya, the Economic Advisor of Nanda Dynasty, was badly insulted by Dhana Nanda. Also oppression of Dhana Nanda became unbearable. He was not concerned about the problems faced by farmers and artisans of that territory.*
[479] *. In later period of history name of Chanakya became popular because of his contribution in the field of Economy by developing a balanced Economic Policy for a State (Arthashastra of Koutilya).*

Strategy of action and its importance was also perfectly narrated by Saint Valmiki in famous Epic the Ramayana. Once Sugreev, one of the warrior from the envoy of lord Rama, as described in the Ramayana, chased Ravana just after seeing him and recognising him through a window. It was absurdly planned and prematurely implemented. The result came in the form of a failure. Ravana managed to escape from the place by making the warrior entirely confused. He was the master of magical powers. With the help of his magical power he had handled the pre matured planning of Sugreev.

During another briefing on the need of planning for developing a strategy lord Rama narrated the need of gathering such a big army and seeking support of the brother of the Demon King for making things materialised properly within least possible casualties. Every action requires a proper planning. Winning the battle against Ravana was not so easy, also it was not impossible. Proper considerations of all aspects of threat from the demon king made Rama and his warriors more prepared, more responsive and more specific.

Even with more powerful army and different magical powers Ravana became the loser because of his poor planning, arrogance and over confidence. Adequate strategy was not worked out by him due to his act of the under estimation of the powers of lord Rama and his envoy.

Victory may not wait for us in the battle field and success may not come on the exam desk instantly without putting adequate efforts. We often ignore the need of proper planning for developing a concrete strategy of organising one for any forthcoming challenges. Because of this reason failures of different degrees and different extent put us in trouble.

It would be better if we start learning form experiences and arrange ourselves properly for any other forthcoming challenges. At this critical point the teaching of the Gita will work properly. It says that one should deserve a right to work, results will come automatically. It would be better to prepare oneself for any other forthcoming challenges without remaining fixed upon the results of any previous action. The instruction is very simple and also easy to understand. One should not stick to the result. The success might make a person full of joy and any failure may bring sorrow. Both the joy and sorrow will create bands of obstacle on the path of ascent. That obstacle supplemented with mental, physical and spiritual crippleness will put a person in a halt. Such halt may become fatal for any vibrant life form.

Planned action can bring a successive scheduled actions followed by one another in a cyclic way. Some of such planned actions often confer the consideration of some of the laws of Nature. That is why it helps in maintaining the coordination and balance of mind, intellect, skills and the body parts. Each parts of an individual work perfectly amidst such a balanced coordination of senses, mind, intellect and body.

Only a mind full of words, ideas and ideals cannot work properly, only a body with a strong physique can also make any action a half dome, only skill can wait for some fretful and coordinated instructions of the mind and only intellect may indulge in some sort of arguments. That is why coordinated actions of all the parts of the individual will be the only way out.

Coordinated actions will open up horizons of the possibilities of culmination of perfectly planned actions with desired state of performance. It may not wait for the results of the previous action to come. It will indulge oneself in the vibrant process of organised actions with an aspiration of feeling one's ascent through the path of spirituality and will power.

Importance of nature in our daily life is a matter beyond the questions and conflicts. For understanding such role, with a clear distinction between acts, conducts and necessity, we may go through a popular story of a beggar and King of all kings.

During one instance a beggar continued moving through the royal path with an expectation of receiving something prosperous from the king of all kings. The poor beggar was standing by the side of a royal path with an expectation of receiving some handful of wealth. The King of all Kings often passes through that path and gives in plenty.

For making the anticipation of the poor beggar true, the band of dust with an admixture of clouds appeared at the horizon. The King of all Kings was moving in through that royal path. The very moment of prosperity and happiness would be there in the life of the fellow beggar. It might bring an end to his wandering status. It may also fulfill his desires.

The dust and cloudy appearance moved more close to the beggar and finally the moment came. A pair of empty palm was there in front of the poor beggar. The King of all Kings was begging! It made him very angry; also the act was absolutely unexpected one. With a mixture of anger and agony he had decided to offer few grains of corns to the King of all Kings.

With happiness, King of all Kings received the gift and moved on further. The day was not prosperous for the fellow beggar. His all faith and contentment on the King of all Kings duly melted. He had nothing to say but to feel, nothing to comply but to hide and nothing to offer but to gain.

Situation turned differently after returning back home. He was to sort things as per its nature and utility. Some glittering corns were of special type. His inmates identified that particular corn as costly gems. This incident made him unhappy. He understood the magical power that implied upon him by the King of all Kings. It was even more annoying to notice that the return was equally countable in terms of identical quantity of the offering. The number remained the same, but in terms of quality there was a tremendous boost. The kind of equally powered boost that he wanted to receive in life made him fully contented and compelled him to change his stand of not to offer things.

Second turn from the side of King of all Kings was about to come. This time he had prepared himself to offer his kind self at the hands of the fellow master having some sort of divine power.

He was not in a position to give up. The kind of incident made him absolutely confirmed about his stand of witnessing the magical transformation which can make him feel the action of the divine power on him. His contentment was also of absolute type because of his capabilities of witnessing the impact of such divine power on grains of corns.

Beggar symbolises a common human being bearing aspirations of progress. The King of all kings symbolises Nature. Nature is the only entity which arranges a living for all its members.

The conservation strategy is gaining a momentum. It is also widening the information gap between people and government. The schemes launched by government often remain off the record of people simply because of their non-participation. Due to this reason participation of people in making the schemes successful often remain off the track. We cannot put a hold on the intrusion of unauthorized hunters and poachers in the referred area of the wild habitat. We, alone on the basis of some legal frameworks, cannot put a halt on any unlawful acts and conducts of people leading to a loss of normalcy in forest biota. We simply adopt a collaborative effort by establishing proper coordination between people, government and environment through ensuring timely participation of people in the planned efforts of the government and conservators.

From evidences available in nature, it has become clear that native Indians are not a threat to the wild population. They prefer living in a harmony as an ideal harvester of the forest resource. Their intended effort is meant simply for harvesting a living without implying any harm to the population residing there. Honey hunters of Sundarban and Kanha reserve forest are of such type. They rarely put a halt in the normal wandering attitude of wild animals. In Gir forest some native Indians even communicate with big cats by producing special types of sound. The fellow lion understands such dialogue and gives a way out. It is a best example of the coexistence of people and animal with an aspiration of sharing the commonly available resources.

Conflicting situation may develop any time and at any place. If we consider the modern mechanized warfare then it is becoming evident that modern wars may rarely last for a couple of days, or hardly for a couple of weeks. On the other hand, it will be so devastating that one can rarely traces out the group of warriors indulged differently in that war. This may happen only because of the extreme mechanization of the warfare.

It is also true that we cannot move on mechanizing any warfare anymore because of the involvement of a huge sanction. People, in the modern society, rarely move on for affording a war. They all imply adequate impetus on ensuring the establishment of peace, prosperity and brotherhood in our society. This effort cannot limit its expansion by any border; it can have a normal confluence through countries and states; even it can have adequate hold on the community living throughout the globe.

There are millions of books and narratives with some noble initiative available for explaining and elaborating the propositions of teachings of Gita. Gita is relevant for both learners and teachers. It has something to say even to a layman having less knowledge about the mysteries hidden amidst the conversations displayed in the holy book of Gita. The term Gita directly links our thinking with the conversation that took place in between Arjun, a Warrior from the side of Pandavas, and his friendly guide Krishna. It was going on amidst a critical situation in which Arjun lost his power of finalising something justifiable to have a sanction of war and killings. A series of killing of such type, in which his beloved ones were at a threshold, made him discontented. Krishna took the role of his charioteer to normalise the situation and to let Arjun understand his own status in a better way. The agitation, as described in the holy book of Mahabharata, was against the stand of his own family members having intention of grabbing all the resources by taking advantage of some conspired game-fares. The game-fare of such type with in infliction of opportunistic ideals was moved on differently and both the segments of a single family took a stand against each other.

Lord Krishna defined his stand by putting himself in the side of Pandavas with a sheer commitment of not to use his weapon at any instances. It was his stand that made him free from direct indulgence of the warfare and made it possible to guard Pandavas through delivering timely relevant instruction. In this way he has secured his position similar to that of the brain in our body. Conversation of Krishna and Arjun amidst the battle field was also an act of holy instructions duly issued for Arjun to signify his timely need. It had linked senses with duties, established correlation between rights and duties, issued bands of things to be done and things not to be done, entangled a spirit with its higher source, conferred the juxtaposition of creation and the creator and finally re-established need of knowing the self.

It will be even more perfectly balanced to contingent human efforts of ascent towards the state of the unification of conscious mind with that of masterly guide. Effort is also made to encompass the segregation of individual differences from the common philosophical knowledge to make it more people friendly and more relevant, as well as time tested one.

Gita, as a common and popularly contemplated term, indicates towards a subject related to the holy book of Gita having bands of knowledge in the form of a conversation in between Arjun and Krishna. This reality made Gita confined to a limited quarter and placed other holy efforts underneath a shadow of ignorance. We rarely talk about Ram Gita, Sanskaar Gita and some other such efforts having a suffix Gita attached to it.

Gita, in its actual sense, stands for some sort of compilation that people can sing. It can be discussed with some beautiful rhythmic tunes. Collective recitation of Gita brings out a collective wave in the form of auditory vibrations for the purpose of cleansing the immediate surroundings. It also conferred essence of collective and community level worship for making the entire effort possible and for keeping the converged senses of cooperation and brotherhood alive.

To a compilation of prayers and songs meant for the supreme lord the World Poet coined a term "Gitanjali" for it. Linking to the practical aspects of life and mission of an individual with the specified spiritual destiny, Saint Vinoba coined the term "Katha[480] Gita (Gita through a series of stories)" and incorporated all the teachings and narratives of Gita in absolutely friendly way. Examples are in plenty. It had not diffused the glory of the original compilation of Gita, also had not conferred replacing the original poetic compilation with millions of

---

[480] Hindi term Katha means Stories. Saint Vinoba Bhave translated Shri Madbhagvadgita in Marathi and also wrote a series of books to explain teachings of Gita through simple stories which were also contextually relevant.

narratives. Waves of vibrations that the chanting of Gita creates is based on the assimilation of collective vibrations of saintly senses that makes a way out through the surrounding of the place of worship and gives birth to an essence of keeping the collective vibrations of cooperation, brotherhood, divine omnipresence and inter-linkages of senses alive.

We, in the same manner, can successfully create hundreds and thousands of such narratives duly inflicted with fundamental human values to make the spark of Gita a confluous one, a vibrant one and a strategic one. It has enormous power of accommodations for incorporating all sorts of socially and culturally relevant directives within the scope of its teaching related to individual refinement impregnated with spiritual ascent. It also makes the relationship of creator and the creation a vibrant one. We can specify any of the particular effort as an initiative inflicted with divine power meant for accomplishing certain works. All such Gita, duly compiled by saintly people, are not with us. In due course of time we have lost many of such beautiful, relevant and time tested compilations due to various reasons. Our mind kept on imbibing presence of such powers tradition by tradition through many of our rituals. Those graceful efforts played a significant role in keeping waves of community worship alive.   Wider dimensions and expanded coverage of the teachings of Gita often make people worried about what to follow and what not to follow in real life. Also in some cases it becomes difficult to think about propositions in the actual ground. Because of lack of timely relevant practical knowledge of the situation, people even keep themselves aside from following and internalising teachings of the holy book in the real life situation. Approach of such religious and cultural teaching, therefore, should have proper considerations of some practical aspects of rituals and worships.

Some people maintain a view regarding Gita is that the entire aspects depicted in this holy book are a confusing one. Saints from olden times worked differently to show that Gita is much relevant in terms of rituals and propositions presented in it. Here also we are trying to trace out a link up in between rituals, traditions and practices that we have in nature to re-establish the age old faiths of the omnipresence of divine within us at its varying formats. We can see things as they occupy a definite shape. We cannot see energy and power due to their in capabilities of occupying space. To feel the presence of such powers in our surrounding, we often take the support of our senses and feelings. In some cases our observations are evidence based, in some other cases it may have some imaginary propositions. Here comes the act of limitations that restrict us to feel Ultraviolet and Infrared [481]radiations which remained off the band of the visible spectrum and duly restricted our sense of vision seven visible waves of light.

There arises another question related to our effort of analyzing the relevance of the teachings of The Gita in present day situation. It was the instructions delivered by Lord Krishna to Arjun during the epic age of Vedic Civilisation. That time war had its presence in the scope of royal management. That time conflicts had a final termination to war for making efforts a result oriented. Sins and sinners had their presence in olden times and are still there with us today; format and geo-locations might vary; arms and ammunitions might differ. Even from the pages of history we can see how Prince Ashoka smashed the Kingdom of Kalinga only because that kingdom had refused to hand-over the murderer of his mother to him. Later on the war and the loss of lives of many innocent people had implied a deep impression in his mind and he had decided to refuse to take part in any other battle simply meant for territorial expansion. Teachings of The Gita have worked differently during different instances of the development of conflicts and agony.

Since conflicts and agony are beyond the scope of any historic time line, we can correlate teachings of any instances to prepare strategic actions of any other present day sectoral management plans. It has the impetus of the absolute knowledge of human actions, wishes, wills and conducts with absolute apprehension of delivering the needful. The reason of discontentment, sorrow and agony of Arjun after entering the battle field was rejected instantly by Lord Krishna through implying a sanction of his indulgence in the war. Killing any individual or creating another one is not the role of any warrior. A warrior can deliver the duty

---

[481] Both Ultraviolet and Infrared Radiations are the parts of the invisible band of spectrum incorporated in the Solar Radiation. Our visual sense organ can feel the presence of only visible spectrum comprising seven different colours.

in time with a clear impetus of making the wiser side victorious. Sinners will lose their lives because of their mis-conducts only.

It is the right place to mention about Upanishads, often referred as Vedantas, as they exhibit doctrines, rituals and worship patters prevalent in later Vedic Civilisation.[482] Those rituals and doctrines were duly incorporated in the great epics to make all sorts of teachings easy to understand. The Bhagavadgita along with majority of Upanishads and Brahmasutra are known as PRASTHANATRAYEE.[483] These three scriptures were studied extensively time to time to inculcate more relevant knowledge related to Divinity and Spirituality. Out of 108 known texts of Uapnishads only a dozen from the initial collection are considered as Primary (MUKHYA).[484] Concluding parts of Brahmans and Aranyaks are also filled with Mukhya Upanishads.[485] Authorship of all the anonymous tests duly collected from the garden of Upanishads is unknown. Group of saints might have collected and represented their lessons in the form of a collection.[486] Conversation between women like Maitreyi and Gargi are also inscribed in the holy texts of Uanishads.[487] Root of all such creations is principally radiated out time to time in different forms and also in different sectorian units from Vedas.

Pluralism of world view was characterised by the Upanishadic age; gradually inclined more towards dualism by combining Sankhya and Yoga doctrines efficiently.[488] The Bhagavadgita moved on a step forward by incorporating Vedanta along with Upanishadic dcotrines with an aspirations of delivering a common pattern of rituals, social formats and political will to the youths of the olden times.

---

[482] Jan Gonda (1975), Vedic Literature: (Saṃhitās and Brahmanas), Otto Harrassowitz Verlag, ISBN 978-3447016032
[483] *Ranade, R. D. (1926), A constructive survey of Upanishadic philosophy, Bharatiya Vidya Bhavan*
[484] E Easwaran (2007), The Upanishads, ISBN 978-1586380212, pages 298-299
[485] Mahadevan, T. M. P (1956), Sarvepalli Radhakrishnan (ed.), History of Philosophy Eastern and Western, George Allen & Unwin Ltd
[486] *S Radhakrishnan, The Principal Upanishads George Allen & Co., 1951, pages 22, Reprinted as ISBN 978-8172231248*
[487] Ellison Findlay (1999), Women and the Arahant Issue in Early Pali Literature, Journal of Feminist Studies in Religion, Vol. 15, No. 1, pages 57-76
[488] Glucklich, Ariel (2008), The Strides of Vishnu: Hindu Culture in Historical Perspective, Oxford University Press, ISBN 978-0-19-531405-2

Maitri Upanishad aspires for attainment of reverence and completeness by human beings with the help of the knowledge of Brahmans and repeated practices of meditation on such knowledge by the self.[489]

Further study of the Bhagavadgita reveals all such studies like the gradual unfoldment of petals of a lotus. In the modern world we have various types of cultural and religious thought process possessing rituals, customs and traditions of different types, which are equally competent to enrich people in terms of knowledge, devotion, courage, will power and dedication. The way we receive each culture to enrich our multiplurality will specify our degrees and ranges of success. Our motive force will guide accordingly to explore possibilities of working out converged cultural segments from all the rituals to move up towards vibrant waves of multi plurality.

India, at this juncture of the development of multiplurality, will be a best example for all of us. Here people learned a lot to live with each other, tolerate each other and enrich each other differently.

We cannot see light. Even we cannot see the propagation of sound through the material medium. Light strikes our eye, reaches our brain and develops a sensation of vision through certain life process of vision. With some sort of illusion, or lack of true knowledge only, we often claim that we can see light. Even all the colours radiated out from the sun are not recognisable by us. If God resides inside the individual, if all mysteries related to the ascent of a person on the path of divinity, then why any devotee search it out for gaining the blessings of any Divine power located outside the physically existing body? Why such a dwindling situation any individual face during the tenure of worship?

Lord Krishna narrated essence of feeling the Divine communion with the physically existing life through witnessing cultivation of knowledge, actualisation of the presence of any supreme power in sub conscious mind and possible ways and means to follow that power. It enables an individual to come across the feeling of the advent of some completeness

---

[489] Hume, Robert Ernest (1921), The Thirteen Principal Upanishads, Oxford University Press, pp. 412–414

in the mind through knowledge transformation. Cultivation of knowledge regarding the relationship of the divine and disciple is enrouted from the age old traditions through the turmoil of the organic evolution. That evolution brought some change in the process of exhibits, but the core remained the same. It was even more perpetual and more profound regarding the ability of harnessing the relationship of matter and energy. We cannot imagine the existence of matter without the involvement of energy, and similarly energy takes a definite visible form to occupy certain space in this universe.

How do people see things and how do they correlate such unavoidable relationship of energy and matter is depend upon the level of understanding that one adheres with. A master of Physics and a master of Philosophy must have varying degree of explanations for putting forth the mystery behind the mechanism involved during inter-conversion of matter and energy. All organic combinations have certain physical and chemical sets of combinations in such a definite ways that they inculcate the abilities of interactions and abilities of giving birth to senses. Even evolution of sensory structures and related orientations became much collaborative in case of human beings. Here occurs a change which brought us near the state of explorations meant for examining the hidden mysteries behind creation and orientation of life forms in the living planet.

These days, things are known to us that earth like situation exists in the universe. Only the matter of concern is that we may not be able to reach the place even after attaining the speed as that of light in a year or two. Only we can admire the presence and orientation of such creations within our visibility. Only we can explore and examine such things with the help of optical and electronic instruments. With an understanding of such limitations human beings never arranged any voyage to explore the inner world of senses that can allow us to explore the outer orientation of time and space. Such an inner world exploration may require a little effort to culminate senses within a confinement for feeling the presence. There also resides a tremendous flux of energy accumulated within such a small space. Those mysterious combinations taking the form of life were explored differently by saints during olden times.

There developed a science of explorations of the correlations of the Creation and the Divine. Matter and energy indulged in a perfect orientation for letting senses flow through them. Arrangement and orientation of all our senses are directed outwardly. That is why we are bound to receive waves and sparks from the outside world. Our inner world remains unexplored in most of the cases. Only adherence of true knowledge and the journey of senses through inner world during meditation can pave a way out for exploring our own self. Meditation is the doorstep where orientation of senses get diverted towards the inner world and bring out mysteries associated to the fact of accommodation of the Divine power inside the living being.

Is that Divine power is restricted to the human beings only? The answer is, obviously and surely without any doubt, No. human beings has gained some sort of evolutionary supremacy in due course of time, but other beings are also of same potential and courage with a domination of animism in them. Dogs are loyal to their master, cats exhibit better vigilance power, elephants are more socialised beings having better memory power and tigers are the masters of their own territory. Taking hold upon the surrounding and defining the role according to trophic [490] level, we can easily arrange these beings and others without any difficulty.

Philosophical and Spiritual supremacy is a step forward that makes a distinction between other animals and human beings. Then also we can witness inhuman acts from human beings and humanly acts from some inhuman animals. The orientation of sense organ and correlation of senses and sensory responses with memory and intellect is the only factor regulating such varying degrees and conducts of animismic and hunmanismic behaviours.

Presence of such a Divine power within the creation is the reason behind the maintenance of an idea of serving humanity with a correlated apprehension of serving God. Only God cannot put a direct access to the feelings of the presence of such immense power within us. It is the

---

[490]. A Trophic livel signifies the food habit of organisms during their representation as they exhibit in a food chain. Green Plants, for example prepares their own food with the help of sunlight and secures the first position in a food chain and basic position in the food pyramid. Second trophic level is occupied by herbivores, followed by carnivores at the third.

approach with which we offer our services to living beings can develop a way out for us to feel the difference.

Once during pre-independent period in Bombay (at present Mumbai) a youth from some semi urban place approached a saint for offering himself at the service to divine. It made the saint happy. He wanted to know the exact reason behind his stand of doing so. Saint also enquired about his capabilities and considered his offering a wise one. Actually the fellow was searching jobs in the city. He was also a normal Graduate from any sub –urban area and his financial situation was also not so good. Perhaps the sacrifice might make him temporarily happy and contented, but will become a burden in due course of time. With happiness saint suggested him for searching out a suitable job and helping the parents and inmates of the family financially. Only After gaining some wealth and knowledge the person can really enjoy the glory of sacrifice. Right now the person has nothing special to sacrifice. Such sacrifice inflicted with sorrow and agony may put both the master and the disciple in trouble.

Even divine cannot allow any individual to put oneself and families in trouble and agony. It is the only state of contentment that helps a person during movement from the physical world to the spiritual world. Offerings of any kind and in any particular form will bring happiness.

Once upon a time, a shopkeeper had a beautiful dream. The dream was so beautiful and so perfectly understandable that he feared of sharing it with others. According to his dream the God himself wanted to visit his shop. It was winter season and more special about the time that, it was raining outside. Amidst such patchy rains he preferred opening the shop. Inmates knew it better about his firmness upon any decision. He prepared some sweet dishes, some snacks and few cakes for the strange visitor of the day. Face of God was appeared in dream and was not recognisable with any clear identification marks. "The Master must introduce himself, or may give some signal so that his poor fellow can recognise", his happiness went on increasing bit by bit.

"Can I have some snacks and a cake?" An old lady was approaching the shop with a can on her hand. "Today, actually I've not opened the shop! If you came then please, have it."

"Guest! Some special or any usual one!" Curiosity of the old lady alarmed the shopkeeper for keeping the matter a secret one.

A cowboy was approaching holding a fruit in his right hand. "That guard is chasing me. Let me come in, please."

"But, you are already inside my shop! Anyway let me see the fellow.."

Cowboy narrated the entire incident behind the reason of his hunger. That fruit was kept aside and the shopkeeper offered him a dish full of sweets, snacks and cakes.

"Don't worry my child, I'm here with you."

The matter settled in an hour. Striking of the noon time bell of the cathedral instructed the shopkeeper to finish his meal. But, what about that strange visitor! There were no traces of such visit amidst the sprinkling of droplets in the courtyard and a shower on the roads.

Evening time visitors were a cobbler, a mason, a hawker and a vagabond. Earning was not the matter of the day that is why he offered food to all the visitors with respect. It became possible because of his happiness. At last the mind refused to support him properly. Entire day and half of the night went on waiting for the master. Ultimately the time came to stop waiting for the strange visitor. His mind was still in a motive of receiving the visitor. May be the master is trying to meet him when calmness mounts the surrounding. With such anticipation he preferred keeping the door half open.

"So nice! So sweet! Really all items were tasty.." , the masterly voice brought his happiness back in dream.

"I may visit you again and again."

Morning time dream mixed up profusely with chirping of birds and silver linings of the clouds.

"God came! Who was that? May be that boy! .. " Series of anticipations and guessing went on for few moments. The entire face of the shop keeper was glistening with happiness. It was the time for feeling the presence of the Master in any nearby position. It had developed a faith in his mind, "My Master must come and visit me again."

We cannot deny the role of a school in the life of any individual. The person gains a lot during school days. S(he) can learn how to impart oneself in the society by redefining ones role in society.

It is not the only aspect of life through which any individual gets an opportunity to expose oneself to the fundamental value system prevalent in society. One's choice factor plays a definitive role in this regard.

Cultural background of an individual is greatly influenced by the immediate surroundings. Human beings, for an example of an ordinary type, is vegetarian by nature, but omnivorous by intended vigil of gaining some essential proteins from the animal sources. Development of canine indicates the biologically and naturally assigned habit to human beings. If we aspire for remaining confined within the naturally sanctioned habits of our own then the acts and conducts related to the killing of animals for the sake of gaining essentials will definitely go at its minimum.

Killing of animals for obtaining food and medicine is perpetually inflicted with acts of animism. It also signifies the place of human beings at a definite trophic level. It has also exposed our relationship with other organisms and our dependency upon the source. We rarely make ourselves capable of trapping waves directly from the sun. It will always reach us through the involvement of producers (such as green plants). Maintaining green plants in nature and allowing them to prosper in our surrounding is, therefore, becoming a non-avoidable activity of the system in which we are confirming our presence. The referred system also limits our ascent and conducts. Within that limit of acts and conducts any human being can explore possibilities of registering the presence of oneself by performing the duties duly assigned to the individual perfectly, perpetually and vividly.

One cannot escape from oneself without performing duties duly assigned by the system designed for ensuring interactions of different trophic levels. If we start claiming that tigers should not be allowed to kill deer, cats should not chase rats, snakes should not feed on frogs and owls should not puncture ripe fruits then our claims will violate the laws of nature. With certain natural instincts, and for maintaining a proper balance in nature organisms ensure their definite role as per the assignments. Human beings are playing a role with some sort of exceptions. One can intend to kill deer for obtaining food; one can trap fishes, kill birds, smash snakes and chase bulls for fulfilling the need of grabbing food. With a modified vigil of registering one's presence in the cycle of energy transfer one can cultivate grains, harvest fruits and maintain mulching animals for fulfilling the requirement of food. For rest of the world the role of that human will be of a protector.

With such dual principles human beings can register the presence of oneself in between the highest and middle order of the trophic level. In another aspect we people maintain our difference from others due to our ductility, capabilities to speak, performance of exhibiting our emotions and affinity of remaining linked with others. Here comes the essence of socialisation and acculturation for the same. On the basis of such involvement in the society parents cannot escape from their duties of nourishing their children, young ones cannot escape from their duties toward elders and seniors cannot escape from their affinity of helping young ones. Escapism of any type and any degree is the affinity of human beings for which the entire community may face sufferings, loss of trust and agony. Escapism of any type can also create individual differences, depending upon which human beings often start ascertaining one's role in society.

Antyodaya

Sarvodaya is the term used by Mahatma and his associates for addressing their plan of constructive works to equip people of India differently during freedom movement.

Central tenets coined for reflecting the philosophy of Sarvodaya are as follows;

1. Individual progress and prosperity resides in the progress and prosperity of rest of the other people.

2. All people have the same right of earning a living from their works without remaining limited to any kind of restrictions or regulations due to variations of their job profiles, or status in society.

3. Life of an individual involved in productivity or farming is the worth living. Rest of other people getting involved in any services depend directly or indirectly on the bottom level of performers.

4. All inclusive development plan for addressing issues and aspirations related to all segments of society.

Post independent India continued addressing issues and concerns related to development plans envisioned by Mahatma through his spiritual successor namely Acharya Vinoba Bhave. Vinoba worked out a strategic plan namely "ANTYODAYA[491]" through which aspirations of poorest of poor were to be addressed first. Various organisations who were working on the same principle continued addressing issues as per the mechanism suggested by Acharya Vinoba. Rest of the other organisations followed the track differently with focus on the development of land, water and forest cover.

---

[491] *Hindi term which means development of the poorest of poor.*

Sarvodaya is the framework through which all inclusive growth of a nation-state will become a reality. It is also a balanced mechanism which negativates the chances of deprivation, exploitation or oppression by all means. It is a reality that society always contains good people and bad people. Bade people never go on increasing in number. We have greater number of people in country who can maintain adequate faith on the constitution and judiciary. They never refer imparting themselves in any kind of lawlessness. They even try their best to safeguard the stability, prosperity, unity and security of their state. They also try their best to deliver services duly assigned by the state. We also cannot make ourselves sworn enemy of our bad segments of society. We have to live with them. It is our duty to win the confidence of such people by making them aware of their role in the community. They should not feel outnumbered or deprived. Any kinds of negative feelings compel them to adopt a measure through which they start disturbing the entire society. If we keep them off the track of main-stream of development then such kinds of people may become more violent and more venomous. Because of that reason also we should adopt a best possible customisation through which their role in society can be ensured. Simply putting bad people off the main track of socialisation is nothing but an act of falsehood which is not admissible in the doctrines of Sarvodaya.

About Me

Name: Chandan Sukumar Sengupta

I have completed my higher studies in Zoology, Information science and Comparative Religion and Science of Yoga. Took part in the comprehensive training programme (Java 2 Core, Web Designing, PC Maintenance) duly organised by Advanced Training Institute of Electronics and Process Instrumentation, Govt. of India.

I am working in the field of Education and Information Science since 1995 onwards. Research projects completed by me are as follows:

1. Enhancement of Critical Competencies through Computer Aided Learning
2. Value aided Education in Indian Context (NCERT 1999)
3. Participatory Learning and Development in Tribal Villages (NCERT 2000)
4. Spiritual Aspects of Spontaneous Education (NCERT 2001)

Cultural Nonviolence [ISBN-13 : 979-8356756771]
5. Relevance of ARTHASHASTRA in present day context (Submitted to Chanakya University)

6. Nonviolence: The Ethical and Spiritual Notions [ISBN: 979-8888837382]

7. Economist of Mahatma [Life Sketch of Kumarappa and Acharya Vinoba] Gitai Mission.

8. Essays on The Gita (Part I, II and III)

Major Initiatives:
1. Took part in Tribal Development Programmes sponsored by Govt. of India in Tribal belts of Santhal Pargana (SInghbhoom, Gumla, Chaibasa , Nowamundi, Tatiba and other adjoining areas)
2. Took part in Alternative Drought Action programmes sponsored by Protestant Mission of Germany. Travelled different areas of Bihar, Bengal and Orissa for project monitoring and Evaluation.
3. Worked as associate of ASTRA Project (in the capacity of Chairman) for the purpose of curriculum designing along with the Dept. of Alternative Schooling, NCERT.
4. Joined Jain University, Dept. of Education as Research Scholar and took part in Research projects.

5. Worked in close association with M.S. Swaminathan in 10 districts of Vidarbha for working out strategic initiatives to address problems faced by fellow farmers in that locality.
6. Became associates of Development organisations at different capacity and continued offering services at different capacity.
7. Took part in the development of Curriculum for Upper Primary segment of Basic Education.
8. Prepared a comprehensive plan of digitization of library and office set up.
9.

Publications:

I am maintaining more than 450 active publications on different themes. All publications are updated and are available at leading market Places (both online and offline).

<u>Present Status</u>: Offering services to development organisations and academic institutions as per need. Maintaining high definition web server, web designing services availed to organisations of well repute. Looking after the publication works of selected organisations is another major part of involvement.